A NEW ZEAL

ᴚD

George Cawkwell in his own words

EDITED BY TIM CAWKWELL

"Vanity has never been one of my strongest points – save when it comes to the products of my pen, in which domain I can keep up with the fast pack." [from a letter of 17 September 1995]

cover: George in Rome ca 1952 posing for Pat's camera

SFORZINDA BOOKS 2022

COPYRIGHT PAGE

ISBN 9 798818 548753

Published by Sforzinda Books

30 Eaton Road

Norwich NR4 6PZ

cawkwell200@gmail.com

set in Sanskrit Text 9 pt

TABLE OF CONTENTS

PART ONE: THE PULL OF OXFORD

PART TWO: LETTERS TO GORGO

George Cawkwell - New Zealand - Authors *et alii*, classical - Authors,
artists *et alii*, modern - Index of persons - Miscellaneous

INTRODUCTION

Is George Law Cawkwell (1919-2019) worth a biography? The case against is strong enough to suggest not. He was a *nomen* of a kind, perhaps even a *magnum nomen* to his family and friends, but the life as a whole is too limited. It starts well enough: an upbringing in His Majesty's Dominion of New Zealand, an early and fierce desire to win a Rhodes scholarship to Oxford, some experience of war ('trifling', to use his word) in the important theatre of the Pacific – even if that war has long been at the margins to British historians – then marriage, then arrival at the Shangri-La of Oxford University, and the special heaven of Christ Church, the winning of a rugby blue and even one game for Scotland, then a Fellowship at University College. Oxford after the war was an exceptional milieu to end up in: he was one of a cohort of undergraduates who had fought in the war and ended up on the winning side, for whom the *pax Americana*, even in a divided world that had invented nuclear weapons, provided a blanket of security. Oxford was veritably the Land of the Lotus Eaters, a taste of whose fruits obliterated all other desires.

And then? Did his life influence national events? No. Is Oxford University at the centre of the United Kingdom? Not if you do not live and work there. Is his chosen subject, Ancient History, the pillar of British public life? The reply can only be dismissive: an irrelevant subject in the latter half of the twentieth century; a 'niche subject' is a kindly but withering description. So – in the end George's life runs out into the sands of time, an obituary in The Times.

From a different point of view, this version of the story is too harsh. He was a Fellow of University College for thirty-eight years, an Emeritus Fellow for a very long time indeed, and the longest-lived Fellow of Univ – in a college whose history goes back to 1249. That is a modest achievement of a kind. Much more important were his gifts as a tutor and as a supporter of the younger members of the College, something conveyed to his family on several occasions, and as witnessed by the flood of letters from many correspondents after his death recording an appreciation of what George had taught them, or the fruits of his guidance.

Yet none of this makes him worthy of a written life. He did start an autobiography, beginning at the beginning in New Zealand, and breaking off in the early 1940s when he is at Auckland University College, which suggests a realisation on his part that his life written in a conventional way would be tedious. Nor was the prose necessary for an autobiography really his forte. He did have writing gifts, but they went into his historical writings, addresses and letters. Furthermore, his real gift was for speaking, and by good fortune in 2002 the New Zealand Rhodes Scholars' Oral History Project chose to do a long interview with him in his own home. This bewitched his family, since so much we had not known came to light, and myself in particular, so much so that in 2005 I carried out my own long interview with him, principally about Oxford after the war. Unedited these tapes have their *longeurs* but a properly edited version, rather than an autobiography, is *echt* GLC.

So, no biography, nor autobiography, no 'me memoir'. However, on his death, my sister Sarah and I rescued a considerable number of papers from his study with the task of considering what to do with them, and while I pondered this, the covid pandemic arrived, bringing with it lockdown. Isolation gave us the opportunity of reading the material, and continued isolation – the pandemic it turned out was not 'over by Christmas' – the leisure to select what might be made into a book. This is the result.

Is it fiction or non-fiction? At first sight it is resolutely the latter, and yet this may be an illusion: first of all memory, that unreliable faculty, may strive to get the details of incidents accurate without always succeeding, a truth of which as an Ancient Historian he was vividly aware. Secondly, the recalling and recounting of events does not discourage artful elaboration to shape and adorn a narrative. Both memory and elaboration push the life story away from tedious literality towards a fascinating sense of the imagined. This book shows that George was alert to these factors. Underpinning the inherent untruthfulness of a life story is the reader's awareness that things have been omitted unconsciously, and suppressed – consciously. I have heard a lot from people who liked him, even loved him, virtually nothing from those who had a dislike of him – or if they did they did not pass it on to his son. To adapt Churchill's words, 'History is being kind to George, for his family and friends are writing it for him.' Yet there is an obvious conclusion to draw. Even if what we have is not true in every aspect, it is certainly *ben trovato*. Rather than anguish over what is true and what is not, much better to enjoy the story as it is.

So why publish this book at all? I publish it in honour of his style, his style of speaking, his style of writing. It may seem at first sight to be the product of mere filial piety, laudable but redundant, but then it will be of interest to many who knew him, both young and old, even if they are now less young and his contemporaries are virtually all departed. It may be filial delusion to think that even those who never knew him or have never even heard of him may find this book, or parts of it, of interest but then no harm is incurred if that turns out not to be the case.

To come back to a starting-point: families are interested in their own history. As my life went on, a New Zealand background seemed to become more important and George preserved a postcard I sent to him in January 2003 – he loved keeping postcards – encouraging him to commit some details of family history to paper. Secondly, I had been the recipient of many of his Oxford stories but lacking his gift for recall, I always fumbled the details. So I was not ungrateful that he kept telling them. My sister recounts how George, in regaling her with something, interrupted himself to ask her, 'Have I told you this before?' to which she replied, 'Many times,' an answer which somewhat disconcerted him without preventing him from telling her again. For my part I felt there was something precious here: there is a particular place for anecdotal history, since it can so illuminate a culture in a way that official history does not, and finding him discouraged in his last decade by the yawning abyss of life without his wife Pat I suggested, reasonably firmly, that he should write the stories down. He seemed dismissive but the idea did bear fruit because it was subsumed into his project to write regularly to his friend, George Engle, published here as 'Letters to Gorgo' (for further details, see the introduction to that section).

George's character – or to use a modern concept, his 'identity' – emerges from these pages. To recapitulate the main points, he had a Presbyterian upbringing, especially imparted by his Scottish mother, in Auckland in the 20s and 30s. This was not stifling as it happened, for it gave birth to his fierce ambition to escape from New Zealand. The move to England brought him from the periphery to the centre of the Empire. He once recounted to me some details of his visit to Lord's cricket ground in 1947 to watch the Varsity Match between Oxford and Cambridge, the details of which now seem fantastical in their way. It had been a one-day outing for him, and quite a number of undergraduates from Oxford went to the game. Keen undergraduates would go for three days, and indeed George did so subsequently, 'keen in a simple way'. They gathered in the drinks tent to the right of the pavilion (as you looked out from it). The pre-war world was gone, and matches after the war less of a social occasion. He remembers a close friend of his reciting bits of poetry, probably 'Gloucestershire come north' and 'I fled him down the night and down the day'.

'The first impression,' he told me, 'was of the beautifully cut grass. The ground looked very beautiful, and if you paid, you could use the pavilion. There was a bar in the Long Room. I found it very engaging, especially in the seats up behind the bowler's arm.' He later remembered seeing Clive van Ryneveld bowling leg spin at Lord's from the top deck of the pavilion which gave him 'some thrill'.

'It was a "college conscious" time. All the undergraduates were wearing college ties, and I wore a Christ Church tie or possibly a Vincent's tie. You looked at the tie and then looked up to see the face above it.

'I stayed until the close of play. The weather had been beautiful all day.'

The world depicted in these pages is a receding one, not just George's memory of Lord's after the war. The intriguing portrait of Charlie Hignett, bachelor don, Fellow in Ancient History at Hertford College, who became a mentor to him when George first went to Univ, evokes a different world. Similarly the parade of figures from the decades just after the war (for example Dacre Balsdon) is both recognizable as part of an unchanging tradition but also curiously far from the twenty-first century. This is another reason to preserve George's acute recall of Oxford anecdotes, specimens in a display cabinet from which he pulls back the curtain.

It is a feature of all societies, including that of New Zealand, that they do not stand still. If he had stayed there George would have enjoyed a very different career, with different emphases and different significances. On the other hand, British public life has a particular dynamism, for better or for worse. Here at its centre he confronted the end of Empire, the end to deference, the onset of radical causes, student unrest even in Oxford, the travails of the 1970s, the advent of Thatcherism (welcome, to his mind), then Blairism (unwelcome, to his mind). Then he was into his last decade when his mortality and how it should be thought about and written about became a major preoccupation. Secondly, his conservatism was therefore both of the small 'c' and the large 'C' kind. He held forthright views, but life and Oxford taught toleration. Above all, he concluded that the individual was of more importance than any cause he or she espoused. Thirdly, there is a narrative thread through this book about his religion, which has quite a conventional twentieth-century arc, since he was brought up in the atmosphere of the Christian faith, but by the end it could be said that he was an atheist. Yet this does not capture it. He was not a card-carrying Oxford atheist; he was essentially an agnostic – see chapter 9 with its two sermons he delivered around 1970; up to the end of his life he assiduously attended chapel in Univ, practising what one might call 'social Anglicanism'. What struck me in studying all this material was his reverence for Philosophy as the supreme subject in Oxford, and his experience of it over several decades caused him to feel that the arguments for a rational belief in God lay in ruins, while not diminishing the pleasure he derived from those ruins.

One other vital aspect of his character needs to be remarked. In a visit to the Château de la Ferté St Aubin in Burgundy he had come across the motto of Catherine de Clermont: *sic omnes, ego non*. It seems to have been a revelation, putting into the pithiest of phrases his own position: 'As all [think] I do not.' In particular it underpinned his conclusion about life and experience: we have to think for ourselves, not be content with purloining the thoughts of others. This idea got crystallised in the bizarre book cover of his selected essays on Ancient Greek History, 'Cyrene to Chaeronea', published in 2011 when he was 92: he chose the figure of Heracleitus as depicted in Raphael's 'School of Athens', the fresco painted for the Stanza della Segnatura in the Vatican. Heracleitus would not necessarily have been among the most congenial figures from the ancient world to him, indeed a 'difficult colleague', but the depiction of him sitting apart in Raphael's painting suited his mood at the end of life, a visual counterpart to Catherine de Clermont's motto.

George's capacity for memorising poetry (chunks of it, not just lines) and quotations was practised to the end of his life, as evidenced by chapter 11, 'Quotations shored against his ruin'. Even if there is a preponderance of the classical, they are at the same time wide-ranging. Their most arresting quality is the constant recurrence of poetic ideas about mortality. This leads in well to the lengthy 'Letters to Gorgo' in Part 2, written between 2013 and 2016 to his friend George Engle. Do they make the book lopsided on the grounds that as many pages are devoted to the last decade as to the eight previous ones? Yet the matter can be considered very differently: the time for action gives way to the time for reflection. Here many incidents from his past life are recapitulated, here are displayed his sheer pleasure at Oxford wit, here his capacity for 'hamming' his life up, here finally, and most movingly, his experience of the perils of old age.

I should give some advice about how to read this book. It will be apparent that while certainly it can be read by beginning at the beginning and ending at the end, it by no means has to be read that way. The list of contents is important as signposting different aspects of his life (and the index may help as well) so that the reader has the liberty to select what interests her or him in what to read. It is even a bedside book which may be dipped into. However it is used, I hope it will offer an intriguing glimpse into a special kind of world, not unattractive at a time when the tectonic plates of the earth shift and grind, a world not to be mourned but celebrated, which is still worth recovering and re-creating.

Note: The initials **NZRSOHP** stand for 'New Zealand Rhodes Scholars Oral History Project' and mark those extracts from the long interview conducted by Hugo Manson for the Project in April 2002.

Other interview extracts marked as **TGC interview** are taken from the interview I conducted with George between June 2005 and April 2006.

Tim Cawkwell / Norwich / July 2022

ACKNOWLEDGEMENTS

My first thanks go to my sister Sarah, both for encouraging me to bring this book to fruition in published form, and for her sensible advice. My thanks too to my brother Simon and sister-in-law Anne for their support. Both sister and brother helpfully defrayed the costs of digitising a substantial amount of material. Still on family matters, Emma Roebuck, George's grand-daughter, designed the cover with her customary flair.

The digitisation of the material was carried out professionally and efficiently by Alice Ahearn and Olivia Thompson, and Alice gave further help in carrying out a thorough proofread in June/July 2022, and in resolving my stumbling efforts at mastering the Greek keyboard.

In the Oxford academic community, Professor Christopher Pelling, first a pupil of George's then a fellow classicist in the University, helped me resolve a large number of queries with accurate and judicious advice. Similarly, his colleague at Univ, Robin Darwall-Smith, the College Archivist (among other posts held in the University), put me right on a number of points. I am grateful to Lucy Rutherford, the Archivist of Hertford College, for information on Charles Hignett which might otherwise have eluded me.

One of the starting points for this project was our family's wish to give wider circulation to the interviews with George conducted by Hugo Manson in 2002 on behalf of the New Zealand Rhodes Scholars Oral History Project. We are beholden to them for their initiative in doing this, and indeed to Hugo's skill in drawing from George a considerable body of reminiscence which might otherwise have escaped his family.

My debt to the Engle family is explained in the introduction to Part 2 (pages 158-61).

Finally, I am moved to praise Amazon rather than bury it, or try to bury it. Without its self-publishing platform and its 'print on demand' facility, this book would have been much less likely to have seen the light of day.

TIMELINE

1919	born in Auckland, New Zealand (25 October)
1928?-32	King's Preparatory School
1933-7	King's College
1938	Auckland University
1941	BA in Latin and Greek (First class)
1942	MA (awarded November 1941) in Greek; awarded Fowlds Memorial Medal (given annually to the most distinguished student for a Master's degree)
1942-5	war service in Pacific with 3rd Fijian Infantry Regiment (NZ Expeditionary Force) – moments of action on Bougainville in the Solomons.
1945	New Zealand Rhodes Scholar
1945	married Patricia St John Clarke, Auckland (17 Oct.)
1946-9	Christ Church, Oxford University
1946	son Simon born
1946 & '47	Oxford University Rugby Blue
1947	one rugby cap for Scotland
1948	son Timothy born
1948	First in Greats
1949	appointed Fellow and Praelector of University College, Oxford
1950	daughter Sarah born

1951-8	Senior Treasurer of College Amalgamated Clubs
1955	first Cawkwell Dining Club (later the GLC Dining Club)
1956-66	Fellow Librarian
1959-60	Greats Dining Club formed
1966-7	Senior Tutor (first tenure)
1967-71	Dean of Graduates
1969-2001	oversaw Bentham Dining Club
1970-4	Senior Tutor (second tenure)
1972	new introduction to Xenophon's 'Anabasis (The Persian Expedition)' (Penguin Books)
1975-81	Dean of Degrees (first tenure)
1978	publication of 'Philip of Macedon' (Faber and Faber)
1978	new introduction to Xenophon's 'Hellenica (A History of My Times)' (Penguin Books)
1980-5	Vice-Master (under Mastership of Arnold Goodman)
1987	Honorary degree from Washington and Lee University, Virginia, USA
1987	retired as Fellow and Praelector
1987-8	Procurator initiating fundraising campaigns among old members
1988-99	Dean of Degrees (second tenure)
1989-95	resumed tutoring until 'second retirement' in 1995

1991	publication of 'Georgica: Greek studies in honour of George Cawkwell' ed. Michael A Flower and Mark Toher (Institute of Classical Studies, University of London)
1992	ceased lecturing
1997	publication of 'Thucydides and the Peloponnesian War' (Routledge)
1998	awarded Runciman Prize
1998	creation of Cawkwell Fellowship in Ancient History, endowed by Univ old members
2005	publication of 'The Greek Wars: the failure of Persia' (Oxford UP)
2008	death of Patricia
2011	publication of 'Cyrene to Chaeronea: selected essays on Ancient Greek History' (Oxford UP)
2019	died at his home in north Oxford (18 February)

[When in the late 1970s George was asked to supply an overview of his career by Faber & Faber, who had commissioned his first book, he could not resist spicing up the dates he listed with the following comments:

'Unlike Philip, only one wife (a New Zealander).
Unlike Demosthenes, fond of wine.
Unlike Isocrates, lectures with vigour.
Speaks after dinners at the drop of a cork.

Enjoys the company of undergraduates and is prickly with those who criticise them.

Loves Oxford with single-minded passion, and is really at ease only with those who share it, but tries with others.

His heroes are Thucydides, Epaminondas and Philip.

Distrusts heroes.

Takes a tempered view of Alexander the Great.

Claims to be the reincarnation of Xenophon.

Would like some time to catch a fish.

Fishes constantly.

Has written a good many articles about Greek history, especially the fourth century, and caused apoplexy amongst admirers of Demosthenes.

Proposes to continue the bad work.']

PART ONE

THE PULL OF OXFORD

1 EARLY YEARS IN NEW ZEALAND

['Nostra Vita' ('our life') is a fragment of a memoir George started but never finished. It only covers the years up to Auckland University, but since this was a period of his life he did not talk about greatly and then only fragmentarily, these pages have a particular value.]

Childhood in Auckland

I was born in Auckland, New Zealand on 25 October 1919, and like the great Julius Caesar and like my sister, Peggy, three years earlier, I was born by Caesarian section. Such an effortless entry into the light of day is commonly supposed to produce a child of notably equable temperament. Caesar was indeed a cool customer. I have never deserved such a description.

We lived in an average-sized New Zealand house, weatherboarded and so in that climate demanding regular and frequent repainting, though I don't recall a single occasion of this happening, and also corrugated iron-roofed so that when it rained the noise was quite impressive. There was quite a large garden with an orchard full of fruit trees, lemons in constant supply, russet apples, Gravenstein, peaches, nectarines, plums in ample supply, and then there was the 'back paddock' as it was always referred to. It too was full of fruit trees, and my father was forever gathering the fruit to take to the Auckland Hospital and to the Knox Home (for the aged). He also had a large henhouse, probably twenty feet by twelve, and another cage for the bantam hens of which he was very fond. For a while he kept guinea pigs. I don't know for what purpose, but probably he just liked the creatures. Population problems ended that and we were back to the bantams, but what with the ducks quacking and the cocks crowing it was quite rural. Between the house and the back paddock there was quite an ample vegetable garden with potatoes galore, kumara, sweetcorn, tomatoes eternally, it seems now, in fruit, beans of various sorts etc. Indeed he used to get up early at 5 a.m. and work in the garden before breakfast at 6 or 6.30. I wish I could see it all so clearly as I saw it long ago. There was a corrugated iron shed, where once the carriage had been housed, as well as 'the back lane' which provided egress for this vehicle, and at the back of this shed there was an outside lavatory which was termed 'the dunny'. Since our house had, I think, been occupied by my grandmother, one has a picture of a late Victorian household, passing into the Edwardian and Georgian. For there was a garage in which the Vauxhall Whippet, or similar economical vehicle, which needed to be cranked into action, a troublesome business for one with a hernia as he had, and once he got the hose of the petrol pump at Gash's garage hooked around a bumper and as he moved off, the whole 'bowser', as it was termed, came down. He was perhaps more suited to the Victorian colony than to the Georgian dominion, no matter how many Dominion Days he lived through or how often he drove along Dominion Road to Sandringham (but not where George V shot grouse). I must not omit the washhouse where the washing was done by my mother. Every Monday 'the copper' was boiled with a fire underneath it. There were two tubs and a wringer. Finally the mangle! Scene of great labours, but typical enough of New Zealand houses in that period. The clothes dried on 'the back grass', on lines held up with props. Finally there was a sort of lean-to at the back of the washhouse where for a period Uncle Willie, my father's brother, slept – of whom more later.

I spent my free time riding a 'bike' on the road or playing with other boys in the neighbourhood. There was every so often the great alarm of a grass fire. The property bordered on the main express line from Auckland to Remuera and all stations southward to Wellington. 'The Limited', as the train that went each night to Wellington was called, though in what sense it was limited I never inquired, would come up the hill from Newmarket station sending forth from its funnel a cloud of sparks which in dry weather and in late summer would set the grass on the bank on fire, not such a danger as I looking out of my bedroom window imagined. On the other side of the railway line was Frankham's timber yard and one dramatic night it caught fire and there was an impressive blaze, 'Götterdämmerung' finale to me, but we survived unscorched.

Occasionally I would go up onto Mt Hobson, an extinct volcano. Auckland had several such, and I would play there with friends. In a field at the foot of it, on Hobson Road, I was scarred for life. A boy picked up a horseshoe and tossed it over his shoulder crying, 'Here's luck.' It got me and I bear to this day its mark on my head. But the luck was not always one way. There was a boy who lived on the Remuera Road. I threw a stone which broke one of his front teeth. Fortunately in those days such damage was not to be repaired in the courts.

Family

I greatly regret that I hardly knew my father. He died in 1932 aged 62 and I was too young to realise what an interesting person he was or even to ask any questions about his life.

From prizes in his library I learned that he had attended Auckland Grammar and had shown ability in Classics, but that is all I know of his schooling. His father, William Joseph Cawkwell, died in 1880 and he may have had to leave school early. Thereafter there is a huge gap. I know he worked for a while in Sydney and at some point he became a pharmacist, but I fancy he learned that on the job. He started a chemist's shop in Newmarket, Auckland, and prospered sufficiently to be able to go 'home', to Edinburgh, very much the centre in those times of medical studies. He qualified at some date around 1910 or 1911 and returned to New Zealand to practise in Auckland. He was, I imagine, a capable medical practitioner but not greatly successful, financially speaking. In Auckland Hospital he was the doctor responsible for infectious diseases, principally scarlet fever and diphtheria, both very dangerous in those pre-antibiotic times. Indeed he had to have the forefinger, I think, of his left hand amputated and he always suspected that the nurse responsible for providing washing facilities at the fever wards had not put in the necessary disinfectant. He used to wear a leather pad over the amputated stump.

Before the Labour government of 1935 set up a national health scheme, doctors had to send out accounts monthly and I remember this regular labour of preparing and posting. He had many 'bad debts' as one can readily imagine and when he died and my mother was not well provided for, she had the chagrin of seeing people getting around untroubled by the fact that they owed him, and thus her, quite substantial sums. One I remember owed £200 which in 1932 was a large sum of money. When the Labour government did 'nationalise' health in the face of considerable opposition from the medical profession, she said to me,

'I'm glad your father isn't alive; it would have killed him.' It would actually have been the saving and the making of him.

He was, I believe, a dear and good man. He got on wonderfully well with the various workmen who were regularly called on to do odd jobs round the house. There was, for instance, Alf Smart the plumber, a Cockney I think, with whom my father maintained a lively banter, principally based on Alf having left a shift-spanner in a cistern. There was endless laughter on this topic. 'Oh Doctor, you are a caution,' Alf would say. Then too there was Gib Wright, the carpenter. He was a follower of the Salvation Army, and was given to homely philosophy. I remember 'know thyself' was given as the root of happiness, though I don't think he had any awareness of Greek philosophy. Anyhow there was always good humour with his tradesmen, a lesson which I laid to heart.

He died a devoted Anglican. He had not always been so, but he was educated in this regard by his family, or rather by my mother and sister. Mother was a Scottish Presbyterian and there came a day when Peggy, of whom he was deeply fond, said to him and her, 'Why is it that Mummy goes to Luke's Church and I go to Mark's Church and Daddy goes to no church?' (St Luke's was the Presbyterian church about half a mile away on the Remuera Road; St Mark's was the Anglican on the corner of St Mark's Road and Remuera Road about three hundred yards distant.) My father riposted, 'Out of the mouths of babes and sucklings cometh forth wisdom. From now on we'll all go to St Mark's.' That was where I would later sing in the choir – which had quite an effect on me. At that time the vicar was the Reverend George Craig Cruikshank, 'Crooky' as he was always referred to. He had been a much-admired chaplain to the Forces in the horrors of France. It is not too much to say that Father loved him and he certainly fixed my father's religious practice for the rest of his life.

My father was bookish, and he used to read me bits of Longfellow, that late Victorian favourite. I remember especially 'King Robert of Sicily'. He was constantly reading and rereading, as if he was painting the Forth Bridge, Thomas Carlyle's 'French Revolution', another great Victorian favourite. Indeed I imagine that the family he grew up in was not unlettered.

In 1932 came the dreadful discovery that he had 'the Dread Disease' as cancer was then referred to. I think he had had a hernia for some time and, as the fashion then was, he wore a truss, and when he was being operated on for that, it was discovered that he had cancer of the bladder. When the news was communicated to me, I simply brushed it aside. I fear I was not deeply touched, and it is only in later life that I realise how much we lost. At the time I simply did not begin to share the misery of my mother and my sister.

The Cawkwells certainly were a curious lot. So little do I know of them that I cannot even get them in the right order. I think my father was the oldest, then came my Aunt Alice, then Aunt Elsie, then Uncle Charlie. Where Uncle Willie fitted in I have no idea. My grandfather William Joseph Cawkwell was born, I believe, in 1837 and lived in south London until he went out to the new colony, on his own I think, and therefore he must have gone no earlier than 1854. What he did in his first ten years is quite obscure, but by 1870 not only had he married and become father of my father but also in October of that year he had begun distilling whisky at the Crown Distillery near the Auckland waterfront. He was proud of his product which was made 'until the axe fell' (the phrase comes from 'The New Zealand Whisky Book' by Stuart Perry) and he was bought out. The 'axe' was the duty imposed on his whisky by the Vogel government in 1871. I don't know whether to bemoan the loss of such glittering prospects of wealth or to be thankful. That is all I know about him save that he was reputed to have played some part in the Maori Wars and indeed to have received a grant of land at Pokeno, about forty miles south of Auckland on the Great South Road, as well as a grant of swampy ground elsewhere, the location of which I never ascertained. (The land at Pokeno, on which no tax was ever paid, was allowed to be swallowed up by a surrounding farm, now rather to my relief, for I would not wish to be in receipt of stolen goods.) I presume he joined the Auckland Militia and Volunteers and did whatever he did in the invasion of Waikato in or around 1863 (cf. James Belich, 'The New Zealand Wars' (Auckland University Press 1986)). That is really all I know. At least I am comforted that his whisky was good.

In Victorian times an estate was not divided up equally in the modern way by valuing the whole and giving each an equal portion. Rather the estate was portioned out in the will. After my grandmother's death around 1910, my father as the eldest received the family house in St Mark's Road, and his sister Alice property in the centre of Auckland, perhaps a leftover from grandfather's Crown Distillery. I am uninformed as to the portions of the others. Uncle Willie spent his years working out on bits of paper what he should have received, and the others may have had their complaints. By the time my grandmother died the values of the various portions had changed considerably. Thus Aunt Alice with her property in downtown Auckland was very prettily placed and there was a fair amount of jealousy. This may have been the cause of the lack of any close bonding in the family. Maybe they were just a contentious lot.

Aunt Alice was the one my father was fondest of. He referred to her as 'Mrs Poof' but that signified little. My father was very given to using nicknames for his brothers and sisters, and I don't think he (or they) put much importance on it. He also for a period called her (but not to her face) 'Mrs Six Percent'. That was because he borrowed money off her and had to pay, as was entirely proper, the market rate, though it was a good lesson to me not to borrow or lend within the family. She certainly lived comfortably and, because of her prosperity, she had time for a weekly excursion into Auckland to the Dickens Club, and I suspect that if I had known her better I would have found her an interesting person.

Aunt Elsie was a bit of an eccentric. Whether she had ever had a man in her life or not, she was always spoken of as an 'old maid', unkindly when one considers how many possible husbands had been killed in the War, and her odd ways were thought to be 'typical old maid'. I only know stories. For example, invited for supper she would arrive at near bedtime and Father would slam the door in her face. Relations were always fraught. I remember going out to Sherwood Rise for afternoon tea on Sunday and Elsie had hidden behind the curtain in the sitting room. 'Come out, you old frump,' cried my father, and as Elsie tried to get out of the room he pulled her nose, with Aunt Alice protesting mildly. At other times he called her 'steak-face'. These names were not to be taken too seriously. I think he and his brother Charlie both went in for name-calling and these verbal assaults were not so offensive as they seem. She lived in a succession of bed-sitters. When she died, she was found not to have made a will and so I received a sum sufficient to take me and Pat to Greece in 1952, and then when I finally succumbed to the desire to purchase the cabinet to stand in our hall and which I had eyed for some days in Audley Miller's antique furniture shop in the High but which I really should not have bought, the next day a further distribution to her heirs arrived precisely enough to cover the cost of my folly. This extra arrived because a further sum of money had been found hidden in her waste-paper basket. She was an eccentric indeed, and she had I fancy a nice sense of humour. I only wish I had known her better.

Uncle Charlie, Charles Augustus Cawkwell, was near in age to my father and indeed in boyhood they had been inseparable. They were 'Cutsy' and 'Pursey', the indivisible cutpurse, but when they grew up they were less close, to put it mildly. I know only what my mother had to tell. The stories tended to end up 'and your father booted him off the premises'. When Father returned from his medical education in Scotland, he was met by Charlie and taken to supper in the Centreway Restaurant, where Father was dismayed to observe the familiarity between Charlie and one of the waitresses, not at all *comme il faut* in Father's book. I think the waitress was Isa, whom Charlie married *en deuxièmes noces*, referred to *chez nous* as the Woman. Charlie uttered some notable *dicta*. He and the Woman sought to divorce. The judge told them to go home and try harder. (They did and lived together not necessarily unhappily ever after.) Asked in court by the judge what was the root of his discontent, Charlie said, 'The woman wants motor-cars and diamonds and she won't get them out of Charlie Cawkwell,' a remark treasured in our house, but the report of the case in 'New Zealand Truth', a sort of 'News of the World', produced shame and embarrassment for Father. Charlie was clerk to the Waitemata County Council and the billboards advertised the case in these words: 'The Carking Cares of County Clerk Cawkwell'. Mother said, 'Your father hung his head in shame as he walked down Queen Street.' We were certainly a family in which respectability was highly valued – as it was generally in 1920s New Zealand. But in truth I know nothing of my uncle save what my not unprejudiced parents had to say.

I come to Uncle Willie. He was deficient in intelligence, and had never done a proper job. My grandmother used to indulge him. 'Don't overwork, Willie. Come home to tea.' But he was simple and she was probably only making the best of a bad job. Father as the senior son felt it his responsibility to look after Willie, and for years he lived with us though I expect he enjoyed it no more than we did. We tried to disown him. He was to be seen walking along, stopping, starting to pick up a bit of paper, thinking better of it and walking on, stopping, going back to the piece of paper, again thinking better of it, finally going back, picking the paper up and putting it in his pocket. I have no idea what this psychological disease was. Obsessive curiosity? Anyhow we children were ashamed of him. After a while, Father arranged for him to go into the Salvation Army Home that was not far away, but horror of horrors on the most direct route for Peggy to go to school. Grave embarrassment indeed. He finally died in that home, though I don't remember when, and Peggy and I and I expect other children of brothers and sisters received a petty sum of money. So lived and died William Dodson Cawkwell. He was a burden to my parents.

Mother

My mother, Isabella Given Kemp, was born in 1880, married my father in 1913 and died in 1952. I owe so much to her that I can hardly bring myself to write of her. She was born, and lived until she left for New Zealand, in Edinburgh. She had two brothers and two sisters and they were all very close. But her father who had a decent position, I believe, in Bartholomew's, the celebrated Edinburgh publishing firm, took to the bottle, lost his job, and finally had to be ejected from the family. Mother always referred to him as 'the Old Man' (a common enough Victorian usage), but her mother, 'Mama', had, I fancy, a hard time of it as the Drink took over. She took lodgers, one of whom was George Cawkwell, and so Bella set off in 1912 for the other side of the world, never to see her native land again. She would sit down every Sunday and write to each of her sisters but that was her only contact with Scotland. I always think of her when I see that painting of Burne-Jones, 'A Last View of England', a family on the deck of a sailing ship looking back at their vanishing past. In the New Zealand of my youth all comfortably-placed citizens aimed to have 'a trip home' some time, but my father was not comfortably placed and Mother had nothing to hope for. She always spoke of Edinburgh as 'the most beautiful city in the world'. It was the only city she had actually seen. She would speak of the Trossachs but I fancy Cramond was her longest journey, about five miles, until she set off for Liverpool in late summer 1912.

She never really took to New Zealand. Partly I expect she was homesick for Scotland and her family and partly she felt the Cawkwells never really took to her. They certainly were an odd lot and she may have been right about it. I have only her side of the story. New Zealand in my youth was quite a class-conscious society though New Zealanders would have denied it. Doctors and lawyers, in the absence of an aristocracy, took themselves very seriously and perhaps she, coming from a humbler world after her father's decline, was quite lowly and felt herself a bit beneath such pretensions. Whatever the cause, she pined for home. She once said to me of New Zealanders, 'They eat meat for breakfast, meat for lunch and meat for dinner. That's why they're such animals.' My father, having set up in practice over the age of forty, was rather odd in the Auckland medical fraternity. He had his friends, but probably felt himself a latecomer and socially he preferred his home. So she did not, I think, have any friends among the medical wives.

When my father died after twenty years of marriage, she was very much alone. She had been left not well off and so she took to letting a couple of rooms. She felt that demeaning, and demeaning it is to those who consider it demeaning, but she had the determination of a tigress to provide for her young, which mostly meant me. Peggy on my father's death left school and got a job as an assistant to our family dentist. So she was on the providing side while I was the consumer. I was sent to King's College and it must have been a struggle to pay the fees and all the incidental fripperies of a boy in the First XI for three years and the First XV for two, during which time Peggy was walking to and from Newmarket to save a halfpenny on the fare. When I think of how little I did to help and sustain my mother in those years I can only blush with shame.

But she coped and, as many men have done, I look back on her with something more than filial piety. In one special regard I am deeply indebted. She had been a teacher, at James Gillespie's school in Edinburgh, and she was an excellent teacher. At home each evening in term she supervised my doing prep. I was, and am, a lazy person and I would have performed in only a middling way if I had not had her teaching. But I always came top in that little world and it was she who set me on my winning way. God bless her memory. God came into it too. She was a devoutly religious person and, before I left the house on a day of examinations, she required me 'to go and commit my ways to the Lord'. I did and, though one might deplore that sort of religion, it worked – though it contributed to my appallingly 'pi' attitudes.

I should mention that she was a decent pianist, and the piano was a central part of our home. On Sunday evenings she would play and I would sing Scottish songs like 'Buy my caller herring', but also Irish and English songs, and this was a large influence on me. There was no real classical music in the diet; indeed apart from an early gramophone no means of reproduction of sound. The only records we had were such pieces as Mischa Elman playing 'Träumerei' and the like, and when my father died I was taken up with silly popular songs. Only when I went to university did I begin to appreciate the real stuff. But in my youth she did provide quite a lot of music of a sort and I am indeed beholden to her for this too.

I had left New Zealand by the time of her end. She lived with my sister Peggy who with her husband Bert looked after her most wonderfully until it came to the moment that Peggy had to commit her to an old people's home, a case of some sort of dementia, I suppose. Sad indeed, and I must draw a veil over her end. She was a good, good woman.

His accent

The great decision in our family – where to send me to school – was not a matter of debate. My parents could have sent me easily to Remuera Primary School, part of the state system and without question a good school by reason of its catchment area, but they chose the private school, King's Preparatory School, a Church of England school. But the choice was easy. They wanted their son to be educated in the habits of a gentleman. In general they regarded young New Zealanders as uncouth and ill-mannered and they detested the New Zealand accent. Indeed they went further and had me go to elocution lessons with the formidable Miss Bruce. She saw to it that I talked 'English' and not 'New Zealand'. I had to read to her critical ear and to recite poetry. (The two pieces I remember were 'Come to me, you with the laughing eyes' and Kipling's 'One man in a thousand, Solomon says...') This had quite an effect on me and

I am never surprised when people say to me, 'You don't sound New Zealand.'

[The matter of George's accent was probed by Hugo Manson in the NZRSOHP, as this exchange shows:

HM: How did they both speak, your parents?
GC: My mother had Scottish speech, though I was not aware of it. People always commented on her. She was from Edinburgh, and she was markedly Scottish, but it didn't strike me. My father was just ordinary New Zealander, I expect. He didn't have an especially affected voice.
HM: And what about the evolution of your own speech?
GC: Ah, now, my own speech... Partly, of course, my parents wanted me educated at other than the state schools. I was sent first of all to King's Preparatory School, and then to King's College, Otahuhu, and I'm not sure what motive there was. I think it was partly the feeling that I should go to a church school and I should have a proper religious education, but more than that it was that I should have the manners of a gentleman. I think it was their feeling that New Zealand was uncouth and crude and so on, so that's why I was sent to these schools, and so getting there, speech was a little bit different. Although I didn't have the extremes of New Zealand speech, there was also this elocution business. My mother had so disliked New Zealand speech – slightly reflecting her attitude to my father's family – that I always spoke slightly what in Britain they call 'posh', I expect. So that cut me off in a sense from my world. I think if I was doing it all again, I would think that it was better for a person to have been sent to Auckland Grammar, to have talked like a true New Zealander, and not been as it were separated out in a sort of self-imagined elite.
HM: You actually had elocution lessons?
GC: I had elocution, when I was about eleven, I think. I went to a woman called Bruce and I used to recite poems etc. That was one thing about my education that I am very grateful for. At King's Prep and King's College, there was a lot of public performance – debates, plays – and I was performing, and you learn a great deal. Of course I longed to be out playing cricket, which I couldn't do; it was rather awful to be missing out on that glorious activity, but I was really getting the neces-

sary confidence for public speaking. I've done a lot of public speaking of one sort or another in my life, and I really did benefit greatly from that at school, and I think possibly the opportunities afforded by King's Prep and College were greatly to my advantage.

HM: Can you remember any particular lesson in the business of public speaking and presenting yourself from those days?

GC: No, I didn't have lessons in public speaking, I just taught myself. The first public speech I made was at about the age of eleven to twelve. I gave a talk to the class about Hannibal. It lasted two minutes. [laughs] But it was my first public speech, and since then I've made many public speeches. I think you just have to teach yourself. Though I could teach people quite a bit now, no one ever taught me; I just had to learn.

But quite apart from these elocution lessons, the whole ethos and values of King's Prep were Anglocentric, and so I grew up somewhat alienated from ordinary New Zealanders and, I fear, thinking myself a cut above them. We were bidden to raise our caps 'to a lady' and give up one's seat on a tram to grown-ups. Our uniform was not markedly superior to that of the state schools, but we had to 'haul up our socks' and to say 'sir' etcetera and our 'best suit' involved an Eton collar and a boater. My father cleaned my shoes every day. As to religion at King's Prep, I went, or was sent, to Matins in the Chapel each Sunday in term, at the conclusion of which I had to rush along the Remuera Road to St Mark's to sing in the choir. I never jibbed or rebelled. No wonder I became 'pi'. At one stage, when in the interregnum between two headmasters the celebrated Charlie Major who had had quite a hand in the foundation of the school took over, every day in Morning Prayers we had to recite what he termed 'the Gentleman's Psalm', Psalm 15. 'Lord who shall dwell in thy tabernacle and who shall rest upon thy holy hill? Even he that leadeth an uncorrupt life; and doeth the thing which is right and speaketh the truth from his heart.' I keep a copy of that too in my diary. This daily recitation too made a strong impression on me. One way or another I was brought up in a very religious environment, and I am grateful to my parents for that.

King's School and King's College, Auckland

From an early age I was smitten with desire to succeed at rugby football, though it was not until the British Lions tour of 1930 that I was really aware of who and what the All Blacks were. Over someone's radio or rather 'wireless', as it was then invariably called, I heard that the All Black scrum half, Mervyn Corner, small in stature, had tackled and laid out George Beamish, a really big (as I realised when I encountered him in 1946) Lions forward, and I and many a New Zealand boy dreamed not necessarily of glory but certainly of success. I began to go to Eden Park to watch club and provincial games from 1931 onwards. I was in a sense quite good, but lacked the ruthless determination of the top players. I can remember that years later when I was playing for the Auckland University side, I would be reciting Greek verbs as I jogged around. That is not the sort of person who gets to the very top of the game. I did play a few times for Auckland Province in the reduced competition for places during the War, and I had, in time, my moments, but basically I was not rough enough, or tough enough. Nor was I one for drinking with the boys. Indeed I remember feeling very shocked at what happened after my first game for the Auckland Junior Representatives in, I expect, 1938. It was in Te Aroha. Before the game all were pretty silent. After it, Lord Beer had taken over, food being tossed around in the dining room, the waitresses were being addressed with shocking to me familiarity, probably to them normal and welcome. In the morning there were patches of vomit around the hotel. I felt as I continued ever to feel that I did not and could not adapt to such society. At prep school, however, all this was in the future and I was full of ambition. I remember hearing the famous All Black, Freddie Lucas, saying on the wireless that 'when the scrum breaks up, the middle and back rows of the scrum must first of all run for their own corner-flag', and so this I did religiously. (It is, of course, all changed in modern rugby.) I meant to succeed and I did in a sense. I captained the prep school First XV and I played two years in the King's College First XV, which seemed glory, and in a sense was. My proudest moment, however, came in 1934 when as a not very large boy, indeed the youngest in the team, I played for Town House in the Inter-House competition at King's College. So I was into the national game early enough.

The real love of my life, athletically speaking, has however been cricket. I was in the First XI at King's College for three years and captain in my last year, 1937. I kept a cricket ball on my study table and I dreamed the game. At the prep school I didn't have much or do much, but that was because I had to attend rehearsals of plays in which I had a part. This did me a lot of good though I didn't realise it at the time, for it gave me practice at public performance and I early learned not to be nervous before audiences. My first public speech was a two-minute piece I had written on Hannibal and that was at the age of eleven, and all through my schooldays I was taking parts in plays. I remember one entitled 'Six Who Pass While the Lentils Boil' [a short play by Stuart Walker, which received its New York première in 1916.] The Queen was a tall boy called Coates Milsom and I was the little Boy. At one moment the Queen said to me in an imperious voice, 'Put it on, little Boy,' and I had to pick up her crown and put it on her head. This caused the assembled parents great hilarity and myself great misery. A similar situation occurred when I sang Nanki-Poo in 'The Mikado', which must have been in 1930 or 1931. The part of Yum-Yum was played by a very small boy called Shrubsell (at the College to be nicknamed 'the Tick') and I had to say to her, 'At last we are alone.' Great laughter from the audience, of course, great embarrassment for me. Public speaking and singing solo or duo in the chapel choir at King's Prep set me on a career of public performance, but back in 1932 I longed to be playing cricket. That came in ample measure once I went to the College and I have never got over my love of the game. One inextinguishable highlight was my watching the great Walter Hammond – oh what a hero he! – make 336 against New Zealand at Eden Park [in 1933], when he drove a spin bowler called Freeman out of the ground and virtually out of the game as he broke the then record for a score in a Test match. I did love it all and used to go to provincial games in Eden Park during my holidays.

In my years at King's Prep I was always top of the class – which is not good for anyone – and it was a pride and consolation to my devoted parents. In 1932 I sat the Scholarship Examination for the College but failed to win the lucrative Horton Scholarship. It was privately reported that I had got the best marks, but the award had been made to a boy from a remote country school who was some sort of descendant of Rutherford, the great physicist, and I suppose the College in fact guessed that he might have magically clever genes. But at King's Prep the Headmaster was greatly upset and it was decided that I should stay on at the Prep for another year and try for a scholarship to Wanganui Collegiate. Then in September my father died, and although I think I was in 1933 awarded a scholarship at Wanganui, it was not financially realistic for my mother to think of me going so far away from home. So at the start of the academic year 1934 I went to King's College as a day-boy.

One minor matter is worth record. In my first year at the College there was some sort of upset over one of the masters at the Prep of a homosexual nature. I had absolutely no idea of such things, but when Mother mentioned these accusations to me I remembered that there was a boy who said that he had been sitting on the master's knee and was invited to take his *membrum virile* in hand! The story had meant absolutely nothing to me at the time. When I told my mother, she said I was to go immediately and tell the Headmaster. I did so and the master was out by nightfall. (Of his subsequent history, I heard practically nothing save that he had married and gone farming. So one way or another dishonour was satisfied.) I mention the affair here, because it reflects the total innocence in which I grew up. I hardly knew the words 'buggery' and 'sodomy', let along having any idea of what they denoted. There were occasional hush-hush scandals in Auckland, but they were veiled from me. As to homosexuality between boys at the College, I never heard of any such thing. Such was the innocence and seclusion of my upbringing. But it wasn't only me. I and another boy were once invited to spend a week in a cottage on the island of Waiheke with the Headmaster and this later disgraced master. We went and had a very happy time and as far as I know no impropriety occurred. But no parent nowadays would avoid the most serious suspicions and no master would dream of proposing such a plan. At a later date at the College I spent a few days with my bachelor housemaster in his cottage at Mairangi Bay. What would be thought or said nowadays? It was a totally innocent world, and when I was in the army homosexual stories were meaningless. There was a song which ran, 'They were only playing leap-frog / When the one staff-officer jumped right over the other staff-officer's back.' It was baffling, unreal.

I went to King's College in 1934 as a day-boy. One travelled by train from Newmarket to Middlemore and back day by day, Saturdays included though not Sundays. New Zealand was in the full flush of the Depression and people were hard up. The general atmosphere of things was depressed and depressing. But it didn't affect me save that numbers at King's in 1934 were under 200 and, though I did not know it, the school was probably not too far from financial disaster. Academically things went along smoothly enough. I was good at Latin, but never in the top class.

I entered Parnell House as a boarder in 1935. It was Spartan. There were about thirty-five boys in the house and only one lavatory, though of course there was a pissoir. Cold showers in the morning. Rather strict rationing of laundry. The atmosphere was pretty philistine, and I was typical. There was one interesting boy, R. H. Parker, who wrote to the Archbishop of Canterbury declaring the Headmaster was a heretic. He got no reply. He said to me of another boy, 'He's an awful ignoramus. Do you know I found out that he had never heard of Aristotle?' Nor had I at that date, but I didn't say so. A friend of his and mine was Charles Wrigley who wrote a constitution. They were exceptional. Most of us knew nothing. Perhaps I was especially isolated because my mother was so isolated, but I heard nothing of the political movements of the time, and only vaguely did I know of Bolshevik politics. When I began to think for myself, I almost inevitably became a starry-eyed Socialist and there was no one to talk with me rationally and to impress on me the important truth that 'angry words betoken a weak cause'. That I learned at Oxford, slowly.

By 1936 I was Head Prefect of the House and a School Prefect. In 1937 I was Head Prefect of the School. In these positions I learned a bit about exercising command. I was in the First XV in 1936 and 1937 and in the First XI 1935, 1936 and 1937, but although I was captain in 1937 I was a poor captain. There was no master tactfully guiding one nor did I receive any cricket coaching. I expect I had some natural talent but also a very unhelpful temperament, which might have been helped by sensible advice. I was also Company Sergeant Major of the School Corps and I did benefit from that. I had to march the school up and down and around on the playing-field and so gained confidence in giving commands. There was also acting. I played Malvolio in 'Twelfth Night' in 1936, perhaps all too aptly cast, and Osborne, the genial and wise schoolmaster, in 'Journey's End' in 1937. At that date 'Journey's End' was quite new (it had premièred in London in 1928) and for the colonies very new. But it was all good experience, giving me confidence in public appearances. In all this I was lucky to be a big fish in a small pool. All I needed thereafter was to face the fact that I was no great fish. Slowly the truth has been revealed to me!

Sport

[from NZRSOHP]

HM: Was sport important? Did you like sport?

GC: Oh, sport was very important in New Zealand. Such reverence for rugby football, that I didn't ask myself did I like it; I did it. You had to succeed, and I was moderately successful – only moderately . . . My highest attainment, I expect, in New Zealand, was to play for Auckland Province in wartime, which was no bloody good at all, all the stars were away.

HM: Well, that shows a certain—

GC: Well, I was quite good in a way, and I got a great lesson there, I may say. And being a literal-minded lad I took it. I was once playing for the Auckland Junior Representatives, one season, and we trained indoors every Monday night, I think, up in the Ponsonby shed. There was a famous All Black called Freddie Lucas, and after we had had a notable win on the Saturday, he said, 'I'll tell you two things. Don't read reports of any game you've played in. And remember you're only half as good as you think you are.' Now I remember both of those things. I never read a report of a game I played in and I never even looked at the programme. I've played against some famous players, but I didn't actually know who was playing.

HM: What position did you play in?

GC: I played, in first-class rugby, every position in the scrum save hooker. So that, yes, I was just useless. 'Get in the pack!' [laughs]

HM: So you were forward rather than back?

GC: Forward, yes.

HM: What is the psyche of the forward?

GC: I expect you hunt in packs, you are violent, you are not expected to have great finesse, you are crude.

HM: Are you saying that was your style?

GC: No, I was a nothing, honestly. But I have played. In later times actually, when I came to Oxford I was a Blue, in 1946 and 1947, which was a big thing then, and then in a loose moment, the Scottish selectors, they came round the dressing room at Twickenham and said, 'Do you want to be considered for Scotland or England?' I said Scotland, because my mother was so very Scottish and I had this strong feeling of Scotland being half my home. And I said Scotland. I played and then we were beaten and so they dropped all the people from south of the border and that was that. But my heart wasn't in it, you see, I was concerned with Aristotle and Plato.

HM: But I mean it's a fascinating contrast, this forward play, rugby, international level and blues and so on, that must indicate a fairly aggressive side, or if not aggressive a strongly-motivated side.

GC: I don't know, one had to do it. The game I loved, and was not much good at, was cricket. I had my moments, but as a matter of fact I had practically no coaching in cricket. One sends one's son to these private schools and you find they don't get any bloody coaching at all. I didn't have any coaching at school, I was captain of the first XI, no one ever said anything to me about it, whether I was doing it wisely or not.

HM: But just before we leave the rugby, I mean, you can't become an international rugby player without having some love for it, can you? It can't all be by the way.

GC: I expect I quite enjoyed it, but it wasn't a love like the love of cricket. I dreamed cricket. I used to keep a ball in my desk when I was at King's College. I had it in my hand all the time. I expect I enjoyed the rugby, but it was very important to succeed. Rugby was the New Zealand religion, and I had to do it.

Eye on the Rhodes Scholarship

HM: Why did you have to succeed? What was that all about?

GC: I should say that at an early stage my eyes were on the Rhodes Scholarship.

HM: From very early on?

GC: From quite early. I remember, it happened when I was about ten, a woman said to me, 'You'll be aiming for a Rhodes Scholarship?' From that moment on I was aiming. It's the only ambition I've ever had, to be truthful. And having got here, like the people who went to Shangri-La, they lost the desire for outside. But I had that ambition, and of course you had to have manly sports on your CV so that was a bit of a stimulus, but most of all, it was a big thing at a boys' school in New Zealand to be in the first XV, and I was in the first XV for two years. I expect vanity was involved. You wanted to be regarded as a hero, or something of the sort.

HM: Or being pushed by your parents? Your mother?

GC: No, she knew nothing. She did once come and see me play, and she was shocked to hear someone say, 'There's that brute Cawkwell.' I wasn't a brute, but still, she heard that. Did me good, I mean, I can't be such a milksop as I really was.

HM: Leading up to say the age of fifteen or so, do you look back on any person who was a key guiding light? Maybe a friend or contemporary or teacher or mentor of some kind?

GC: The headmaster of the prep school in my time was a man called Beaufort. He had an effect on one. And I expect there were good masters at King's College who had an effect on one. I must say that I was very well taught, in that I was taught by good people, and they did have an effect.

*

HM: Going back to that very interesting point of what put you on the trail to Oxford was this woman by chance saying to you, 'I suppose you'll be going for a Rhodes Scholarship?'

GC: That started me, and of course you've got to remember that in those times in the thirties, there was no way out of New Zealand other than by the Rhodes Scholarship. There was a thing called the Commonwealth Scholarship, which I did actually get at a later stage and had to resign it when I got the Rhodes, but in general the only way out – to come to England – was by the Rhodes. Nowadays of course they go off to America, but that's a very significant shift in New Zealand life that that's a source of education and money, etcetera. That wasn't there in the thirties. I also had the feeling that I had to get out. It was a suffocating world. When I go to the Oxford railway station now and I'm saying goodbye to someone, I'm always saying privately, 'Thank God it isn't me.' But in Auckland, when I went down to the harbour, the wharf, to see someone off on the boat, I came away with an awful feeling of loss and desolation, because I wanted to get out, I wanted to go. And that was characteristic of the time, I think. I remember someone saying he couldn't wait to shake the dust of this country off his feet. Well, I thought that was very irreverent talk, that a New Zealander shouldn't talk like that, but there was some sort of feeling like that, you had to get away, had to get overseas.

HM: Were you unusual, do you think, amongst your peers in feeling this?

GC: Well, most of them hadn't the opportunity. I was going to have a chance of getting the Rhodes Scholarship, but those who didn't would just have to settle down and be there. The war made the difference.

. . . It was exceptional to be a boy at King's. Most people in Auckland were grammar school boys, either Auckland Grammar or Mount Alba Grammar or something. King's was exceptional. I mean, in a way I expect people thought that it was a bit of England, it was based on an English public school. And it was, in a way. It was inspired, I think, basically, by Rugby School. And Rugby School inspired schools all over the Empire. Bishop's College in Cape Town, South Africa which has a tie that is virtually the same as the Rugby tie, the colours a little bit differently combined. But Rugby was a great exemplar. And this affected King's. Though not so much I think Christ's, but King's was like that. And there was a feeling that it was different, and, I'm sorry to say, a feeling that it was a superior situation, I mean, people superior socially or superior something.

HM: So then going through school you were top of the class?

GC: Yes, I was very successful at school, I'm afraid, I was academically reasonably successful. I was not brilliant. I was at the top, but the top wasn't very high. There were boys who were cleverer than me, certainly, yes. But overall I was pretty successful. And then I was very successful athletically, as far as the school went, and after all King's College in the thirties was bloody near the rocks. Numbers were down because of the Depression, it was under 200. Of course that was a great opportunity for me . . . It was very bad for my character to be so successful.

*

HM: So as you were going through school, going through King's, apart from this quiet ambition to get the Rhodes Scholarship, what were you going to be when you grew up?

GC: Well, I'm sorry to say I was going to be a Rhodes Scholar. I expect I thought I was going to be a schoolteacher. My mother had been a schoolteacher, and I think there is something about genes and teaching. Far too didactic, my character, and so I think I was much impressed when young by reading that maxim of Bernard Shaw's, 'Those who can, do; those who can't, teach.' There's a great truth in that. But I was glad to have had a few moments—

HM: Is there a truth in that? I mean, that's constantly quoted and teachers get furious about it.

GC: It's absolutely true, it's absolutely true. The doers don't teach, they do. I do think that's so. But I was very glad therefore to have had a very trifling amount of war, which gave me a feeling I'd done something and now I could settle down and do no— and just teach, or study and read and so on. My greatest happiness in life is being in this room with these books. It always has been. All the games I've played, and I've played quite successfully, but they were nothing compared to being at home with my books, and in later times matched by being in the college.

Auckland University College 1938–41

[from 'Nostra Vita']

It was the best of times and it was the worst of times. Plainly enough there was going to be a war. One saw ominous programmes in newsreels of Germany's rise to power. There was the background of the Spanish Civil War, not very real to us and hardly ever discussed, but German and Italian forces were assisting Franco and even we could not avoid the feeling that this was a dress-rehearsal. There was constant talk of Spain amongst left-wingers at the university and some of it rubbed off. On the other hand there was the glorious feeling of being liberated. One was free to loaf and I did, alas. I spent quite a lot of time and effort on the student newspaper 'Craccum'. I enjoyed the insight into printrooms with the great trays of lead, a single piece per letter, for every piece was hand set. Then there were all the societies and evening meetings, very distracting but engaging. I played rugby for the University First XV and cricket for the so-called Senior B Side (and this greatly disappointed myself). Altogether it was an excitingly full life.

The idea of trying to win a Rhodes Scholarship had been put into my head when I was about ten, and I never wavered in my aspiration. Of course, once the War began in 1939, such ambitions were put in cold storage but I continued to hope that after the War I would go to Oxford. It is therefore surprising that I did not apply myself to my studies with more resolution. I certainly worked very hard when I got to Oxford, but previously I was very dilatory. I think that I thought all these extra-curricular activities were necessary but I neglected the central thing.

*

[from NZRSOHP]

HM: King's College 33–37, and your father had died, it's the world situation getting—

GC: Well, that's an interesting thing to me, that the Spanish Civil War, which was such a crisis for many people, it was never mentioned in our very restricted home in the 30s. My mother didn't know anything about it, and it wasn't till I got to university that I began to hear about it. I remember in the 30s I began to be very aware of the crisis in Europe. There was a series of newsreels in the cinema, 'The March of Time'. I remember seeing one about the occupation of the Ruhr, and the Rhineland, and a general feeling that things were coming, and of course when one got to the University one began to be very taken up with it, and like all young men of course I was very socialist, with no understanding or knowledge, but you know what Clemenceau said, 'The man who isn't a socialist by the time he's eighteen has no heart, and the man who is after he's twenty-one has no head.' I had the heart there, and it didn't amount to anything, I didn't know anything, and it would have been better if I'd been properly instructed. But I had a sort of snobbery. Not Labour, that would be appalling.

HM: Because yours was an interesting situation, wasn't it, that you had been brought up in this lifestyle to believe that you were a bit up there

23

rather than down there, but your actual life conditions were no holidays, and not a lot of money.

GC: That's right. It was like the Cheshire Cat, the smile remains after the cat has gone.

HM: So the Spanish Civil War rather passed you by?

GC: It passed me by, but of course when I got to the University in 1938, it was almost over. I didn't know about it. Though in those times there were the Left Book Club books published by Gollancz – I know there was a book, 'Fallen Bastions', those sort of works had some effect on one. I think the really important thing is that going to the University was breaking away from one's social background in New Zealand. It was a great liberation. One went there and the sort of talk of the professors was wonderful. Not the sort of talk that ever happened in respectable circles. Not that they said anything very much, but they did talk ideas, and I remember there were one or two people there. Arthur Sewell, whose name I shall reverence into eternity, he was the English professor but he was wonderful, he was intellectual, he had ideas, and he talked about things in a way that was greatly inspiring. And then there were others too. I know now that they worked in very adverse circumstances, in the sense that they were physically cut off. People didn't go to New Zealand very much, and they didn't get away very much. They had a sabbatical every so often, but [to go away was] a huge excursion for them. And the libraries were very inadequate – there wasn't all this library service that there is now.

HM: This is a very key point about academia in New Zealand, isn't it, that isolation in those years, and yet they could still sustain that level.

GC: They lifted up my life, and they lifted up my wife's life too. We met at the University. She came there in 1939. It was a transforming world. New Zealand was a very stodgy respectable society, and the values of respectability and the comfortable middle class – that was all thrown aside and people were free. It was a great liberating influence.

HM: And students in those days, perhaps more than they do right now, did express an alternative view, didn't they?

GC: Yes, they did, and it wasn't up to much, but still, it was something. For me, it was a great excitement.

HM: But now what about the stream of your actual work? Leading to what you've studied all your life? Where did that begin?

GC: Well, I did Classics at Auckland University, simply because it was a thing I was good at. Not all that good, I may say, but I was reasonably good.

HM: You'd done Latin and Greek?

GC: I had done Latin at school but I hadn't done Greek. But anyhow I did Classics, and so I got onto that. It wasn't till I got to Oxford that I found out about Ancient History. I am a dud, but God meant me to be an Ancient Historian, I see that. And I took to it – I meant to be a philosopher when I came here. I quickly found out that I was unfitted by God or anything to be a philosopher.

HM: Why? What do you mean by that?

GC: Because I wasn't clever enough. I'm not intellectual enough. Philosophy is a very high-powered thing. I remember from a memorial service for Gareth Evans, a great philosopher who died young, in University College, he was a wonderful man, but he said on his deathbed, 'In a way I'm glad. I find philosophy very difficult.' Well he was a very very clever man. It's a bloody difficult subject and not to be dealt with by duds like me. I'm interested and I go to things, but I couldn't possibly have been a philosopher. I haven't got it in me. But I found here that I took to the ancient history and I can remember a crucial day, I was engaged in a very good tutorial in Christ Church with a man called Urmson [JO Urmson] who was a very good tutor. The hour came, and he was rather put out when I said, 'I think I've got to go, because I've got a lecture in St John's.' It was on Tacitus, and that showed I preferred Ancient History to philosophy. But I found I had ideas, and in a modest way it was a thing that I was suited to. So I discovered that here; in New Zealand I hadn't. Although there was a great deal of apologia about Classics, I didn't actually really think that it was the great thing that it was professed to be. And it was only when I got here that I learned what a big thing Classics is.

HM: Still back in New Zealand, you completed the degree in Auckland?

GC: I did the BA and I finished that in 1941. And then the War was on. And I was very anxious to finish my MA, because I didn't see my ever going back, so I went on and I did that in 1941, and I went into the services in 1942. This of course created a tension in my soul. By not volunteering in 1940, and going to the Middle East, and possibly not being killed, I lost out. When I read about the New Zealand division in

Crete, those were heroes of a sort that I wasn't, and I feel that it cut me off from my countrymen. I wouldn't go back there, I don't think I deserve to belong in the world with these people.

Religion

[It is worth ending this section on his earliest days with a footnote from 'Nostra Vita' in view of the preoccupation George felt through the rest of his life with questions of truth and the value of religion, in his case the Christian religion. See also chapter 9.]

It was in my time at the University that I became taken up with Anglo-Catholicism, by now an outworn creed I expect, but then flourishing. I don't know how or why I first went to St Thomas' Church in Freeman's Bay, what I regarded as a slum area, but the vicar was a very remarkable priest, Arthur Russell Allerton. Father Allerton, son of a Liverpool pub-keeper, was totally devoted to High Church practice and I came under his spell. He was very fond of the drama and had staged a notable 'Murder in the Cathedral'. His Catholic services were themselves drama. He was, and led me to be, a great admirer of TS Eliot (I still am). But he was also a Christian Socialist and he had influence on me there. One way or another he was a dominant influence. He had done some sort of degree at Keble College in Oxford – perhaps a Pass Degree – after the Great War in which he served in the Artists' Rifles, a battalion of congenial souls. He had a great influence on my life and when in the 1950s or possibly the 1960s I saw him in All Saints' Margaret Street, old, feeble and blind, being led up to the Communion rail, I wept.

2 CLASSICS AT AUCKLAND UNIVERSITY

[This address was delivered in 1978 to Auckland University College. George refers to Charles Cooper, Chair of Classics at AUC from around 1933 to around 1947 and to EM Blaiklock (1903-83) who was Chair of Classics from 1947 to 1968. In 1940 a division of responsibilities was made between teaching Greek which became Blaiklock's domain, while Latin teaching was granted to Cooper. Reference is also made to WA Sewell (1903-72) who had been born in England and appointed Chair of English at AUC in 1933 when he moved to New Zealand. He remained in Auckland for twelve years.]

General

Before talking about Classics and the Classics Department, I would like to record in general terms the large sense of obligation that I feel for AUC. I remember a master at King's (who had been to Cambridge) talking contemptuously of the place as a 'jam factory' and I expect there was much to contemn, but it was at any rate jam for the bread and butter of New Zealand life and I found it all enthralling and indeed inspiring. The degree courses were so structured that one did quite a diversity of bits and one might suppose that the single year spent on English including Anglo-Saxon (for which in an effort to make us learn the grammar we were required to translate suitably paratactic bits of English into Caedmonesque) or on French might have been better spent on Latin and Greek. I do not think so. The school education I had was extremely limited and these extra 'bits' permanently enriched my life. For one thing they brought one into contact with people like WA Sewell, whose memory I will cherish to the tomb, a man who was above all an intellectual. I still remember a brilliant lecture he delivered on Hardy's 'Woodlanders' which inspired me to read a good number of Hardy's books. There were others too like Julius Stone, whose performances at undergraduate societies provided general intellectual stimulus. All in all, 1938 to 1941 had an immense influence on me, and I am most grateful

27

for all that AUC provided. If I say anything in criticism of the Classics Department, it must be judged as minor compared with the great benefits of what I received both in general and in the Department.

Atmosphere of the Department

Those teaching us had two great impediments in their work. First, we came to university study of the Classics very ill-equipped indeed. In my home Latin was honoured. My father (born in 1869) had been educated at Auckland Grammar School and he loved Latin – not that we discussed it (for he died when I was not quite thirteen), but I knew that Latin was important. (I still have Becker's 'Gallus' and 'Charicles' which he had won as prizes. ['Gallus: or Roman scenes of the time of Augustus' (1844) and 'Charicles: or illustrations of the private life of the Ancient Greeks' (1845).]) It was natural enough therefore when I began Latin at King's Preparatory School when I was nine or ten, [to use] Longman's Latin Primer and Kennedy, and for a decade I was at [*sic*] translating into and from Latin. But it never got much beyond that. When I was at King's College, the reading of texts was very fitful. I remember Horace 'Odes I', begun and never completed, and (most unsuitable) Cicero's 'De Senectute' ['on old age'], again not completed. But nothing else remains in my memory with one exception – some extraordinary classes with an extraordinary man, ME Bardsley whom I mention *honoris causa*. He took us in the sixth form for Cicero's *Pro Milone* and was a wonderful example of how important enthusiasm, no matter how   freakish, is in educating the young. However, I left school with practically no sense of Latin literature, though I was moderately good at grammar and sentences, and so the Classics Department at AUC had very little to build on. I do not think King's was unusual. Most of us beginning in 1938 knew very little indeed about the ancient world. There had been some mugging up of Roman antiquities from a little book 'Res Romanae' and some Roman history but, compared to what candidates to Oxford knew, even now, it was ludicrously small. The reason was, I think, the system of public examinations, which required no precise knowledge of set texts, to my mind essential in getting the young properly started. Whether this is correct or not, we were certainly very raw material for the staff of the Classics Department to have to work on.

As to Greek, until I got to AUC I found it hard to credit that anyone should deem it worth devoted study. I remember my headmaster at
King's mentioning with due awe the name of Plato, but when I was in
my sixteenth year and a boy said to me that 'so-and-so is an awful
ignoramus – he hadn't even heard of Aristotle', I too had not heard of
the now hallowed name. ME Bardsley a year or two later told us about
Homer, and even recited bits of the 'Iliad' as he bowled (badly) in the
cricket nets, but, when I arrived at AUC, I had really no fund of the feeling that all properly educated men knew, or desired to know, Greek,
and Professor Cooper's persuasions were not readily heeded. One could
hardly have been a very inspiring pupil.

Secondly, the staff of the Classics Department had to engage in a
good deal of *apologia* for classical studies. Not only in schools but generally in New Zealand society the 'dead' languages were deemed to be a
worthless matter for study. We students faithfully repeated the voiced
arguments, but one was not really convinced. Not until I got to Oxford
did I begin to believe in the supreme importance of Greece and Rome in
education, and this scepticism must have been a considerable impedi-
ment to our teachers. They were, to my mind, brave men and deserve
high honour for all they did, but it cannot have been a very happy
atmosphere for them to work in.

One other matter must be mentioned, *viz.* the celebrated wrangle
between Cooper and Blaiklock. Others are more competent to describe
its genesis and development, but I will set down what I understood of it,
which may be far from accurate but may be of some interest in showing
how far it impinged on the students' consciousness. I was perhaps exceptional in that I got to know both of them quite well and was privy to
matters not generally known about, but it was plain that Cooper
despised Blaiklock and Blaiklock detested Cooper. Cooper was a suave
little man, whom one would never guess was a professor. I remember he
used to lecture in plus fours (as I now do myself often enough) with
those white and tan shoes so prized in the 30s, and the combined effect
of manner and dress was odd. If he was in a rage, he didn't show it but
became even more suave and so the more infuriating. He was very
prickly and, I imagine, got on very ill with most of his professorial
colleagues, but, whether that was so or not, he was a complete contrast
with Blaiklock. Cooper was a sceptic about religion, Blaiklock a rather

embarrassing evangelical who tended to judge men in relation to their devotion to or lack of Christianity. Cooper had 'odd' tastes such as a liking for the detective stories involving a character called Lemmy Caution; Blaiklock had, and professed, no such contemptible frivolities and was much taken up with French literature in which he was certainly well enough read. Cooper looked back on his Scottish education at St Andrew's with great piety and mouthed the honoured names of Burnet, AE Taylor, WM Lindsay, D'Arcy Thompson as if they were the gods on Olympus. Blaiklock had never studied abroad, having thrown up the chance in order to marry his admirable but sensible and unacademic wife; his only academic god was Professor Paterson, a man on whom Cooper passed the judgement of silence. Worst of all, Blaiklock was a disappointed man. He had been led by Paterson to believe that he would succeed him in the chair. Paterson died, I think, early and Blaiklock was passed over.

The conflict began, according to Cooper, before ever he had set foot on New Zealand soil, for *en route* he received a letter from Blaiklock explaining how things were done which betrayed no suspicion that the new man would not necessarily do the same as his hallowed predecessor. Cooper was no man to overlook such presumption. From then on things went merrily from bad to worse. On one occasion, according to Blaiklock, in Cooper's room they faced each other across Cooper's desk and Blaiklock declared, 'Say that again, Cooper, and I'll hit you,' possibly adopting a suitably aggressive stance. Cooper's methods were not physical. He preferred to wound with the suave tongue, and he did. There were faults on both sides. On one occasion, when Cooper fell ill, Blaiklock had to take over his class on the 'Agamemnon' and chose to begin again at the beginning of the play! I was not at AUC when the final divorce was effected, and Latin and Greek became virtually separate, but between 1938 and 1941 the great conflict was ripening.

How much did it affect the students? I think it did not in fact directly affect us very much. One tended to take sides and because Cooper was incomparably the better scholar, though not necessarily the cleverer man, I rather sided with him. I see now that this was unfair. Things I have learned since about Cooper suggest that he really was an intolerable person in many ways and after all Blaiklock was essentially a very nice man for all his weaknesses. But harmony within a small department does seem to me now a very important part in getting and keeping students interested, and one can only regret that the two parties could not respect and express respect for each other's merits. A more lively interest in the ancient world must have resulted.

Both Cooper and Blaiklock were however admirable in their care of and for their pupils – as I now know by experience of what happens elsewhere. Both entertained me most generously. Blaiklock took me for walks round Titirangi ending up with lunch at his house. When I was in the army, he took the trouble to write me letters, one of which I still have, quite witty indeed. Cooper had me to dinner several times and once I stayed too late for the last train and slept the night. I must have seemed a very brash young man but he and his fiery-tempered red-haired Scottish wife, Alice, put up with me. I don't think I was exceptional. Perhaps both rather courted the support of their pupils, but I don't think that was really their motive. Cooper, unable to get on with his equals, resolved to make the most of his pupils. Blaiklock was trying to help us as best he could. To both I am very grateful. (There was one irony. As I said, I had rather sided with Cooper and spurned Blaiklock, but when I named the former and not the latter as referee for the Rhodes, Cooper was having a period of sabbatical leave and working at home. Alice rang AUC and said Gordon would not do references when he was on leave. Blaiklock was asked to write on my behalf and did, and did not damn me. I now write references at all moments even when I am far away from Oxford and consider Cooper's conduct monstrous. I think the story shows something about both men.) It is important that students know their teachers and feel cared for personally. Both the conflicting parties by no means failed in this respect.

Somewhat irrelevantly, I will mention one aspect of life in the department which I include solely for amusement . . . It hardly deserves mention, though it was a factor. Blaiklock was a man whom women much admired. That is not unusual. One's pupils generally admire one, and one's female pupils are often very devoted. Such personal hero-worship is important in moving students to work and Blaiklock was the more successful for it. But there was one girl, who made a dead set at him and was bent on adding him to her list. I remember that through three terms of 1938 she sat about six feet away from him as he lectured on Livy IX and the disaster of the Caudine Forks and she without cease kept jiggling her thighs. Blaiklock affected not to notice. In later years as classes became more rarefied and smaller her efforts were intensified, until on one occasion she trapped him in his room by blocking his only egress between desk and bookshelves, put her hand on his shoulder and said, 'Kiss me, Blaikie.' The pillar of the Evangelical Union stood firm. Finally in 1942 they faced each other in a class of which she was the only member. History does not relate the consequences, but I have no doubt there were none. So she too received some sort of education outside her formal studies.

My own course

I began on Latin I and Greek I in 1938. For Latin we did Livy IX under Blaiklock and [Virgil's] 'Fourth Georgic' under Cooper (which marvellously illustrated their different methods on which I will enlarge below). That was unsatisfactory enough. But I could not get on with the Greek. It was lectured on by a nearly blind man called Doric Algie, whether that was his given name or a classical nickname – neither seemed probable. There was no personal encouragement, and I simply could not keep up conscientiously with the work. So I dropped it, a fatal mistake and despite Cooper's efforts to persuade me to persist. I think now that the fault was largely Algie's. The young need a great deal of encouragement and he did not give it. He disappeared from the department that year, either by retirement or, as was said, disposed of by Cooper.

In 1939 I did Latin II and started again on Greek I, this time under Blaiklock and he did encourage us. Under his tuition I read an atticised version of the battle of Salamis from Herodotus VIII and a bit of Euripides' 'Troades'. But my Greek remained second to my Latin, and so it has remained even though it is now my life. If one is really to know a language, one has to begin at a very early age. Memory fades but I think that for Latin we read a selection of Juvenal's 'Satires' under Cooper and Cicero's 'Second Philippic' under the newly arrived and universally liked Peter Crawley, though I recall that he didn't express much liking for Ciceronian invective. The truth was that it was an ineptly chosen text. One has to know a lot about the background properly to enjoy such a work and of course we had absolutely no such background.

In 1940 for Latin III I read [a selection of] Seneca's 'Letters' under Cooper, and what else I hardly remember – perhaps it was then that I read Lucan VII under Crawley (who again did not like the text with its gory descriptions) and possibly some Virgil read on my own or Horace 'Epistles I' under Cooper. For Greek II I read Demosthenes' 'Olynthiacs' and Euripides' 'Alcestis' both under Blaiklock, whose tedious methods were by now rather weighing on me. I graduated BA at the end of the year. Through all of course we had proses and unseens.

In 1941 I went on to read for MA Honours in Latin (single) and to do Greek III, which included Thucydides VII, Sophocles' 'Ajax', both under Blaiklock, and Herodotus IX on my own. For Latin I read a great and greatly satisfying amount – Virgil, Tacitus, Martial, Plautus, Terence, and plenty of Cicero I seem to remember. I took the final examination in November and became an MA.

I have listed perhaps tediously and probably inaccurately what I read to show how little I had read of Latin literature before I got on to Honours, and how little Greek in my three years up to Greek III – no Homer, no Aeschylus, no Plato, no Aristophanes. Unseens partly supplied the gaps, but it was all fairly low level. Compared to what I later found that English boys coming to Oxford had read, it was as nothing. When I first became a don, I set a piece of Lucan for an unseen only to be told that most of the candidates were likely to have read it. Indeed clever English boys probably read more at school than a New Zealander would have done if he had done both Latin and Greek single Honours. That is no longer the case, alas, but it shows how low our standard of attainment was. It was partly this that made Classics seem less than respectable as a university course in New Zealand. I think more could have been required of us, but only if more had been required generally, which it was not. I did, for example, Philosophy I, and passed by mugging up my lecture notes over one weekend. Of course I do not exempt myself from blame. I should have set my own sights higher. No one suggested that I should, however, and in general for all its virtues the standards of the University were sadly low. Apart from proses, I was never required to write anything for my Classics course. Not until I got to Oxford did essay writing become a regular part of my work. In other subjects in New Zealand an essay a term was required. But in Classics never. I expect the labour of teaching us the rudiments of the language was heavy enough, but some essay work on the texts we were reading would have been helpful, and its omission was a serious defect.

In view of my own professional interests and of the now widespread concern with Ancient History one might ask whether I now think that the lack of Ancient History in my course was regrettable. I do not think so. The climate has greatly changed. As competence in Greek and Latin declines, interest in things ancient grows at an enormous rate, and Ancient History is now particularly appealing. So study of that aspect is a good, if not the only good, way to encourage the young. It was not so in the 1930s. If we had been put on to periods of Ancient History, I think our efforts with the language and literature would have been much diminished without great compensating gain. One would not have done Ancient History by, with and from the evidence, and it would have been largely distraction from our real business. I did do some for MA Latin and by then I had read quite a lot of Latin. That was rewarding even though it was mostly mere mugging up of the 'Cambridge Ancient History'. Earlier what I needed was the reading of texts and more texts. So I do not think those who drafted our syllabus were at fault.

Teaching methods

Cooper was a very exact scholar and he prepared for lectures with enormous thoroughness. He once told me, and I have no reason to doubt him, that to take a class of fifty lines of a text he knew well he would spend three hours in preparation. He was a distinguished translator and he furnished us with an admirable version, but he also delivered a lively commentary on points of interest. He was at his very best on grammar and metre and explained the text in the most illuminating fashion. Similarly with proses and unseens. There was nothing casual or thrown off. An unseen became the means of illustrating Roman life and literature, and I much regret that the division of labours between him and Blaiklock deprived us of his excellent instruction in Greek. But it was not all gold. I recall that when we were reading Seneca he delivered a lecture on the topic of *sententiae* – literally so, for he read out a cyclostyled piece that he distributed to us to follow. He was not pleased when some unrest with this sort of thing reached his ears. But all in all he seemed a very good scholar and was a quite admirable pedagogue.

Blaiklock was, by contrast, extraordinarily lax and dull. He simply did not share Cooper's standards of thorough preparation. He would on occasion bring to the lecture-room various commentaries from which he would read out bits. I recall tedious excerpts from Lachmann's Lucretius provided in this way. But most tedious of all was the constant references to paragraphs of Goodwin's Greek Grammar. One suspected that this was Paterson's method and Blaiklock knew neither other nor better. As a result his lectures hardly inspired one. But he made up for these defects with his personal kindness and niceness. For he was above all humane. The tragedy of it all was that if only he had gone abroad and had experience of a different academic world he would have seen that these methods were not good enough. He certainly had a very good brain and could have been an outstandingly good teacher.

However, between them they kept the flag flying – or rather the flags from their separate bastions. Because Blaiklock was so amiable a man, he kept Greek going, to his eternal credit. Cooper was a glimpse of Olympus.

Finale

One point must be made. Academic life is solitary, and one desperately needs the stimulus of other scholars in the same field. As far as I know, those who taught us laboured on alone. There was every inducement to lower their own sights. The library was good enough for undergraduates, but for professional scholars it was simply inadequate. I do not think that in my time any of my teachers produced work of their own, but they had little stimulus and certainly not the instruments to do so. When I was in New Zealand in 1971, I was struck by the change. Departments were all bigger, sabbatical leave and conferences of Australasian scholars regular, and despite the remoteness the subject was on the move. That was hardly to be expected in my time. Just keeping the subject going was heroic enough.

In my experience criticisms of the system and the teaching come most readily from the less satisfactory. I was no Syme [who became the pre-eminent 'New Zealander in Oxford' in the twentieth century – see below pages 59-61] nor any shadow of him, and my criticisms probably prove that. So I must finish by saying again how grateful I am to AUC and to the Classics Department and to its staff, which laboured over people like myself, far from worthy of all they did for us.

3 LEAVING NEW ZEALAND

[from NZRSOHP]

War

GC: What did you do in the war, Daddy? I didn't go. And in 1942, I had actually enrolled, I mean volunteered for the Air Force, and by the luck of the draw, I wasn't called up. And then in 1942 I was called up and went into the Territorial Army, still maybe on the list for the Air Force, and there came a glorious day when I was marched out of the Third Auckland Battalion, which was up at Warkworth or somewhere like that, and I was going to the Air Force. Free! Liberty! And after a week's final leave, I got a telegram saying, 'Come back, the name was Cawkhill, not Cawkwell.' By God, I went back with my tail down, and probably my life was saved by that mistake [laughs]. So I didn't get to the Air Force. And I was not such stuff as heroes were made of. But I have a bad feeling that I didn't do what a decent New Zealander would have done. I should have been in.

HM: By carrying on with your degree, you feel that was—

GC: By finishing my degree. I should have chucked up all and got in. Of course by that time there was conscription. So I can't quite remember, but by not being in the New Zealand Expeditionary Force at an early stage, I feel that I've missed out in the mainstream of being a New Zealander. So I wouldn't be comfortable at home there. I feel in a sense that I failed. You see, in New Zealand life in the last forty years, fifty years, those who had been in the war and done things were an elite. Those who hadn't were outsiders. Whether they were in fact, but one felt it. So I'd missed out on the great New Zealand experience. When one reads Antony Beevor's history of the Cretan campaign ['Crete: the battle and the resistance'], you really do feel tremendous pride in the New Zealanders. They were wonderful and good, and one missed all that.

HM: Yes, although also since in recent years there's been quite a lot of writing by people who for whatever reason did miss out, like conscientious objectors, and other people whose circumstances kept them from—

GC: Yes. Well thank God I wasn't a conscientious objector. I don't have much respect for conscience either. I don't have much respect for high-mindedness and high ideas, I think it's been a bloody nuisance in history [laughs].

HM: And would you back that up with ancient history?

GC: Yes, I think our high-mindedness is just a bloody nuisance. When you think Sparta was undone by high-mindedness. There was this great influential king, King Agesilaus. He had these bloody silly ideas about fighting Persia, and it was absolutely lunatic. They couldn't do it, and they didn't adapt to the changing world, and they were stuck being little Sparta, and it was ruined.

HM: So having got your MA, we're coming back from Sparta to you, that was in '42—

GC: That was in '41, I took the final examination in '41, and early '42, while I was waiting to be called up, I taught at King's College for about four weeks, which I enjoyed. But then I went into the Territorial Army, waiting to be, as I hoped, for the Air Force. It never happened, and so I somehow was moved to the Third Division New Zealand Expeditionary Force in New Caledonia. I got there, but I wasn't in the battalion, I was in the base camp, and that was no bloody good. One was full of heroic ideas that one hadn't really got the guts to carry out. But they came, they called for volunteers to go to the Fijian Infantry Regiment, and I went. There were about five of us. One of us was the All Black Ron Ward, and he had a pretty short war, that fellow. He was out with his platoon, the first day, and a Jap shot him from up a tree. They shot a boy, and Ron went out to pick him up, and he got shot too, in the shoulder, and so he was a casualty. But no, I went to the Fijian Infantry Battalion. I joined them actually on the boat in Noumea, and I knew no Fijian, I knew nothing. But there we were on this boat full of Fijians and American troops going up to the Solomons, and I couldn't communicate. Officers had to have our turn down in the hold, because there was a danger that the Japs would attack, that the submarine would hit one at dawn, that's always the thing. And we'd be going up through the Solomons at night with the bloody lightning flashing, and the Japs know we're here, of course they haven't got any aeroplanes left, but I was down there at dawn, at the dawn stand-to, and I'll never forget these chaps, the great rows of naked bodies, and Americans shooting crap down below. If anything had happened, I'd have been swept away in the rush. But we were there. I got to Bougainville, I had had thoughts that we would go ashore and walk up a track, but not at all, there were great ruddy trucks going round in the road. But we had no real place there, the Fijians; we did a sort of scouting job. And I had a few trifling moments for which I am grateful to God, when one might have been shot. I am very grateful that I had that minor experience of war, and it was very slight.

HM: But why are you grateful for that?

GC: Well, it gives me a sense of war. Presumptuous, but as an Ancient Historian, I find again and again that people who haven't had any experience of war, they don't understand. And I don't understand, but I have a sense of logistics and what it's like, and that did me good. But also it made me feel respectable in a sense. To have been there, when they could have got one, but they didn't. I won't describe the petty actions but they're branded in my soul.

HM: Sorry, can you describe one?

GC: Oh, well. There, we – the battalion – the first time we went out, there was a big fat New Zealander called Volker, who was the battalion commander. He was a bloody dud and ignorant. And he was walking up the trail, which was wide enough to take great GM trucks, but we chaps were getting through the jungle on each side, which had been shelled by American artillery and the tops were all off the trees and one was fighting one's way through. I was a platoon commander and my chaps were absolutely exhausted. We called for a halt, and we got down on a ridge and we found out afterwards that the Japs had been dug in just the other side, probably within twelve or fourteen feet of where we were. The British army always thought of commanding ground, but the Japs got down low and shot you as you came over the top.

On that occasion we were pulled back, and the battalion used to bivouac in a four-sided formation on the trail. In the course of the night, some of the American mortars landed in the battalion and did a bit of damage. The boys were pretty shaky the following morning, and I thought, I'd better be with the front section as they go out, they're in a pretty shaky state. So we led out, and my company was on the right-hand side, my platoon was up on the front of that, and I was with the front section, when suddenly there was a scampering, and I thought, 'By

God, a bayonet attack! The Japs!' Just before that I had gone up and said 'Stop it,' and the boy was pointing at me and I couldn't speak any Fijian, but 'Don't be bloody silly!' And then I realised bullets were pinging into the tree just above me! Suddenly there was this scamper and I thought, 'By God, a bayonet attack,' instead of which there was a row of startled Fijian faces coming through the jungle, and it swept away the back sections of my platoon. We were left out there on our own, and I'd sent my batman back to headquarters to tell them where we were and what was what, so one of the boys at headquarters chucked a grenade at him, and I thought, 'Oh God, I have left the New Zealand Third Division for this bloody rubbish. How terrible.' I was really in a dejected state.

Well, there was that. They might have killed me there but they didn't. The other one was a minor thing, and I behaved very improperly. We were going to sort of lead an advance. I took over one of the Bren guns myself. Well, a platoon commander shouldn't do that. I took on a Bren gun and was shooting round the bloody jungle, and I saw some little eyes looking at me from a slit trench, and I chucked a grenade and, anyhow, I got them, they didn't get me. And so that was a very minor bit of war.

HM: What was your feeling about that? I mean, you did kill them.

GC: I shot them, but I didn't have any feelings about that. It was the interesting thing about the war: you were almost without feelings on the battlefield. I have seen things, minor things, that would be very shocking if you were not keyed up to see them. I remember seeing a chap shot in an awful state. It didn't move me anything like the spectacle of some Fijian kids in Fiji who had gone out and picked up off the reef on the mud flats some unexploded shells, and they blew themselves up. It was a terrible thing, and I remember that, because I wasn't ready for it. On the battlefield, one expects these things, you're all psyched up, as they say. But I had very little war, I don't want you to think I had anything much, but just enough to know I'd been there.

HM: And to know what it was like to have the possibility of your being killed.

GC: The possibility. It gave me the feeling, well, I can now settle down and be a stodgy old teacher of some sort.

*

[In 1998, neatly half way between the second Gulf War, which marked a high point for the USA as a military power, and the Iraq débâcle in the first decade of the new millennium, came two films that signalled that high point. One was Steven Spielberg's *Saving Private Ryan*, the other was Terrence Malik's *The Thin Red Line*, both appearing in 1998. While the first of these concerned the D-Day landings, the other was set in the Pacific War about American troops fighting the Japanese on Guadalcanal in the Philippines. Since George had been involved in the Pacific War, I took the opportunity to ask him whether the latter film portrayed the truthfulness of battling the Japanese on a Pacific island. On 4 June 1999, George wrote to me as follows:]

'The only action I saw was in Bougainville (and I must make plain that it was trifling), and the terrain of that island, or rather the vegetation, is different from that of Guadalcanal. Bougainville, or at any rate the parts I was in, was entirely jungle-clad. One moved along trails expecting to be shot from behind trees or even from up trees. Guadalcanal has quite large tracts of grasslands (as the film properly represented, no doubt being made there) and so the fighting must have been very different. [Guadalcanal was scouted as a location for shooting, but there were logistical difficulties and so the film was shot in North Queensland, the Solomon Islands and California.]

However, I fancied the machine-gun post sited on the top of the hill was symbolic rather than real. They [the Americans] had to be striving to 'get to the top'. The post had a good view mayhap but if the Americans had set out to destroy it they would, I am sure, have attacked it from the air (the aerial photography was very full).

Again, maybe for reasons of cost, the action in the film involved about two battalions. Island landings involved at least one whole division. (I seem to remember that it was the America 1 division, but there may have been a second division). Before they went ashore, there was the most terrific aerial and naval bombardment. The Japs had machine-gun emplacements on possible landing beaches. These were made of coconut palms (which are very tough) and often the Japs survived the preliminary bombardment and had to be dealt with by the troops involved in the landing. But the film presented a quite different picture –

a comparatively small force making an unopposed landing and being bullied forward and up to an improbably placed post. It was, to my mind, all symbolic – good men, subordinate officers caring about soldiers' lives, an ambitious and insensate commander disregarding all considerations other than the attainment of his glorious success, cost what it might.

I expect supplies could go wrong, but in general the US Army was abundantly supplied. It seemed to me pretty improbable that the water-supply should have been neglected. As we went by boat up through the Solomons, I fancied we would be landing on a beach and walking inland! Instead, we found great big roads with a huge amount of transport going hither and yon. When the Yanks went in, they quickly built up a powerful base amazingly supplied with everything, and this was because their army was very strong on logistics. Of course, the film depicted the very early days, or even the first day, on Guadalcanal, but the US Army was in general not unprovided. I bet they would have foreseen the water problem. (Of course, fear makes one very dry and the need of water is very great.)

Altogether, I am no expert on jungle warfare or on Guadalcanal in particular, but the film was concerned with recognisable types of men in a pretty largely imagined situation. Why I didn't like it was that I found the tension too much for me. I was and am an innocent lad."

*

Getting the Rhodes Scholarship

GC: And I got the Rhodes Scholarship at the end of the war. I'd thought that I'd missed it, and then I got married right at the end of the war on 17 October 1945.

HM: And that was in New Zealand?

GC: In New Zealand. They suspended the rule that Rhodes Scholars couldn't be married, and so I went to the interview in Wellington. Judge Smith, I think he was, said to me, 'Will you be able to keep a wife in Oxford?' And I said, 'Very much better than if I didn't have a wife.'

HM: I just wanted you to tell me in a bit more detail about the lead-up to the actual award of the Rhodes Scholarship. Because from the age of ten—

GC: I had been bent on it. And the war came and I thought I'd lost it—

HM: What happened? Was it advertised again?

GC: Yes, I applied and it was said that one can be married, you see. And so it happened.

HM: Who were the other contestants when you were going through it?

GC: The others who were elected were a chap called Bruce Harris, who became a Classics professor in Australia. And the other was a chap called Jack Ridley, who was in Univ actually, I think he was an engineer, and he's something in New Zealand now.

HM: I think he became Commissioner of Works, or something like that?

GC: Yes, something like that.

HM: So you were called to Wellington, to Government House?

GC: I don't think the Governor-General was there, for some reason. It was chaired by this judge, Smith. And there it was. They were mad, but I was a natural, I think. I mean, I had, as it were, the qualifications, except for a heroic war, which they overlooked.

HM: There's an excessive modesty in this whole thing, isn't there? [Pat Cawkwell enters room. Hugo Manson addresses her.] You were there, when he applied for his Rhodes Scholarship?

PC: Did you do it from Fiji, or when you got back to New Zealand?

GC: I think I did it when I got back to New Zealand, didn't I? Yes.

PC: I think you did too. Obviously you wrote at the end of the War and said, 'Perhaps we'll get married, shall we?'

HM: Was that the proposal?

PC: Yes. And about a week later, or some time later, you wrote and said, 'I see the Rhodes scholarships have been restarted. What about marriage? Perhaps it's not on.' And I asked somebody at Auckland University, and in no time at all he rang me and said, 'It's all right, they've decided to waive that.' And you could be married if you wanted to be. When George came back he said, 'We'll get married quickly in case they change their minds.' [laughs] And we got married in six days or so.

HM: You got married in six days! For you, George, the prospect of being an impoverished Rhodes Scholar over in Oxford, what about that?

GC: Not at all.

PC: I didn't think they were impoverished.

GC: I must say that Pat is a woman who has never thought about money in her life. She'd have put up with any hardship to put up with me, which was a greater hardship still.

PC: But people were coming with this money. The Rhodes, as far as scholarships go, was a very good one.

GC: But one needed a bit of extra. The theory then was that you weren't fully covered.

HM: But Rhodes was the top of the tree in scholarships.

GC: Yes it was. The world has changed, because Rhodes Scholars came and did BAs in Oxford. Whereas now, they come very often, generally speaking, to do doctorates. And when the faculty is looking at graduates that they're going to admit, they don't give a damn whether he can kick a football. They choose someone who is good on his written work and his academic ability. I would never have made it. [laughs]

HM: I don't suppose there are too many people who had had this clear ambition from the age of ten.

GC: No, that's right. And lack of ambition for anything else, that was the worst thing.

HM: Well, it was a very focused ambition.

[After Pat has left room.] HM: You went for the interview, and the Governor-General wasn't there.

GC: Oh yes, there was a committee.

HM: Was the interview a difficult process?

GC: No, I expect that I didn't find it difficult. Sensible people think that interviews do you no bloody good, but actually I was reasonably good at interviews. I've been ready with words and so it was all right; it didn't cause me any miseries or soul-searching. I expect if I had been rejected I'd have been downcast, but I didn't expect to be. It's terrible to be so arrogant, isn't it? I just took it quite naturally.

HM: And what happened after the interview? Were you told straight away or did you go away?

GC: I can't remember.

HM: And there you were, with the scholarship.

GC: Yes. I think my wife was with me down in Wellington, I'm not sure. We went back to Auckland and I did a bit of work at Auckland University, just reading thises and thats, and we set off. By this time, she was pregnant and we had meant that she would have the baby in New

Zealand and then come over, but by the hand of God we were deprived of the flat we were in. So we just packed up and came, to the shock and horror of a cousin of Pat's, who was over here. It was not a place for people: England was worn out at the end of the War. They had been very short of food, they were tired, undernourished. The thought of someone choosing to come here was horrifying to this quite old woman. But we got on very well, and we were the only people on the ship who had a flat to come to. Another cousin of Pat's, who'd been a prisoner of war and was living in Oxford, had got a flat for us. We went straight to the flat. I settled down in Oxford. We arrived in June 1946. I remember coming up the beautiful Woodstock Road, things were in bloom, and it seemed to me paradise. We had come through London, and the ship had been delayed because there was the victory parade: they thought it wouldn't be fair to discharge their passengers in the throng. (By God, you can imagine what it would have been like getting by taxi from whatever.) We landed at Tilbury, came up those awful backs of houses. It was like *This Happy Breed*, you know, that film of Noel Coward's, mile on mile of it. We got into London and we got over to Paddington and we came to Oxford. Fancy trying to do that through the crowds of the victory parade.

HM: You'd come over on what ship, by the way?

GC: We came on the *Akaroa*, which had been converted as a troop ship. We didn't have a cabin. I was in a cabin of about six men, and she was in a cabin of about four women.

HM: And so you got here to Oxford. How had you gone about choosing or being selected for a college?

GC: Ah, now, when you were awarded it, you were then sent a form by the Rhodes Trust in Oxford, asking you to name eight Oxford colleges in order of preference. Now, frankly, in my ignorance, I knew of only one college: Balliol. So there was a man who had been a Rhodes Scholar from King's College called JD Lewis. I sent him a telegram, saying 'Send me your eight Oxford colleges in order of preference.' He had been at Christ Church. Christ Church came back number one, and that was how I went there, I'm glad to say. It was a curious telegram that came through. I remember Merton was the eighth. University College, I'm glad to say, was somewhere on the list. But Christ Church was head. It seemed very chance, but I recognised the hand of God, if there is a hand of God. Christ Church suited me wonderfully. I loved it, it was perfect, and I still love it.

Getting married

GC: My wife's name was Patricia St John Clarke. She was the daughter of a woman called Lilian Buick, whose father had been a Conservative Member of Parliament for Palmerston North. They were comfortable enough, I expect, as farmers were in those times.

HM: And where had you met?

GC: We met at the University. That great liberating ground. It was liberating for her to be away from the stifling milieu of Auckland polite society.

HM: And the meeting point for you?

GC: We met at a philosophy lecture. She did Philosophy 1 and I was there. And so I was no great catch, but she took to me. Sixty-three years since we met, she is still putting up with it. Bloody fool. [laughs]

4 CHRIST CHURCH, OXFORD

Arrival at the House

[On 26 June 1998 George gave the address at the Christ Church Gaudy recalling his arrival at the House just after the War.]

Mr Dean, honoured guests, fellow members of the House.

Shortly after 11 p.m. on 11 October 1946 a porter made his way across Tom Quad to the last staircase of Meadows. He disregarded a future Professor of Chinese who lived on the ground floor. He ascended to the first floor where, living opposite to the Lord Cherwell, lived a fresh-faced and tuneful lad called Armstrong, and he went on up to the next floor and woke up a bloke from one of Her Majesty's remotest dominions, and told him that his wife had just been delivered of a son. I should make it clear it was the bloke's, not the porter's, wife. The porter didn't show it, but he can hardly have been thinking 'things were getting back to normal'. They certainly weren't. Not only had the Head Porter only recently returned from active service, that Admirable Crichton, Joe Borritt, Captain of Marines, much admired and respected. But on every staircase there were men with tales to tell, a bit elderly for youthful frolics. In Kilcannon, or thereabouts, for instance, was an Australian Rhodes Scholar who had lost a leg at Tobruk, and, nearby, a man who had been the guest of the Japanese army, the wonderfully gifted Tony Chenevix-Trench. There was, in short, a right old mix-up, fairly serious about making up time lost. Gone were the days when a man had to pack his bags for writing in the examination called Divvers, 'Lot's wife was a pillar of salt by day and a ball of fire by night.' Gone too the days of 'Brideshead', which in truth had for most members of the House existed only on paper. We carried our rations of butter and jam to breakfast and returned to the study of Plato or whatever.

In Oxford generally the House was thought to be full of 'Brideshead' types. Inside, they were scarce indeed. A better distinction could have been made of us as of Plato's Dialogues – 'genuine', 'doubtfully genuine', and 'can be confidently rejected as spurious'. These last, of course, were we colonials amongst whom one did, in a forgiving or forgetful mood, count the Americans. We certainly had much to learn. I remember one genuine type quoting at me a remark of the poet Cowper. 'A very athletic habit seems inconsistent with much sensibility.' I maintained a stunned silence. So did he, when I knocked him down. Much later, I was still being 'improved'. In the middle 1960s I went to a dining club as the guest of the Steward, the late DV Hill, 'Hooky', of honoured memory. The young man who presided had assembled a number of vintages of a swagger claret, the youngest being 1953 and the oldest 1929. After dinner he sidled up to Hooky and purred, 'I hope you liked the '29, sir.' 'It was very good, Jock. But I'll tell you what. You want to keep it for a bit.' The lesson was not wasted on me. As Kipling's Mr King remarked, 'It sticks. A little of it sticks, among the barbarians.'

Bliss was it at that time to be out of uniform, but to be in the House was very Heaven. I cannot omit, but cannot do more than allude to, some of its glories – not least that great oddity, straight out of Rowlandson, Canon Jenkins, who was wont to begin his sermons with the proud flourish 'In this eleven-viceroyed House'. In the middle of the Great Freeze of Hilary Term 1947 – will we ever forget it? How the cisterns froze, the lavatory pans froze, the water in the jug and the basin in one's bedroom froze, one's towel froze, one slept in one's balaclava, one's head under the blankets, and oneself froze – in that Great Freeze we could hardly keep warm but Canon Jenkins did. I recall seeing him arrive for Matins just in time to join the procession as it rounded the corner and turned up the aisle, in full sail. Under his surplice and cassock he had cardigans the sleeves of which covered his mittens, below his trousers his pyjamas hung down to his carpet slippers, an unforgettable view of a great polymath eccentric. Then, there were the late appearances of that shy denizen of the night, or rather of Friday night, Grant Bailey. He and his pupils had many a problem to sleep over. I mention finally the incomparable RH Dundas who tutored me for Greek History. I couldn't really hear him, but I know it was Greek History, for he abstained in the case of married pupils from ensuring that they knew the facts of life. My great regret is that I did not make a collection of the cards Dundas sent me, wonderful lessons in economy of language. Many of us had them, and most of us will know well this celebrated sample, but I do not apologise for repeating it. He once sent a note telling an undergraduate to cease playing his piano out of hours. The young man sent back a chirpy note saying, 'If I am as good a player as my friends think I am, I should be allowed to play whenever I like.' Dundas replied, 'You're not. They don't. You mustn't.' It is a measure of the man that one feared to be thought ill of by him.

Save for those one encountered in University clubs, one knew hardly anyone outside the House. (I exempt the interchangeable Palgrave Browns, whose tutors never knew which was reading whose essay. They were the exception that broke the rules.) The House was not exclusive. It was just separate. I remember a remark made in Trinity Term 1947. The serving of lunch in the cricket pavilion had not yet recommenced after the War, and we cricketers used to come up to the Hall for lunch, and I defy any House man to sit in this Hall without feelings of, at least, satisfaction. One of us said to one of the opposing side, 'Of course, there's only two places to be in Oxford, Balliol and the House. But at Balliol they try.' He was himself a 'Brideshead' type and saw no reason to try, but he had got that right. Experience as a tutor over almost fifty years has shown me that a great deal of effort is often devoted to the attainment of effortless superiority. But he, and we, *had* effortless superiority. To be in the House was heaven. Where higher could one be?

Ah, Christ Church, 'with all thy faults I love thee still', only I didn't then know of any faults, and despite fifty years of scrutiny from just down the High I still don't. It is certainly most generous to its members, and, Mr Dean, we thank you all for your hospitality both in time past and tonight especially. I, and I doubt not all members of the House in this Hall tonight, feel a great debt of gratitude to Christ Church which we can never pay off, though we will, when called on, do what we can.

Let us all rise and drink a toast.

'The House.'

Christ Church remembered in interview in 2002

[from NZRSOHP]

HM: And how were you received, as a New Zealand Rhodes Scholar?
GC: I was received very well. I don't have any of these feelings like Chris Laidlaw about feeling a fish out of water. I was as happy as could be. I must confess, that first night of term – 11 October 1946 – on that night,

my oldest child was born. The porter came up to deliver this unusual message. Of course, one wasn't going to let little things like the birth of a child deflect one from one's calm, but still, I lived in college and I do confess that I used to long for people to stop at my door instead of going up and down the staircase. I mean, many people feel lonely like that, but I never had the sort of uneasiness of not belonging or anything. I expect I was a fish out of water, but I didn't know it. And of course I was a rugby player, and those playing rugby for university were thought to be superhuman.

HM: But what about your wife, then, where was she?

GC: She lived in this flat in North Oxford. And it wasn't an entirely sexless life, I may say, because I was free to come and go, and I used to go weekends and so on. But we had agreed before we left home that I would have the full experience of Oxford life, in so far as it was possible, and so I did live in college and I worked very hard and I was playing this game of rugby and travelling around with them and so on. So it did quite work. And I had the bliss of sitting in my room in Meadow Buildings, looking out over them as I read Plato, lovely.

HM: It sounds blissful.

GC: It was a very blessed time. And of course being a coarse-grained fellow I didn't fuss about food or anything. I ate what I was given. And the scouts used to give me a double portion. I was playing for the University, they thought they ought to feed me up. So I did very well.

HM: So you were fully into the life of the University. You were talking about the different colleges: was there a hierarchy when you got here, of quality or in any other sense?

GC: One thing about Oxford at that time, which isn't true now, but you didn't know people outside your college, except in so far as you played games with them, or you were in the Union, or maybe had known them at school, but I think that on the whole one stuck inside one's college. Christ Church was really quite a world on its own, and there's one story told, I've heard various versions of it, but the Master of Pembroke in those times, a man called Holmes-Dutton, was in the habit of asking young lordlings to dinner in Pembroke. And one young lordling in Christ Church, this was in the thirties, had received an invitation from Holmes-Dutton to dinner in Pembroke. So he went down to Tom Gate and asked the porter to call a taxi, not realising that Pembroke was just over the road! But it was a very self-sufficient world. So I didn't feel any comparison with other people. I remember a friend of mine with whom I played rugby football, he was in Balliol, and he said to me coming home from playing a game in Wales, he said, 'Come on, admit it. Don't you wish you were in Balliol?' And I was amazed. I had never even thought of it. I'd never physically been into it, save once. And I had no thought or envy or anything. Christ Church was all in all to me. I didn't think anything about anywhere else.

There were a certain number of aristocrats, but they kept to themselves. There was a Peers' staircase over in Canterbury Quad, and they were grouped there together. And some of them were quite grand in their behaviour, but many of them were perfectly ordinary nice people. I mean, finding aristocracy in England is not easily done. It was then a sort of upper-middle-class place, into which I fitted very well.

*

HM: And your studies were being done in Christ Church?
GC: In Christ Church, I was tutored in Christ Church. I must say that the experience of the tutorial system was interesting to me. I'd had to do very little writing in New Zealand. And then to be producing two essays a week, one History and one Philosophy, it was taxing, I wasn't used to it. And that was very good. The great merit of the tutorial system is that it makes you work, and what you do for yourself is what counts. And after all, you've got all the books, you've got all the lectures, you've got everything. I must confess that my Greek History tutor, who was a famous man called RH Dundas but not famous for scholarship, to my mind he was a hopeless tutor. Paradoxically very good, in the sense that I thought, 'This is hopeless, I'll have to get on and do it for myself.' And I did. His selection of essay topics were absolutely ridiculous. They survived from the previous century, I think.
HM: So it was at this point that you were moving towards ancient history?
GC: Yes, it didn't take me long. I had some ability at it, and I should think it was after three terms or so, I knew what I wanted to do. Of course we had to do both, History and Philosophy, and I'm very grateful for doing the Philosophy and my life is enriched by it. It breeds intellec-

tual resource like nothing else. And it was a wonderful course that I had in Greats, and I enjoyed it, I did my best. I was no good at it, as most people are no good at it. You've got to be very good. I've seen that with examining, you see. The Philosophers hardly ever give more than an alpha-beta, when people are very good. I remember JL Austin said of a man I knew, 'I'd be content to give him a First if he gets an alpha-beta on his Logic paper.' I got good second-class marks but I was never going to be a Philosopher.

HM: But what is it about Ancient History that attracted you, I mean, apart from what you've said?

GC: Partly – I think I can say it without offence to myself – there is an element of originality about my mind. Terrible thing to say, but I think there is that. And also just the milieu suited me. I was able to cope with the evidence. My mind isn't very big, but I was able to cope with the evidence, fit it in and churn it out in a new form. So it did suit me.

HM: It's an interesting mix of your great activity and involvement in everything that was happening and your interest in contemporary matters. There's a rebellious element about you, isn't there?

GC: I hope not! [laughs]

HM: I mean, this kind of independence.

GC: I'm independent, I am independent, yes.

HM: I mean, going your way, and thinking of the Rhodes Scholarship idea from ten.

GC: Of course Greats at its best was meant to be a course that encouraged people to think for themselves. Paradoxical it is, because it was the great breeding ground for civil servants in England, and they are notable for not thinking for themselves. Not allowed to by the system, I expect. But Greats suited me marvellously, and I enjoyed it greatly. There are very clever people doing it, and really very talented, and I was the least of all, but it was a very pleasing environment to be in.

Daily routine at Christ Church

HM: What was your daily routine?

GC: I got up early in those times, and one had lectures, and then I worked in my room. I didn't work in the library very much, I always got things to my room, and one had to get the essays written. In the afternoon one played games. The first time I went to Iffley Road, to rugby football, the captain, Oswald Newton-Thompson, put us through such a rigorous time I thought, 'Oh God, if this goes on I won't be able to keep it up.' We ran full speed up and down the ground three times first, thinking I was doing a sprint, and then it was turned into another sprint, and then another sprint. I thought, 'I can't go on with this.' But I did. I was often pretty tired when I got back to my room, so that I used to sleep before dinner. But I worked, and in the vacation I worked extremely hard. People thought it was very remarkable, having a wife and family and doing all this, playing all these games and so on. The truth is that I was very much better off having a wife and family. I went home, I had my books there. She, the goddess, arranged everything for me to work. I used to work extremely hard in the vacation, much harder than any undergraduate I know now works. Although in term I was a bit distracted, in the vacation I did a great deal of work at home. When it came to the summer term, we were playing three full-day matches of cricket a week, starting at 11.30 and going on till 6.30. But it happened, and it was lovely, and we travelled a bit.

HM: And what were you aiming for?

GC: Full enjoyment. I don't know. I was going to get a First, I was aiming at a First, and I got it, by the grace of God. But I hadn't any thoughts, I didn't know what I was going to do.

Getting to University College

When I came to the end of the course, I was sitting around a bit, and I thought, 'Well, I'll have to go school teaching.' And I remember I had an interview with the headmaster of Harrow, and that didn't come to anything.

HM: Were you surprised at that?

GC: I wasn't really. I think I just thought that it'll be all right. But then the job was advertised at Univ and I applied for that.

HM: At University College?

GC: At University College. And after a long period of delay when they were interviewing people and so on, and after I was dined at Univ a couple of times, I got it. I don't know what I'd have done if I hadn't got that, but I did it, and I think there was a sort of presumption of being in the Lord's keeping. Maybe there isn't a Lord, but he was certainly keeping me then.

HM: He was around then, yes. And that was a job as tutor?

GC: As Fellow and Ancient Historian, yes, Ancient History tutor.

HM: Right, and as far as you were concerned, that was a lifetime job?

GC: Lifetime job, yes. I was frankly quite unworthy of it. There were very able people who applied at the same time who didn't get it. I don't know what they were thinking of. There was one chap who was my fellow candidate, a man called Brunt, who became a very eminent Roman historian. I can't think how I beat Brunt, except that maybe Univ had just won rugby cuppers and they thought they'd get a rugby coach. [laughs] It paid off, they won rugby cuppers again after an interval of only thirty years. [laughs]

HM: So you didn't get involved in college rugby?

GC: Well, I used to see the young. They did want people who'd be about the college. And I enjoyed all that. I was too much given to playing games and feasting at dining clubs etcetera not to enjoy that. I took to all that part of it and gradually became a college figure.

HM: And there you were for—

GC: I'm still there in a sense! I'm an Emeritus Fellow now, but I have lived my life around University College. And having this facility of remembering names and events and so on, I've always been quite useful to the place.

HM: So this really was a natural home for you?

GC: Yes, I was meant by the Lord God from the beginning of Creation to go to Oxford, settle down there and never go anywhere else again. [laughs] Which is rather shaming. Rhodes Scholars are expected to go – the founder expected people to go out and rule, govern the world and bless mankind.

HM: Had there been any suggestion that you ought to go back to New Zealand, or to do anything?

GC: That was implied in the whole thing, but of course it was countered by the fact that the subject I had taken on was done only in Oxford in the way that Oxford did it, at that time – of course that's no longer the case, so that I couldn't really have done it elsewhere as I did it and wanted to do it here. So that I was slightly excluded from that. As I've already said, there was this element of feeling sundered from New Zealand as a whole. I hadn't really had a proper war.

HM: And yet there you were, one of its greatest achievers in accomplishing this—

GC: Achievement was success, courage in war, having been through it. I hadn't been through it, that was it.

HM: What about University College, then? What was it like compared with Christ Church?

GC: Frankly the contrast was almost comic. Christ Church was what they would now call laid-back. People did what they wanted to do. Univ was much more like a public school, with everybody going down to watch the rugby team playing in the cup matches and so on. Christ Church didn't do that sort of thing. And Univ was a very close-knit society, quite small physically, and they all lived on top of each other and they loved the college dearly and they loved each other and it was very close, while Christ Church was much more widespread and separate. And so it was very different in that respect, and where Christ Church was big, Univ was comparatively small, at that time – well, it was probably only half the size of Christ Church in numbers of students, and physically Christ Church was very widespread. I had in the first year rooms in Meadow Buildings. That was 300, 200 yards away from Peckwater Quad, where people live, and then there were those few who lived in Tom Quad, in separate places there. It was all spread out. There was Canterbury Quad with the Peers' staircase, etcetera. It was a much more spread-out place, whereas at Univ we're all concentrated, all living on top of each other, a small Junior Common Room. Univ actually has always been a very good college. You've got to be an absolute troglodyte not to be happy in Univ. You know, anyone who feels lonely in Univ, there's something wrong with him. That used to be so, I expect it still is in some degree.

5   LIFE AS AN ANCIENT HISTORY DON

[Inspired by the NZRSOHP I supplemented those interviews by conducting further interviews with George in 2005 through the summer, starting in June.]

Charles Hignett

TC: Just say something about Charlie Hignett [1896-1966, fellow of Hertford College 1924-1959], who in my mind is a mentor of a kind to you.

GC: Well Charlie followed the old-fashioned thing, of inviting all new appointments in the sub-faculty to dinner. And I went, and I asked him back, and we had a very pleasing exchange. It was very important to ask him back.

TC: What was his position?

GC: He was Ancient History Fellow of Hertford. He told me he couldn't get on with CE Stevens, the Ancient History Fellow at Magdalen   College. Stevens hadn't answered an invitation, but he sent him a telegram on the day when he was due to say he was coming! Charlie sent him back one saying no you're not.

Charlie was a very colourful character in his way. I remember the first time I went. He said come at about 7.13. I got there at about 7.13 and a quarter. And he said, 'Pity you're late. We'll have to wait until X goes in.' And he stood at the window looking to see the Fellows going up into the Hall, and when X had gone and was suitably surrounded with people, he went. And I'll never forget that first night.

TC: What age was Charles Hignett at this stage?

GC: He must have been about fifty-two or something. He'd been a Fellow of Hertford for some time, and knew the Oxford ropes. He was a very special character, you see. He had been taught by Grundy [Ancient History Fellow of Corpus Christi College, 1903-31], whom he regarded as a source of great misinformation. And he insisted on being correctly reported. He dictated his lectures. They were carefully written out, with the time, twenty minutes past and so on, written in. So he'd know where he was up to. It was a very odd way of lecturing, and I was very glad of it, because it was very hard to settle down after the War, it had been an unsettling time. So I went to his lectures and took notes on them. The Athenian Constitution was the basis of my felicity. But many people thought to dictate lectures was not quite the thing. But I used to go and see Charlie, we had afternoons together, you know, for an hour or two, and we'd discuss things. And the great triumph of my life was one afternoon, he pulled down a copy of JHS [Journal of Hellenic Studies], and wrote in pencil beside a note, 'Doubted by GLC' [laughs]. On another occasion, we had been discussing something – in those times the Messenger Service between colleges was very good – and I had only been back in college about an hour when a note was delivered, saying, 'Sorry we couldn't agree about Diodorus. Still, as Socrates said to one of his stooges: if we find the answer we lose the problem' [laughs].

He regarded Wade-Gery as a man preaching nonsense. He would say to a pupil, 'Did he say that?!'

TC: So do you think you gained from him the necessity to be sceptical about everything, in a way, even in Oxford? Because Wade-Gery would be a very elevated name, wouldn't it?

GC: Wade-Gery was much more my style. I thought his lectures were really *mar*vellous. I greatly admired Wade-Gery. And the styles in which he wrote his articles, masterly, I think. Not everybody thought so, but I think so.

TC: Did Wade-Gery combine that ability to do all the detailed study with getting the bigger picture?

GC: Yes, so he never wrote. He was signed up to write a history of Greece, by Methuen. And he never did it.

TC: The work I remember is the work on the Athenian Tribute Lists. Is that not an example of something unavailable in the nineteenth century, but in the twentieth century, ancient historians would then have a proper record of these immensely valuable 'documents'.

GC: That was because of the Americans. The work was done jointly with Benjamin Dean Meritt – B.D. Meritt – and Malcolm McGregor. And it was American money, because Americans spend a lot of money on archaeology, and it's all beautifully published. And I had ATL [Athenian Tribute List] Volume 1 as an undergraduate, quite unusually.

TC: Did Charles Hignett ever publish?

GC: Oh, yes! Not only his history of the Athenian Constitution. And then he did his book on Xerxes' invasion of Greece. And that was very interesting because it's full of very careful topographical discussions but they're based entirely on maps and what other people said. *He* never went there. He never walked around.

TC: Which is something you've done.

GC: I haven't *really* done it. Not like Americans. They get around. I mean, Charlie was not a traveller. The first time we met, I said something about, 'Are you going abroad this summer?' thinking that a single don would be able to go off to Greece each summer. And he said, 'No. I haven't been abroad since 1934. I haven't been to London since 1936.' And later in the conversation I said to him something about Cambridge. He said, 'I've never been to Cambridge' [laughs].

He died in 1966, I think. And he retired in about '59, and I used to look up his references for him. They were always absolutely dead accurate. He'd copy them all out very carefully, but I'd check them. I used to send him cards. And this was a source of great interest to him and his sister Fanny, counting up the number of words I could get on a card. He was astonished.

TC: Was there an element of eccentricity about him?

GC: Oh yes. He didn't live in college, he lived out in Frenchay Road in digs there, because, as a young don, he had been sort of tackled by the rugger louts or some rowdies on the Bridge of Sighs in Hertford and debagged. He wasn't going to have that sort of thing.

His life was dull, it was all very carefully regulated. The first time I went, when Common Room was over, he said, 'Let's go upstairs for a while, there's still time.' And then came the moment when, at about five to ten, he had to go and change, because he was going to change out of his dinner jacket, to go home to North Oxford. And I used to accompany him to Cornmarket.

TC: Pat said that she had no contact with him?

GC: Yes.

TC: And secondly, he would ring up and Sarah was in the habit of answering the phone. And Charles Hignett called her 'Telephonic Sarah'.

GC: Yes!

Oxford Ancient History in the 1950s

TC: Who were the great names in Ancient History in the 50s?

GC: The great name in a sense was Hugh Last, H.M. Last. He was a very striking figure. He always wore striped black suits with spats, and talked in a very ponderous way. His lectures were very good, and I was able to get every word down and I worked them up and made them my basis for my work on the constitution of the Augustan principate. Of course, all that stuff was utterly out of date, because Ronald Syme had taken over, and the world of Von Premerstein, because they all observed the rise of the Nazi party, the fascist party, those of allegiance, we knew what that meant.

TC: Is it true that Syme had read the German scholars in a way that perhaps an old guard at Oxford hadn't?

GC: No. Last's lectures were full of Mommsen's first edition, and then Mommsen's third edition of the '[Römisches] Staatsrecht', but he was so constipated, and he didn't actually have original ideas, I think. There was a lot of constipated stuff about the scholars' world, scholarship etcetera. He was a really powerful figure, but he was nothing intellectually, compared to Syme.

TC: Did Syme follow him as Camden Professor of Ancient History?

GC: Syme followed him as Camden.

TC: What year would that be, can you remember?

GC: 1949.

TC: If Last had stepped down in 1949, you had heard him as an undergraduate?

GC: Yes. Syme and Last didn't get on because they were totally different people, and whereas Last was very ponderous and serious about affairs, a man of judgement, Syme was naturally lightweight about affairs. He was flippant. I remember one story about Ronald Syme: he went to Congregation with Isobel Henderson, and when the house divided into the *placets* and *non placets*, with a huge number of people going out *placet*, i.e. approving the motion, Syme said, 'All these people can't be right, let's go out the other door.' There was a sort of flippancy about him, and I found he didn't really apply himself to business. But of course, he was a great scholar of a special sort. He had this extraordinary knowledge of all the details and all the people. Prosopography was his big thing, and he knew them all, as it were, and whom they had married.

He had a huge memory, with a great vision. And he assumed that everybody in history thought as he thought, and he thought as the characters do in Balzac's 'Cousine Bette'. He was constantly talking about Balzac.

TC: His output was prodigious, wasn't it?

GC: Oh, his output was prodigious and his public utterances were pretty lightweight. The thing was that he could narrate, and with subtle hints and so on, give the reader his point of view. He could not argue out a case, like Peter Brunt. He didn't argue a case for the decline of the aristocracy or something, that wasn't his style. It's not surprising that in Greats he had done very well in the Ancient History side but rather feebly on the Philosophy side. That wasn't him.

TC: What was he like as a lecturer, do you think?

GC: I went to his lectures on inscriptions of the Roman army, I think, and that sort of thing. I don't think he was a good lecturer. I've heard him deliver one or two papers at conferences. I heard him give a paper at a conference; it was lightweight, I thought. And the sort of things he said when he was on tour overseas were shaming.

TC: Really?

GC: He thought anything'll do for these people. He'd come along with a few ideas jotted down on the back of an envelope, and it was embarrassing. When we were in Otago he arrived and his address was really pretty flimsy and inferior.

TC: But his genius went into his prose?

GC: Yes. And his genius was to write like Tacitus. He was more Tacitean than Tacitus, really. Of course his great book, 'The Roman Revolution', really made him a millionaire. When he died, he left about a million and a half pounds.

TC: Because it had been read round the world?

GC: Yes.

TC: It's not an easy book, but it's riveting.

GC: But it's *narrative*. Syme thought narrative was the job, and I don't believe that's right. I think professional historians ought to be arguing about important principles etcetera, and asking important questions. He didn't think that. He did narrative with sly hints on the way. I once said something to him about Tiberius. He didn't deny it. But a minute or two later in the conversation, he kicked back in a sly way.

TC: What do you think will happen to his reputation?

GC: It will stand, but after all, Peter Brunt, actually, gave it a bit of a thumping because of his scepticism about prosopography as a method. And Peter wrote one or two devastating articles on that.

TC: But 'The Roman Revolution', one thinks or hopes it will be read in the next 100, 200 years.

GC: They never are! But it will be read, yes.

TC: But will that be because it so interestingly reflects the condition of Europe?

GC: I don't know. His idea is that the principate of Augustus was in fact a violent revolution with seizure of property and murder of people and so on.

TC: And the Roman ability to dress up these terrible things in legal words...

GC: That had deceived Last.

One interesting thing about Syme is, you see, he was always Professor Syme, or Mr Syme. He never did a doctorate. In those ages people didn't do doctorates. Now the one man who was an exception, Nicholas Sherwin-White – *he* did a doctorate before the war, in that he did the thesis; 'The Roman Citizenship' is his book; and it was all approved and so on. But he never took the degree. Because he felt he couldn't take a doctorate when people like Syme and Last and Wade-Gery were just ordinary Misters.

TC: And Peter Brunt followed Syme as the Camden Professor?

GC: Peter followed Syme in 1970.

TC: You were a close friend of his by then?

GC: I knew Peter reasonably well, yes. He was at Oriel. We used to exchange hospitality and converse.

TC: He was a great one for anecdotes, wasn't he? Like you, of course.

GC: I'm feeble! He had a wonderful range of stories about Oxford, with a slight touch of mimicry in his voice, which he does extremely well. Ronald Syme liked to mimic. But Peter did it very well. I've asked him whether he wouldn't write them down, but no, he won't. They'll die with him.

TC: Better even than writing would be to have him talking.

GC: I know. He's an old man now, and I think he's beginning to feel that death is at hand. He wishes it were.

Anyhow, a notable character was Dacre Balsdon at Exeter, a very good tutor, and a very generous entertainer.

TC: He liked the young, didn't he?

GC: He was very good with the young. He liked them, as I like them. I don't think there was any homosexuality. That was just the way one did it.

Balsdon had his merits as a historian. He wrote good articles. He wrote one rather lightweight book about the emperor Gaius that was quite enjoyable. And then he wrote a book about Roman women. But he didn't write books very much. Whereas you see Ronald Syme wrote great books. 'The Roman Revolution', 'Tacitus', 'Sallust', 'The Historia Augusta'. There were important works there. His mark is very considerable. Whereas Dacre will be forgotten. But he was still a notable character. I did have a tremendous row with him.

TC: Was that ever made up, that rift?

GC: Not really, no. He had many rows in his life.

TC: Oxford being a close, intimate society, that must have gone on quite a lot.

GC: I expect so, yes. Dacre didn't take any pains to conceal his feelings. I met him in the quad of Exeter just after he had come back from a period of sabbatical leave. He said, [flamboyantly] 'Oh it's maaarvellous to be back! The only thing I can't *bear* is my colleagues!' And they took against him. And they wouldn't have him as Rector, and he had more or less decided that he was going to be Rector, or should be Rector.

TC: So he made enemies easily.

GC: He made enemies. People detested him. I remember, there was a young Law fellow called Buxton. He said to me, 'You must come and have dinner and meet Buxton our new Law Fellow, he's very ...' then after about a year he said, [with venom] "*Buxton!*" [laughs]. And like William Greig Barr, who became Rector. He thought that Greig Barr was the golden boy when he was there, living in college. But when he married his Greek wife, Eleni, and Greig lived out of college and didn't come in very much and so on, he fell right out of favour. I was at dinner in St Hugh's one night when Balsdon was the guest of the Principal or something, across the table, and he said to his host, 'Is it true that Exeter have elected *Barr*?' He knew perfectly well. Well the man they did take on of course was Kenneth Wheare, in the 60s, and Kenneth Wheare was a really very wonderful, able man, you know.

TC: One of the things I remember you saying, I hope I don't misremember, Oxford was a place for gossip because it was intimate –

GC: Oh! Endless gossip, yes.

TC: And the rule was, you can gossip, but just be careful what you say to someone's face?

GC: Yes. Say anything you like about him behind his back, but not to his face.

TC: Or her face, now.

GC: Yes. It was tremendous gossip, nothing was secret here. I mean there were things *I* didn't know, I didn't know until I read Nicola Lacey's biography of Herbert Hart, that Isaiah Berlin was Jennifer Hart's lover! Herbert didn't know, either! Anyhow, we're getting off the point here. You want notable Ancient Historians.

TC: Yes, that's right.

GC: Well, a notable Ancient Historian was Michael Holroyd, a Fellow of Brasenose. When he died in 1953, I read in The Times that although he was widely read, he never wrote anything. Except an article. And I thought, my God. In those times *all* Oxford dons got an obituary. (They don't get it now.) But in The Times. I thought, they're not going to say that about me. So I sat down that very day and wrote my first article.

TC: One of the merits of 'Georgica', the *Festschrift* in your honour published in 1991, was that it's got a bibliography, and I must say I was struck by how many items there are in it.

GC: Yes. It's longer now.

TC: So, your first article was ...?

GC: ... published in '56. And I had the patronage of Stanley Robinson the great numismatist.

TC: So it was on coins, was it?

GC: Yes, and I remember Russell Meiggs wrote to me and said, 'We generally give First XV colours to those who publish in numismatic journals.' Meiggs is a man I ought to talk about.

TC: He was Greek History?

GC: Well he did all Ancient History at Balliol. He was very good. And a very good tutor, and a very notable figure. But he was a big man, and he had this extraordinary mop of hair hanging back. It wouldn't be anything now.

TC: It was very striking.

GC: Looked like a prophet.

TC: Let me remember something about Meiggs from around 1969 or '70. When I met him, he remembered seeing the Fritz Lang silent films, German films of the 1920s, and *Doctor Mabuse the Gambler* which was a sort of mythical film, not available. And I thought that he'd seen it, he remembered it, that was terrific.

GC: He was a man of great depressions. But he wrote some very notable things. He wrote a very important book about the history of Ostia. He wrote a very worthy and admirable history of the Athenian Empire. And he wrote a few articles, but not many. But he was a really very considerable force. He was very kind to me. He looked after me in my early days in a way, and I owe him a great deal. There was one day when I thought I was going mad, trying to get round the Callias decrees before the Peloponnesian War. I rang him up. And he took me for a walk in the Meadows and told me, don't worry, none of us know. I was really getting into quite a state about that.

TC: This would be in the 1950s, would it?

GC: Yes, it could have been 1952, '51.

TC: Oh right, you had a lot to learn, didn't you?

GC: I knew *nothing*, Tim, it was all a bloody scandal my being a Fellow.

TC: But you seized your opportunity to find out, and got stuck in.

GC: I don't know how I got the job, I think it must have been the hand of God. In my retirement speech, I said that one of my fellow candidates at that time was Peter Brunt. And I said this to Miriam Griffin, she said, '*No!*'

TC: You were interviewed by the Fellows collectively, not a *small* interview panel? That's extraordinary, isn't it?

GC: It was a pretty inferior way but they took me on. I think they took me on because Giles Alington thought I'd be a good chap for the boys.

TC: Univ didn't know what they were getting. But they got something in spades.

GC: They did. But they got it through Alington's perception.

TC: Those things are important at interviews. Peter Brunt is the great scholar, but Peter wouldn't have been the great college man that you were.

GC: He would have been hopeless.

TC: Univ needed that, that was part of the ethos. Russell Meiggs was interested in looking after people. You might have the great figures like Syme and what have you, but you need people who'll take an interest in people, don't you?

GC: Of course, Meiggs was good at that, and it was a Balliol tradition, really. Balliol dons cared for their people.

And there were *other* people, they were all very distinguished and able. CE Stevens was absolutely dotty. He had a lot of dotty ideas, but he was all great fun.

TC: Martin West was not a historian, but you always speak glowingly about him.

GC: Martin West. He is a most distinguished mind. He is a real *Wissenschaftlich* scholar. He was frankly a poor tutor, because he has these tremendous silences in conversation. And the young *hate* silence above all in a tutorial, it makes them feel stupid. He'll just look at you and say nothing. But he's a very good scholar indeed, and, I must say, he was also a very good picker of academic horseflesh. Of course Stephanie West [his wife] is a tremendously clever woman.

TC: A most high-powered couple.

GC: That house is an absolute powerhouse. And they just sit, reading books at breakfast.

Martin West is the real thing. He won the prize for most distinguished classicist recently [probably the Balzan Prize for Classical Antiquity awarded in 2000], he won a tremendous sum of money. It was well deserved. He probably wouldn't have been suitable for the chair [Regius Professor of Greek] because that's not his thing. He's rightly placed now, when he became a Fellow of All Souls. That's the sort of Fellow that All Souls ought to cater for. And they did.

He was a delightful character. He became the secretary of the Governing Body – he couldn't take proper minutes, you know? He wasn't good at that. I used to run a Greats dining club, and he'd suddenly be seen with a great spider on his shoulder.

TC: Good Lord!

GC: Some sort of toy thing. He didn't say anything, it just happened. So when he went to All Souls, it was natural for him to lead the great mallard business, where they go walking around the roofs, and crying 'quack quack'.

TC: That prompts me to ask: what about [Edward] Fraenkel, [Paul] Maas, and [Felix] Jacoby?

GC: Reggie Burton of Oriel called them the front row of the scrum. They were very formidable, and they too represent a quality of *Wissenschaftlich*.

TC: They'd been refugees in the 1930s?

GC: Yes and were still here. I never taught Maas, but I once sat beside Jacoby at a feast and talked to him, just after he had published his book entitled 'Atthis', and he really did look βοῶψ, he looked like an ox. Ox-faced. Fraenkel I really never talked to, though I must say that – it's one of the things that I wouldn't confess to anyone else, but ... – in the general summation and condemnation of the non-literary dons of Oxford Classics, he exempted me. When I was Chairman of the Sub-Faculty in Ancient History, in which role I had to go before the Franks Commission etcetera, there was a famous meeting when Robin Nisbet and Donald Russell were present representing the literature sub-faculty. The question was about the reform of Greats. And Dacre Balsdon said about them, 'They've ruined their subject and they want now to ruin ours!' and I gave him a public ticking-off, and said, 'This is a very serious matter, the whole future of the subject is at stake.' I was really gratified, I shouldn't confess these things, but Robin Nisbet recently gave a talk entitled 'Retrospects', in which he said that I played an important part there. It was very gratifying.

TC: But coming back to Fraenkel ...

GC: Fraenkel had said he condemned the whole lot of them, 'except Cawkwell'.

The Franks Commission

TC: What was the Franks Commission?

GC: The Franks Commission was about the reform of the University, and Maurice Shock was on it. This is 1965. I had to go before them and give evidence for the Ancient Historians. And Franks was the most lordly man, a really Rolls-Royce intellect. He would ask one a question, at great length, amazing lucidity, and at the end of it, all you could say was yes or no.

TC: Socrates!

GC: He was a really great man, Franks.

TC: The Franks Commission Report had a great impact on the University, did it?

GC: Well, it should have, but like the reforms proposed by John Hood, they wanted to sweep it all aside. I remember my countryman, I'm ashamed to say, John Owens, Senior Tutor of Lincoln, declaring as Chairman of the Senior Tutors' Committee – he said, 'Totally unacceptable.' But of course, they should've thought about it seriously, and they've spent time getting round to that. Some of the reforms proposed by the present Vice-Chancellor, John Hood, are actually Franks Report reforms.

It was all rather irritating to Maurice Shock. I mean Maurice really wrote a great deal of the Franks Report. It wasn't taken seriously. And that's an Oxford thing. The great thing about Oxford is complacency. They think they are incomparable. They mustn't be compared to anybody else because they're incomparably good. Which they're not.

TC: And the politics of these things are so important. If your things are rejected at first, how do you do them in such a way to get them back in some other way ...

GC: You do them like Julius Caesar: present them partially. Bit by bit you get them done. You've got to be persistent.

TC: Can you say something about the timetable of the proposals?

GC: The first thing was to make a literary option in Greats. That began something like 1970. And for the life of me, I can't remember what exactly was on the agenda at the famous meeting we held. We wanted to have some sort of reform, getting literature into Greats, I think. Anyhow, I played a part there – that must have been back in about 1964, '65. I perceived, and I believe rightly, that if we didn't change, we would just lose out. If all people who wanted to do classical literature went elsewhere, our subject would die. When I'm dying I shall think that that was not a bad moment.

TC: And what was the first year in which undergraduates could come up and do Greats with no Greek?

GC: That is later. I think it would be something like 1979. One of the first girls in Univ did that, Janet Williams – got a First, very clever girl. But she came up in 1979. It must have been late 70s that that change was made. But of course, they've got to be bloody good, to do it. If you're not, it's too much work.

TC: The other thing that I ascribe to you, correctly or not, is the idea of bringing in a *modern* history option.

GC: Well I had quite a hand in the introduction of Ancient and Modern History. And my purpose there was simply to create jobs for the boys. I could see Classics going, declining. And I wanted History – Ancient History – to be hooked into Modern History. It *is* appealing, people do do it.

TC: Do you think that has been a success?

GC: I believe it has, yes. I don't know about the numbers doing it, but I think it *has* been a success. People want to do it.

TC: Is it wrong to say that part of the appeal of doing Ancient and Modern is that they relate to one another? Syme could see Roman history and could see Europe, Germany in the 30s and think of Rome, and you studied fourth-century Greek history for its own sake, but you were constantly surprised by these repeating patterns of behaviour later on.

GC: That's true. Anyhow, I have done useful things in a minor way.

His books

TC: Now, 'The Greek Wars', published in 2005. That's material you've had in your drawer for a long time, and pulled together, is that right?

GC: Well, a lot of it's been written for about twenty years, anyhow, and slowly rewritten. People may say it's very remarkable for a man of eighty -five to produce such a book, but of course, I've been going at it since 1985. Practically everything I've published has been lying around in the mind and actually in the drawer for a very long time.

TC: Which is the book you're most pleased with, 'Philip', 'Thucydides', or 'Greek Wars', do you think?

GC: I think probably the Thucydides was good. The Philip was good too, of its sort.

TC: How did that come about?

GC: A chap from Faber's called on me, and said, would you write a book for us. And I said yes, without thought. I have never wanted money or anything, I didn't think I was worth any money. And I thought I ought to look for a prestigious publisher, like the OUP.

TC: But Faber's was good.

GC: Faber's were all right. They publish it, they sell it, and that's the end of it. Routledge's with 'Thucydides' was a small book, but I thought it was a good book.

TC: It won the Runciman Prize. How do you think that happened? You've no insight into that?

GC: I think that the judges are told to read the following books, and they read them.

TC: Is it true you were a bit disappointed in the reception of 'Thucydides'?

GC: Very few reviews, you know, very few. There were some. They were all right. But I mean, it's amazing to me, it was never reviewed in Classical Review for instance. I think it's partly the great slackness and laziness of people. The English are very lazy. They ought to be made to brace up a bit, you know?

TC: If I may say so, I think it's the most difficult of your books.

GC: It is.

TC: Because it's so densely argued! And Thucydides is a difficult author.

GC: In a way, I think one of the best things I did was the introduction to the Penguin translation of Xenophon's 'Hellenica' [1978].

TC: Why do you think that?

GC: It was well written, I knew it. I expect it's now getting a bit rusty.

TC: The attraction of a book is to be able to write? You like writing prose, don't you?

GC: I do enjoy writing, yes, though it's a great labour.

TC: Did you labour over passages at all, to try and sparkle them up?

GC: No, no, I didn't.

TC: Because one of the rules of Trevor-Roper was to avoid purple passages lest they rise up to shame you in old age. [George bursts out laughing.] That's one of his ten rules of writing.

GC: He writes beautifully, you know.

Eric Gray

GC: We've got off the point: Oxford scholars. I could say something of my tutor, Eric Gray. He was a man of tremendous ability and it came to nothing because he had been appointed just before the War. He went off to the War for about five or six years, doing pretty hair-raising stuff. He was with the Greek Resistance. They called him Hercules, he was very strong. And he was a brave man, but of course, he then came back to Christ Church to find himself appointed Censor, which runs all the administrative offices. He was a Senior Tutor, and Admissions Officer, and so on, all sorts of things, and Dean. It used to be all one in Christ Church. That took up six years, I think, when he should have been spending time getting back to his subject, and he didn't. And I think the Professors, Ronald Syme in particular, were at fault. He should have encouraged him. I remember Eric lending me a piece that he had written about the Tabula Hebana. It was excellent. And it was very much better than the piece written by AHM Jones and published in the Journal of Roman Studies. But he never published it. And in his old age he had become very diffident – he would ask *me* my opinion. God, I was a nothing compared to him.

TC: We formed the impression, that's my cohort of Christ Church Greats pupils [late 1960s], that he was afraid of being contradicted.

GC: There *may* have been something in that.

TC: If you are saying he had lost the plot, as a result of the War, that's a shame, isn't it?

GC: He lost the feeling that he had to get on and publish something. I mean, he knew a tremendous amount about Asia Minor. But it never came to anything.

TC: He was good on archaeology, wasn't he?

GC: He was very good. Mayhap, he was not a good lecturer. He was not a good tutor. He talked. He just started talking after you read your essay, well that's not right. The points that I would make about good tuition are: first, undergraduates want their essays answered. Secondly, they don't want to be chucked out on the hour, they want a proper discussion. I always allowed an hour and twenty minutes on average for my tutorials, and with a very clever person it was two hours. I used to sit

taking notes of what they said, you see. I always made them read it, because it's a literary production, I want them to hear what it sounds like –
TC: With your notes you can then refer to what *they've* said.
GC: And my notes are concerned with their *argument*, I wasn't concerned with the details of what they said. And I never interrupted someone, unless he used some trendy language. In which case I used to trip him up. But I tried to hear it as a whole and argue with him as a whole.
TC: Did you find that stimulating? With the brightest?
GC: Oh yes, with the brightest, it was indeed.
TC: Did it make you think, 'This chap's got a point I hadn't thought of,' every now and then?
GC: Not very often, because originality is a rare thing with undergraduates, and in a way, I had an original mind. So generally they were more shocked by my ideas! But no, coming back to Eric Gray, he talked on and on, and I remember making points to him, but he would sort of take a note of them, but he never actually wrote a considered reply.

The Wykeham Professor of Greek History

TC: What is the succession of Professors of Greek History through your time?
GC: In my time, there was H.T. [Theodore] Wade-Gery, whom Syme called the Holy Theodore. And then there was Andrewes, Tony Andrewes, a very good, admirable man. Good scholar. He didn't have some of the qualities of Wade-Gery, but he was a very weighty, considerable person. And then, after that, there was George Forrest. He was a man we all liked very much.
TC: Forrest got it in about the mid-70s, did he?
GC: It must have been about 1977. It was a death sentence for him. He'd been the most brilliant, wonderful tutor, and he was a good lecturer. But he was not suited; partly, he didn't, to my mind, have enough knowledge of the subject! His knowledge of Greek history stopped with the fifth century. And that wasn't very satisfactory. And he didn't have a good critical mind. Now Peter Brunt has very good critical faculties. Brunt can sit through a paper and make some very pungent criticisms at the end. Forrest didn't do that. It was a great tragedy for him and for the

subject. Then David Lewis took over, and he was very worthy, followed by the present one, Robert Parker.

TC: And that's when Simon Hornblower should have got it?

GC: I don't know that he *should* have; in my mind I wish he *had*. He's got this tremendous polymathy. Read everything! He read my book on the Greek wars in a day as soon as he got it. I've known him do it before with that book of Sallares ['The Ecology of the Ancient Greek World' by Robert Sallares]. He read the whole bloody thing and it would take me a month to read it! He read it all in a day or two.

TC: Did you think you might be in line in the 1970s?

GC: I might have been considered if I had applied, but I didn't want it, I wasn't good enough. One thing, at the bottom, my Greek isn't good enough. No, it wouldn't have done me.

TC: In a way, your blessing has been that you've been able to pursue your original ideas?

GC: My blessing has been that I was in the job that I was equal to, and greatly happy, it all suited extremely well.

Masters of Univ

TC: Could you cast your mind back and do a list for me of all the Masters you've served under?

GC: I went to the College while John Wild was Master who had come to the College as a Chaplain, and in the War he had been Domestic Bursar, very amiable; the Fellows were all getting old and retiring; and so they committed the folly of electing him Master. It was too much for him. He was a very nice man, but his mind wasn't big enough for the job, and his wife [Margaret] was such a young woman bravely trying to be hostess. They were ill paid, I realise now, disgracefully ill paid. The entertaining was bad. After the War, everything was difficult – rations and so on. So, one had sympathy for him, but he really wasn't up to the job. And it was Clem Attlee, he solved the College problem really, since he was an Honorary Fellow and was really devoted to the College. I don't know whether this was so – but it was generally assumed – that he had Wild appointed Dean of Durham. And that was a very happy issue. He was very good there; he was at his very best in dealing with problems of fabric, which even by that time Deans had really become much involved with. He's a nice memory, I liked him. Anyhow. He was followed by Arthur Goodhart, and Arthur was to my mind a great man.

TC: What year?

GC: 1951. I sat through that election, which was very interesting: we all sat around discussing people, I remember someone nominated Roy Harrod, but most interesting was that Giles Alington was persuaded that we ought to have some big name, and he got on to the idea of TS Eliot. And it was very funny, in the early stages, Arthur Goodhart had no thought that he would be asked to be Master. (Arthur was Professor of Jurisprudence, greatly liked and admired and so on. But he *commented* on the suggestion of TS Eliot by saying he thought he was an awful bore, the fellow had tried to read him his poetry on the *Queen Mary*.) When he was actually asked to be Master he said, 'Don't they know I'm a Jew?' He had assumed that the college would *not* be electing a *Jew* as Master of this Christian establishment. I think, all in all, Arthur Goodhart was wonderful. Of course, he became probably the biggest benefactor of the College's history. He was a big man, he was highly respected by leading lawyers and moved in the highest circles there.

TC: So he'd made his money in the law, or was it family money?

GC: It was family money. His name was Arthur Lehman Goodhart, he was one of the Lehmans. He was very rich, but he was very generous, and he had many charming idiosyncrasies. Although he was rich, he just had an ordinary Vauxhall car, which he drove very badly. However he was instrumental in founding the Pedestrians' Association – to protect pedestrians against his type of driver!

TC: Was he good because he was good at entertaining, or in understanding the College?

GC: He was shrewd. He had a good sense of finance, and it's really very important in a Master. He had this wonderful wife, Cecily, whom we adored; she was a wonderful woman. And Arthur decided that if there was going to be a viable College in the post-War world, the wives must have a place in the College. And he started a wives' dinner, and he did things for the wives, and bluebell parties up on Boar's Hill. He did all that with such spirit and generosity, and really, I can't speak highly enough of him. He quickly fixed on Maurice Shock, who became Bursar when Norman Marsh went off to Amnesty International, or the Hague or something. Arthur had a tremendous regard for Maurice Shock, and rightly. Maurice understood about money but also he has great skill in approaching people about things.

Arthur was due to retire in 1961, but because the Goodhart Building would not be completed, the College extended him by two years, changed the statutes so a Master can have an extra two years. And he was able to stay there as Master.

The staff passed from liking him to loving him. He had his foibles. He had a secretary etcetera, but you'd see him going up the High every night with his letters to post them, because he could give evidence in court that he'd posted the letter in the letterbox! I reverence his memory.

TC: The fact that he'd been Professor of Jurisprudence would have given him an inside view, wouldn't it?

GC: Oh yes, he knew the College, but of course, when he ceased to be Professor of Jurisprudence, that was another great blessing because we got Herbert Hart.

TC: Arthur steps down in 1963 and after him?

GC: Sir John Maud became Master, having been quite a figure in the College in the 30s. He went off to Birkbeck as Master or something, just before the War, and then he went into the Civil Service in the War, and had a fairly illustrious career there. He had great merits, great personal charm for people who couldn't see through it. And I would say he was a good Master, you never get everything. He had his merits, he also had grave defects, but that's not uncommon. He was the only serious candidate at that time, though. George Paul proposed Herbert Hart! And one didn't think very seriously of it. But when Herbert became Principal of Brasenose in 1973, it was clear that he would have been marvellous. There was a great change, though, because between 1961/'63 and '68, Herbert had done the Hart report into junior discipline, and he got an interest in the running of the University. He took to it. And he had a sort of innocence about him, he found it very interesting, and he wrote a very notable piece about it, and a special report was published. And that got him going, and I expect it was that, slightly, that moved Brasenose to invite him to be Principal.

TC: Sir John Maud.

GC: We've got Sir John Maud. They came, and he had to go through a process of learning that Oxford was a very different place from when he'd been Dean.

TC: And his wife, Jean, was very grand, wasn't she?

GC: Slightly, yes. She was quite strong meat, in a way, but she served the College most wonderfully. She loved the College. And she was very good with the music, and cared for the undergraduates. The College was very lucky to have had Jean Maud in the Lodgings since she did a great deal. And we have to honour her memory because through the bad period of student unrest, when people were being bloody and silly, they took to ragging John Maud, just because he was raggable, and she held the place together. She had a very precious part there. One of his defects to my mind was that he was not good on finance, in the sense of being unrealistic. And the College did get into financial troubles over the Staverton Road building. Caring about the finances is to my mind an all-important part of the Mastership, because, if anything goes wrong, he will finally carry the can. It's not a Bursar, it's not a committee or anything.

TC: So who came next?

GC: Arnold Goodman. I voted for Goodman because I thought, as a city solicitor, he would be able to read a balance sheet, and see the College had to be more serious about things.

TC: Did that turn out to be true?

GC: He had never read a bloody balance sheet in his life! If there was a shortage of money, he'd set out trying to find it. He was *not* a good money-raiser and that was one of the great disappointments.

TC: Lord Goodman started when?

GC: He started in 1976.

TC: So Sir John Maud had quite a good stint, didn't he?

GC: Yes. He had thirteen years. I think he probably was disappointed not to be extended. Not that he'd really wanted to do it, but it's a sort of mark of success. But actually, when the College made an extension for Arthur Goodhart, it said, 'And the next Master will not be extended.' I don't know whether that was explained to John Maud or not.

But Goodman was just, frankly, inadequate. He had no idea what the whole place was about. It turned out, when he retired I think in 1986, at almost one of the last Tutorial Committee meetings that he was

75

at, it emerged that he didn't know what the 'awards' item on the Tutorial Committee *was*. He knew nothing about it, and he didn't try.

TC: And was Goodman a Wilson appointment? Did Wilson get involved at all?

GC: No, Wilson had nothing to do with it. In fact, at that time, people were saying that Harold Wilson wanted to be Master – well, he couldn't – and he'd let it be known that he couldn't. Nor could he *possibly* have thought that, because having a reigning Prime Minister [as Master] has political implications of great importance. So anyhow, Arnold came, and in many ways he was endearing. He was very generous in a small way; undergraduates who got into trouble financially and so on. He said, 'I think I know a fund that could help,' or something – it was actually his own money, I realise. It cost him a good deal to be Master of Univ. And he was, in his way, generous.

TC: Did he carry on his legal practice, while he was Master?

GC: He probably did, yes. He was a notable character, but I think he had no idea what Oxford or the College was about. He never learned the first names of most of the Fellows. You know, it's really important to get on rather personal terms with people nowadays; he didn't do that.

TC: And was there some resentment about this?

GC: No, it was just felt to be him. People really admired him because he knew all the great. And dons will do anything for a rich man, and for a man who has important connections.

TC: Don't we all?

GC: I think I less than most.

TC: That's true!

GC: I wouldn't cross the road to meet a famous man, I'm too proud.

I don't think Goodman knew where the College playing field *was*. He never got to the river. We were in Cuppers finals a number of years in his Mastership, he never *went* there, no idea what it was all about. And I had a to-do actually: there was a New Zealand graduate who came to do a doctorate in Jurisprudence. He was assigned to Dworkin as supervisor, and when he got there at the start of Michaelmas Term – he was under his own steam financially – when he got there Dworkin was not around. Dworkin didn't arrive till well into the second week of term. And this chap wasn't complaining, but *I* was complaining. I said, 'This man has come from New Zealand, he's spending his own

money, I think he's entitled to find his supervisor *here* when he comes.'
I was Dean of Graduates and I didn't write to the Law Board about it
since I was wrong to do that: it would have been for the College to do
it, so I put it to the Tutorial Committee of the College. They were
frightfully good at avoiding awkwardness at these things. The decision of
the College was that Arnold should talk to Dworkin himself. Well,
Arnold finally caught up with Dworkin in London, in the sixth week of
term, and Dworkin took about ten minutes to persuade Arnold that he
was doing absolutely all that could possibly be expected of him. Because
Arnold hadn't any IDEA of what the duties of the job *were*. So that was
a not uncharacteristic incident. He had some reputation as a fundraiser,
but it wasn't just. He had friends, and the friends gave a bit to the
College. But I had hoped he'd bring in big money, you know, and he
didn't really apply himself to it in the mind. I wanted to make an appli-
cation to the Wolfson Trust to get £600,000. And he didn't give any
guidance in that. When I finally took him the letter to sign, he said,
'Well that's a big sum of money.' And in the end we got about £20,000.
Well, he should have been actively involved at least.

TC: Because he'd have known trustees?

GC: He knew Isaac Wolfson. But he wasn't good at it. And he was a
desperate Chairman. He didn't read the papers. You could see him reading the papers *at* the meeting. And furthermore, his word was worthless.
You would see him about something, you would have the Tutorial
Committee; a week later, in the College meeting, he would take a quite
different line, he's totally forgotten what it's about. And the last person
to go and see him would be able to get his ear. It was a lack of constan-
cy, and when I became Vice-Master [in 1980], he just didn't back one
up!

For example, one Fellow told me that he was not going to be
back in Oxford till the second week of the next term. And I said, 'Look,
you can't do that, the people coming, it's not just tuition, it's being
about and being accessible and so on!' And I wrote and said, 'I wish to
make clear that I think it would be very improper if you didn't come.'
Well that was a mistake on my part. [Trouble ensued] and Goodman
didn't support me. I must say, he was feeble.

TC: So this is in the thick of College politics. You had your own allies,
presumably.

GC: Yes! But my real ally was that I knew the undergraduates and they knew me, and that was successful, I think.

TC: You could understand immediately from them if there was something amiss.

GC: I think so. And I knew the Old Members, and I had this gift of memory: I could remember things about people, little things from thirty years before. And they always liked that; they liked to come back to College and be remembered. And that's, in a way, been one of my chief usefulnesses to the College. Because I do remember people. And I like people too.

Arnold Goodman took a very rich man out to lunch, who said he'd give the College £50,000. And so, on the strength of that, he was invited to a dinner Arnold was having for Armand Hammer, the great oil tycoon, very rich man. And the aim was to get money out of Armand Hammer. And there were present a notable company including Princess Alexandra, because Arnold was a great friend of hers. And there were other people there, there was Clarissa, Lady Avon – widow of Anthony Eden, and there was a lot of curtsy-dropping and so on all round. But this man was there, and I stepped up to him, and I thanked him for his generosity, and he said, 'Oh, don't worry, it was nothing.' Well that's what it was, because it never came! Arnold wrote to him, a couple of times, and he finally wrote and said, 'We will quite understand if you can't afford it.' Well he's as rich as Croesus. I have suspected that people sometimes thought that Arnold could get them things, and people liked titles.

TC: So you're Vice-Master through all this, and Lord Goodman steps down in 1986.

GC: 1986, yes. I ceased as Vice-Master in Easter 1985. I wanted to get on with my work. They then set about electing a successor, and Dworkin persuaded them that Kingman Brewster, one-time President of Yale, would be a very good thing. He was hopeless. He knew *nothing* about the job, he was only going to have *three* years, he'd only deal with *one* lot of undergraduates through the college, through their course, then they [the College] said, 'Well, we could extend him,' but you don't extend people until you *know*! It was *absolutely* terrible.

TC: So that was a failure of the collegiate system for electing a Master?

GC: It was a disaster. He was amiable enough, but he had a stroke between being invited and his coming. As far as I know, the College was not informed about this. I expect they'd have said, 'Oh, you'll be all right,' but it was quite clear from the start that he was a spent force.

TC: Is there a weakness if you got heads of colleges in position who have not had involvement with Oxford?

GC: That's a great weakness, and now, they do engage head-hunters, so that situation is less likely to arise. But it was a very bad, ill-conducted affair to my mind. Anyhow, he didn't last very long: he became Master in Michaelmas Term 1986, and he died in 1988. And *then* the College elected John Albery, whom you knew.

TC: Yes.

GC: Now, on the face of it, there was much to be said for it since he'd been a *wonderful* Tutor for Admissions. He had raised the College's academic performance enormously, and put us at the top, by his attention to whom we admitted, you see. And he really did us extremely well, though it was a very bruising business. Anything he was involved in was bruising. I was once asked by St John's whether he would be suitable as President – this was before he was on the table at Univ – and I said, 'I can't think he wouldn't do the college good, though you'd know you had him!' Fortunately that didn't happen for St John's, and we got him. And really, I thought he had all the qualities necessary for the Mastership – except judgement, good sense, wit, tact [chuckles]. He had the most tremendous ego. He could only think of his own ideas, and he couldn't consider anybody else's. He was tactless and crude, and he took to the bottle. It showed me that Masters ought to be married – going home to the Lodgings, and saying, 'The Fellows were bloody to me today,' and the wife would say, 'Well it's all right, my dear, let's have a drink and not worry about it, they're small people.' Instead of which he went home and had the solace of the bottle.

TC: Was he any good at the finance side?

GC: No. He was crowded out.

TC: I ask because, with Sir John Maud, Lord Goodman, Kingman Brewster, and then Albery, you did not have a Master really thinking about the finances in the way they should.

GC: No, we didn't but the way he should think about it is a different item. I mean, he's got to be aware of it, and he must be on good relations with the Bursar, but he must sort of keep hands off. It's a delicate thing. Anyhow, poor Albery came to disaster finally by making a speech at a Boat Club dinner – I wasn't there for that. The only Fellow present was the Chaplain. But he said something very offensive; I said afterwards to the President of the Women's Eight, the captain of the Women's Eight, 'What did he say that was so upsetting?' and she said, 'I'd be too embarrassed to tell you.' So he had to go, and he was virtually dismissed.

TC: Right. When the Master's appointed, the Statutes say they can do it up to a certain period, is that right?

GC: Yes.

TC: But there had to be a bit of a palace revolution to get Albery out?

GC: Well, the Fellows knew, and they did [terminate his Mastership], but I had ceased to be a Fellow by then. And then they got Robin Butler, who's there now. Jill Butler has been absolutely marvellous, really superb. And he is very good in various ways. In the Civil Service he had great power, he would just give orders, there wouldn't be a question of tact or anything. He is a very tactful person, *but*, in a college, the problem is, and it's a problem of Oxford generally, that the man at the head of things has no *power*. I say the head of a college is the opposite of the harlot in history: he has responsibility but no power. And so he doesn't see that really his work begins when there's an awkward decision to be taken. Though I'm not there now, so I don't know, and I don't go collecting information, I would say he has been an outstandingly good Master.

TC: That's encouraging, because I was going to say, would there be any truth in the notion that when you were a young Fellow, the Master had more of an aura than when you'd seen it all? Butler slightly gives the lie to that.

GC: The Master, in my mind – you see I've been there so long – the Master has aura. If the Master asks one to do something, you bloody well do it. And that's not the attitude of the young Fellows now. They don't know about this.

Univ philosophers, and others

TC: Have you got any other names that are worth saying something about?

GC: I have known a good number of people, or I've encountered a good number of people, like John Sparrow of All Souls. Isaiah Berlin I encountered a bit. Freddy Ayer I encountered a bit. One little thing of Freddy Ayer: when he was in New York once, he was asked something about Oxford, he said, 'Oh in Oxford everyone's so much cleverer than one,' but of course he was a very, very clever man himself. And I rather got on with him in a strange way. He was a tremendous egotist.

TC: Because you liked the philosophers, didn't you?

GC: I got on with them.

TC: You've mentioned Herbert Hart.

GC: Yes.

TC: Can you pick out two other names of Fellows whom you felt to be outstanding?

GC: Peter Strawson. A great name in the history of philosophy. One of the greatest philosophers of the twentieth century, no question. A man for whom I came to have a great regard. I didn't terribly like him in early days, but at the end I saw. I could tell you a lot about Peter Strawson, but he was outstanding. The other man that I thought was really outstanding was Leonard Hoffmann, now the Law Lord, Lord Hoffmann, a very clever man. But you know, quite a number of the people in the College are very clever. And I think the standard's pretty good, it's only duds like me that they've got saddled with. You need a few duds in the College to do the jobs.

TC: Is it true that in a way you thought Philosophy was the supreme subject?

GC: Yes, I did. I still do. I mean it's the architectonic subject, but then one sees that Peter Strawson's first step into fame was an article entitled 'On Denoting' – [TC laughs] – some people got rather contemptuous of it. But that's where the subject was going at that time. I think it's the central subject.

TC: Lennie Hoffmann was not Professor of Jurisprudence ...

GC: No, no, he was just a Fellow. A Law tutor.

TC: So you've had some very distinguished legal people.

GC: Oh yes, and you see, John Finnis, who's there still, he's very distinguished. I mean *very* distinguished. But we had Gareth Evans, the Philosopher. Brilliant star, died young. He was very, very clever, outstandingly clever. We also had John McDowell. I never heard him say a bad thing in his life, but then he didn't always say very much. He was a bit remote but a very able man. When I was Vice-Master I shielded him from being asked to take college offices, because I thought he was too good to waste.

TC: On the mundane?

GC: On the mundane things. But I never said that to anyone, but that was what I did.

TC: And John Mackie?

GC: Well John Mackie was a notable Philosophy tutor. We had this tremendous Philosophy team, you see. And before that there was Alasdair MacIntyre, and of course there was Herbert Hart having been Professor of Jurisprudence, then succeeded by Dworkin, another great name, and now Finnis. I should mention my friend David Wiggins, he was very good too.

TC: And of the other Classicists, Frederick Wells?

GC: Frederick Wells was a very gifted amateur with a *wonderful* feel for the Latin language, a very gifted composer of proses and so on – he was very good at all *that*, but he had, I think, limitations of mind. He didn't have big ideas, he had little ideas. But he was very considerable, he had a wonderful knowledge of English literature, and I think he was a very special thing, he was a *very* good tutor; very good Dean, oddly enough, when Giles Alington died. Wells was a man whom one must speak of with the greatest respect. But I remember John Wild spoke at his funeral or memorial, in which he compared Frederick to AE Housman – that was ab*surd*. But he was a considerable person. Talking about philosophers, we had George Paul who came in about 1945, I think. He got Strawson in, that was his great service to the College. But George was a very clever man indeed, but I think he lost the light. He became Domestic Bursar.

TC: It's interesting that Univ should've developed such a strong suit in Philosophy.

GC: It was tremendous, yes. I think it derived from George Paul and Peter Strawson.

TC: Right, things came together. You're not bound to continue it, because you need to find good people.

Oxford's future

I was going to try and conclude with this. Let me make a broad generalisation which can provoke you into disagreement if you like, that the 1950s were a very good period for you as a young Fellow, doing the teaching, and you had your sport, well, the cricket. Then in the 60s, the advent of difficult students was not to your liking. I remember you saying to me, you thought that there *was* a type of undergraduate that had got very earnest, and that persisted a bit possibly in the 70s, but with the advent of a new Prime Minister in Margaret Thatcher, the cultural life of this country changed quite significantly. Did the young become more congenial in the sense of more keen on the traditions and what have you?

GC: The thing about tradition in Oxford is that boys who have been to public schools where tradition is valued, they never ask about it, they just observe it. Boys from a state school can feel uncomfortable, they don't *know* what it is to understand this, and so they don't accept it. I mean Oxford has changed so much, it's painful for me to think about it.

TC: Yes.

GC: But I've known many most delightful and admirable people in the College, I think so well of the young.

TC: And that's throughout every year?

GC: Throughout, yes. There were troublemakers round about 1970, funnily enough they were in PPE, and they behaved pretty badly towards Maurice. But no, that passed.

TC: So your worry at present is the financial position?

GC: Well, there's the *big* question of finance, people are not paid enough, and talent will go where the money is. Inevitably, America is attracting the talent. That's just a hard fact about history.

TC: So what's your view of the Campaign for Oxford?

GC: They're just getting going under John Hood. The colleges are getting their act together. For instance, last year, the Director of Development told me that we got in a million and a half pounds in one way or another. In view of our not very great riches, that's quite an addition.

TC: And that's a change from the Lord Goodman days.

GC: Yes, we didn't get those amounts, but it's been built up. And I had a minor part in starting that.

TC: It means putting things in place that that could start to happen?

GC: Yes.

TC: Because these things take time if you're waiting for legacies?

GC: No; it is that people's attitudes have to change, they have to realise. But people learn. *Are* generous. And well, there it is.

TC: Perhaps this is a good point to conclude on: the Cawkwell Fellowship was set up, say a bit about that.

GC: When I retired, there was no university appointment, and so the College could only afford, or said they could only afford, short-term Fellows. Money was collected, and I think the Ancient History fellowship has been more funded than any other in modern times. A lot of it is in legacies, but still, it's pretty big. They kept changing the goalpost as a way to get in more money. But it's there, and now we've got the fully funded thing, and Robin Butler has tried very hard to get it all.

TC: Would people be coming three years, and then they were thinking, 'Well I must move on'?

GC: Yes. But now, we're getting a full-timer, an American woman who's quite a name [Lisa Kallet, George Cawkwell Fellow in Ancient History], but whether she will stay, whether it'll be to her satisfaction, I don't know. [Kallet did in fact remain as the Ancient History Fellow until 2021.]

TC: Did you not also set up a little fund for undergraduates to travel?

GC: When I retired I wasn't going to give something to the Common Room; they don't value it, they don't go to it, they forget about it. So I gave £1,000 pounds, and Sarah gave, I think, £100 or so, and that set up the Cawkwell *Prize*. I set it up in such a way that it'll last as long as I last. And it's about £100.

TC: And the undergraduate who receives it is obliged to do a report for you?

GC: No, that was a different thing. There were Masters' travelling scholars, and Mrs Rose of New York, whose daughter Emily had been in the College, gave money each year, quite a sum of $5,000 or something, and called it the Cawkwell Scholar. That has now come to an end, but she was very good to them, and very generous. That was a sort of one-off operation that's now come to an end. I don't care at all about the title, I just wanted these things to go on. Particularly the subject of Ancient History, I think it's a very good subject. I wanted that to go on, well it *will* go on, whether there's any pupils for it I don't know. Colleges are very good at forgetting what they've promised.

TC: So the independence of Oxford from people wanting to put Classics into the dustbin of history is important, isn't it?

GC: Yes, it's absolutely essential. But where are we going to get all this money from, a huge sum? People have said, Oxford colleges should go independent. But the government could still squash you in a minute. We've got to get big sums of money, and to pay people large salaries, and keep them here.

TC: We're running to the end of the tape, so, I know that's a slightly sombre, sober note to end on. Is there some final thing you're burning to say?

GC: Oh, I love Oxford. The only thing I've never been able to forgive people for is not loving Oxford.

TC: You meet those people on occasion?

GC: Well, people complain about it. If they do, I just wipe them off.

TC: Okay. Well there's plenty of people left who do love it.

GC: Yes. Right.

6 ANCIENT HISTORY AS A SUBJECT

Fourth-century specialist

[from NZRSOHP]

HM: I know you wrote a book, 'Philip of Macedon'.

GC: I was a specialist on the fourth century. I would like to suppose that there was some grandeur in my choice. Ronald Syme wrote an article in which he explained how he had got on to the Roman nobility, and it was in reaction against the constitution of the Soviet Union, published, and the sham, it was a façade and the real truth, the hard truth, was the dirty villainies going on behind. And that's what he saw in the Roman – well, I didn't have that at all. I took up with the fourth century simply because nobody else was lecturing on it. When I began lecturing, there were these great stars all lecturing on fifth-century Athens, and I couldn't honestly say to anyone, 'Come to my lectures instead of going to theirs,' so I took up with the fourth century, and gradually became used to it and it used to me. I must say, I wouldn't pretend any grand motives therefore for my taking it up, but I did in time develop a strong antipathy to what I might call moralism: the general feeling that life, history is goodies and baddies. I had wrangles with colleagues over this – Sparta was such an evil society, it must fall because of its own evil. If people fell because of their own evil, the world would be a very different place, but they bloody well don't. History shows that evil prospers. I remember when I was young, my mother, who was very religious, would say, 'Be sure your sins will find you out.' Well, if sin found you out in history, it would all have been very different. Villainy prospers, that's the history of the world. Dirty villains prosper. And don't say that because a man is villainous, he comes to disaster because of his villainous character. The truth is all the opposite. So I dislike that sort of moralising. To my mind, the history of the fourth century is in large measure military. The Greeks were beaten because they came up against a better general.

HM: But this moralising thing, before we lose sight of that, have you found amongst your colleagues a great deal of that?

GC: Yes, I have a strong antipathy to moralising. Such a moral man myself [laughs].

HM: But history in the sense of contemporary history recording, as happens through journalism, there's a strong moralising element there, isn't there?

GC: Yes, isn't there? As you see in the present thing about Palestine. And I can't exclude it from myself. I don't believe in rights, I'm a great opponent of rights. The Israelis have the notion that they've got a God-given right to that land, and if they've got a God-given right there's no need to think about it. There are no rights. Occupying something – possession is nine points of the law. There's something to it. The Palestinians have been there for a long time. They want their stolen goods back again, and the Israelis should make a calculation. 'Can we go on being shot at by these people? Are we going to have settlers out here for the rest of history being kidnapped or caught in ambushes and so on? It'd be better to get back inside our own territory and put up a big wall.' They don't but they ought to think like that. And I try to remain neutral but I have very strong feelings in support of the Palestinians. I think the present thing is very disgraceful. I had a pupil actually, called Austin, the daughter of the great philosopher JL Austin, and she was a pupil of mine for a term or two, and she married a Palestinian philosopher called Sari Nusseibeh, and she gave an interview to the Daily Telegraph within the last year, in which she talked about it all, and she said, 'My people are desperate and angry,' and that is what the Palestinians are, and desperate and angry people are dangerous. What else can they do? But you don't want a sermon for history on the subject of the Palestinians.

HM: But it's interesting in the context of your own specialised area, that these sort of judgements are being made.

GC: Yes, they're moralising, and I'm afraid I tend to slip into them myself, but I shouldn't. I should say, 'On a cool appraisal of the interests of the state, Israel ought to get out,' but I don't say that. I say, 'On behalf of the Palestinian people, for God's sake stop this present bloody murder.' But it's not consistent.

HM: In your work over these years has that been a problem, taking the moral line or not to take it?

GC: We tend to take it. I mean, I would try to take a Thucydidean line, the cool appraisal of states' interests and so on. Have you read the

Melian Dialogue? It's all set out, about how you approach the problem of relations with Melos. And I would like to be able to think like that. I'm not always equal to it.

HM: And then in your book on Philip of Macedon, what were you wanting to say?

GC: Essentially it is that Philip defeated the Greeks because he was a better general. The military art was more highly developed there, he was the great general. The Greeks had had their great general in Epaminondas but he was dead and gone, and when Philip came on the scene the Greeks couldn't measure up to it. There was an inconsistency there, it was necessary for them, if they were going to fight Philip, they had to have a much more unified system. They needed to have a unified army. And of course my own feelings about the European Union now are contrary to those. Though people neglect the fact that the situation has changed enormously in the last fifteen years, with the fall of the Berlin Wall and the end of the Cold War, the *raison d'être* of the European Union for many people, namely the need to unite against Russia, has gone, so that that makes it a somewhat different situation here. But the Greeks were going to fall if they couldn't do better against this show militarily.

HM: But what about [modern] Greek interpretations of the fourth century, Philip and so on?

GC: I have shamefully to confess that I don't read modern Greek. I don't think there's much to read on it either. Of course, the great question for them is not the rights and wrongs of Philip; it is whether the Macedonians were real Greeks, and they can't admit they were not, because the Bulgarians might be in to snatch it. And it was a tremendous scandal, you see, there was a province of the Turkish empire, a *vilayet*, called Macedonia, and that took in all the northern part there, and they're outraged that there should be a state called Macedonia, capital Skopje or somewhere. They're all in a great heat about that. That's the thing. And they must maintain that Macedonia was a Greek country and they were Greeks. Well, I think they were. But that's the thing that really interests them.

HM: Yes. But I was wondering about your links and comparing notes with colleagues in Greece.

GC: In Greece? Well, there are archaeologists, but I don't actually know of a single Greek ancient historian whose works on the fourth century would have to be read. They're wonderful people, but they rather guard their little patch of archaeology jealously. There's a man I know in Oxford who wrote a wonderful piece about a site, he can't publish it because the Greeks won't give him permission to publish it. If he did publish it, they would cut him off from ever going there again. There's a sort of prickly chip on the shoulder about things to some degree.

HM: So that's interesting, that kind of direct link between the present-day feelings and something of so long ago that really just from somewhere like Oxford you can unreservedly go in and say what you feel about it.

GC: Yes, it's true.

'The Credulity of Ancient Historians'

[Address delivered to the Classicists of Oriel College in 1988-89]

Though I am only in my sixty-ninth year, I am at heart and in mind truly a γέρων and can no longer play the Demosthenes. That great man never spoke extempore but he never used notes, let alone a script. He learned it all, and if you think that nothing much, just try and learn the 'De Corona' [about 100 pages of the Oxford Classical Text] by heart. I've done that sort of thing in my time, but no more am I to be found, like Demosthenes, trying to make himself heard above the roar of the surf and with a mouthful of pebbles, no more am I to be found pacing the High trying to make myself heard above the roar of the traffic and with a mouthful of truths about Greek history – a very Hornblower. Now I am become like Isocrates and can only write my thoughts and read them to a keen circle of sycophants from outlying places. So I come to Oriel.

But, Classicists of Oriel, I imply no disrespect: your lineage is impeccable, your industry known to all, your genius undoubted, your opportunism a warning to unwisely fulsome tutors. At the end of a Matthew Harvey essay, I was moved to remark, 'That was such a good essay I am minded to deny you nothing,' thinking that he had been known to accept, when pressed, a glass of sherry. But quoth he, 'Great is καιρός. Will you please address the Oriel Classicists next term? Nothing serious of course, or you'll see for yourself some of the wide open spaces of Oriel life, I mean some of the yawning chasms, which make the Oriel library resemble a mass dental surgery.' I could only reply, 'μακαρίσαντες ὑμῶν τὸ ἀπειρόκακον οὐ ζηλοῦμεν τὸ ἄφρον.' [Thucydides 5.105.3 – 'in blessing your simplicity we do not envy your foolishness'.] He said, 'You'd do better than the Melian Dialogue [where the quotation occurs].' *Touché*, Harvey.

As to your academic lineage, it is too well known to need more than the merest allusion. Is not Oriel the college of Sir Ronald Syme? He is a New Zealander, of course, but what a one! He is the man who matched the hopes of the great Gibbon himself. 'Such reflections tend,' he wrote, 'to enlarge the circle of our ideas and to encourage the pleasing hope that New Zealand may produce in some future age the Hume of the Southern Hemisphere.' Though you might not guess it, I am a New Zealander myself, but of the humbler and the more athletic sort. *Je ne suis pas la rose, mais j'ai vécu avec elle.* I was not an All Black but I have played with All Blacks, those men 'of violent technique but epic style'. I am the sort of barely educated New Zealander you should think of when you read Plutarch *de malignitate Herodoti*: 'If there are Antipodean peoples, as some say, who dwell on the underside of the world, I imagine that even they have heard of Themistocles and the Themistoclean plan.' Themistocles's plan was how to win the World Cup. I don't allude to my article on Themistocles and how he was alleged to want the other side to win. That is decently buried in an unobtainable Antipodean publication [reprinted in 'Cyrene to Chaeronea']. As one of you remarked in Michaelmas Term, 'Good.' But to return to your lineage, not only Syme, and Tod of 'Greek Historical Inscriptions', a book 'most dear to me' as one of you said when I mentioned its price – Syme, Tod and the supposedly deaf Sir David Ross who was once heard concluding a tutorial with these words: 'No, I'm not happy about pleasure,' a remark which he would enjoy making, but also PA Brunt, the great academic labour-saver – I mean, whenever he turns his hand to a subject, he leaves nothing for anyone else to do. I drop no more names. Macaulay declared, 'Every schoolboy knows who imprisoned Montezuma and who strangled Atahualpa.' I declare, less exceptionably, 'Every Orielensis knows his or her two Ms.' No doubt you keep mum – fully informed about them – I mean 'Miasma' (by RCT Parker, the

Classics Fellow) and 'Mausolus' (by S Hornblower, the Ancient Historian). What an unhealthy couple! Like Suttee and Thuggee. 'I don't mind a moderate amount of Suttee but I draw the line at Thuggee,' as a Dean said to the captain of the Rugger Club.

As to your industry, I cite only one overwhelming instance. In Michaelmas Term I had the privilege of riding into college in the car of Mr Stephen Lawrence. 'But where will you park?' 'I always park in Oriel Street.' 'But aren't there double lines there?' 'Yes, but the police never bother me. I just leave a notice in my windscreen, "Working in Oriel College".'

As to the genius of Oriel, I quote Kenneth Grahame, 'The Wind in the Willows': 'There is nothing, absolutely nothing, half so much worth doing as simply messing about in boats.' I quoted this to Clive Cheesman, who said, 'We don't mess about. We're not like the Wadham boat as described by FE Smith on a famous occasion. "Why is the Wadham boat like Noah's Ark? Because it moves slowly over the face of the waters and is full of strange creatures." At any rate we don't move slowly.' 'Yes,' I said, 'the analogy breaks down in that respect.' (Proemium concluded.)

*

So, Classicists of Oriel, here I am. But where was I? 'You were gathering wool on the slopes of Vesuvius.' Oh yes. How things have changed: when Oscar Wilde got a First in Greats 110 years ago, 'some of the questions,' to quote his latest biographer, 'played into his hands. For example, he was asked about "the geographical position and military importance of the following places – Potidaea, Heraclea, Plataea, Naupactus, Mantinea".' One wouldn't have to be an Oscar to write a brilliant answer, like that famous brilliant one-line answer of a hero called Peter Ralli in the History Schools in 1922. 'Her subjects wanted Queen Elizabeth to abolish tunnage and poundage, but the splendid creature stood firm.' Pure Thatcherism you will say. So let us stick to the point, whatever it was, but no matter what it was, for it is impossible for a φύσει ['by nature'] Greats man to stray off the point, if, that is, there is anything in the argument from design. Everything has its true function. Consider the famous judgment of Benjamin Franklin, 'God wants us to tipple because he has made the joints of the arm just the right length to carry a glass to the mouth.' Indeed in 1581, one Bartholomew Batty 'praised the wisdom of the Almighty who had made the human posterior in such a shape that it could take much correction without suffering permanent damage.' Thus Greats men or rather Greats persons cannot err, though of course we must be careful in our use of language. It is salutary to be reminded of the story known to practically everyone concerning Dr Webster, the great lexicographer. His wife came upon him in the conservatory embracing a housemaid. 'Dr Webster,' she exclaimed, 'I am surprised.' He replied, 'No, Madam. You are amazed. I am surprised.' That's a nice way to talk, I must say. And one must practice Socratic irony. I like the remark of one of our professors about a recently retired and famously idle Fellow of his college: 'He is the man to whom in my experience retirement has made the least difference.' And pray, cultivate ambiguity, as in that comment on a handsome young man exclusively devoted to the society of other young men. 'He will never want a wife.' Which puts one in mind of that kind comment on a lesbian lady, 'She was one of Nature's gentlemen.' And please remember that Stoic maxim, *nil admirari*. It is quite clear that Mrs Woodrow Wilson did not read Greats. She was heard in a lull at a dinner party to say, 'When Woodrow asked me to marry him I was so surprised I nearly fell out of bed.' In what I have just said there is a very great deal for you not to think about – though, I must say, Oriel is not what it was. Once when a reputedly prosy fellow was mumbling an undeniably prosy speech at an Oriel Gaudy, an Indian Old Member called out, 'Louder and funnier.' Yet I hear not a word.

But, Classicists of Oriel, where was I? Oh yes, Mrs Woodrow Wilson's dinner party. I'm very grateful for a very decent dinner tonight. When one is a pensioner one is very keen on one's sportula. But I particularly like dinners as a philosophic subject. Oscar Wilde remarked that 'a Conservative is a man who has never thought; a Radical is a man who has never dined.' The first part is utter bunkum. *I* refute it. I am a Conservative and I sometimes think. Indeed I had a thought the other day when I was reading The Telegraph, though my thoughts are not really political. I am like that Headmaster of Eton who said, 'I have no politics. I vote Conservative for the good of the country.' But the second part of Oscar's dictum is all too true. A good dinner is a powerful disincentive to Radical opinions. As Saki said, clear soup is better than a clear conscience. Of course some will say, 'I prefer my high principles to haute cuisine.' I warn such people that a lack of dinners can undo even the most high-minded. There was a distressing incident in Shanghai but a year or two ago, which was exposed in a front-page letter to the Liberation Daily. It was written by catering workers at the Shanghai Exhibition Centre and was headed 'An Uncivilised Buffet'. Apparently 'hundreds of Chinese economic officials and factory bosses descended on a buffet reception before it was due to start, gobbled up most of the food and stuffed the rest in bags or their pockets'. The letter went on, 'They could not wait any longer, and all swarmed to the dining tables. Clutching chopsticks, forks and knives, their motion looked like rain pelting the ground. Some stuffed whole chickens into plastic bags and pocketed fruit. Others took a whole dish of lilac-flavoured ham to their dining table. In an instant all the sumptuous food on the table was swept bare. Those who reaped their bountiful harvest gorged like wolves and tigers.' The letter-writers thought all this a mockery of the Communist Party's propaganda efforts to promote social etiquette and 'socialist spiritual civilisation'. How much better if they had been used to a good dinner such as you have given me tonight. I thank God it was not a Spartan diet which consisted almost entirely of porridge-like goo – nor for that matter the meal consumed by the Great King at his accession. According to Plutarch, 'he had to eat a cake of figs, to chew some turpentine wood, and drink a cup of sour milk'. Plutarch adds, 'Whatever else is done besides this is unknown to outsiders.' Readers of Aristophanes' 'Acharnians' will readily guess that it was a quick visit to the Golden Hills with an attack of schizophrenia. But I must say something in defence of the Boeotians. Polybius tells us there were many Boeotians who had each month more dinners than there were days in the calendar, and you might have an idea of obese Boeotian swine, and think it better to be a discontented Socrates of the Oriel JCR than a Boeotian from the Oriel High Table. That would be quite unjust. Boeotian dinners were probably no more filling than a Continental breakfast. But, good Cawkwell, what of that list of Boeotian goodies in the 'Acharnians'? Permit, I reply, permit Aristophanes to make a joke, or I'll report you to de Ste Croix for not having read and believed every word he has written and he will mark you down as a bad man and 'unprogressive', that pregnant word in radical vocabulary. No, dinner for a Boeotian was probably just

93

a lot of garlic. That is why no foe could face them. Xenophon's saying they breathed fire was just a euphemism. The Boeotians never were in the difficult position of the courtiers of Philip IV of Spain. 'The struggle between the urge for reform and the tradition of conspicuous consumption, between economy and opulence, therefore tended to be uneven. Occasional modest victories were no doubt won, as in 1630, when the court was reduced to a mere ten dishes for lunch and eight for dinner, with a maximum of four chickens, or fifteen eggs, to the plate.' The economies of the Oriel High Table are *not* unprecedented.

But, good Classicists, I know you are practically impervious to the pleasure of the flesh. You will quote to me from Plutarch's great treatise 'The impossibility of leading even a pleasant life on the maxims of Epicurus', you will quote to me those celebrated words, 'And what man could be better pleased with the embraces of the most exquisite beauty than with sitting up all night to read what Xenophon said of Panthea?' The very name, Xenophon, reminds me of what I proposed to talk about. Was Herodotus too credulous? He didn't believe that a man could swim ten miles underwater but did he really think a man could with one fierce clean blow slice off the flat of his foot to escape from the stocks, and hop away to Tegea by night? Ladies and gentlemen, Herodotus was not a senseless brute. He was a conscientious historian. You just need to understand what a conscientious historian is, on which matter I quote Mark Twain, who said of Herodotus, 'Many things do not happen as they ought, and the best things do not happen at all. It is the duty of the conscientious historian to correct these defects.'

Now, our conscientious historian ranges widely and wildly and I am moved to cite a piece I noted some years ago in the TLS.

> Frederic Prokosch's books *The Asiatics* and *The Seven who Fled* minutely described landscape in both books but this novelist had never been anywhere near Asia. The geography he rendered with such confident and exhilarated concreteness, as his picaresque hero wanders through Lebanon, Tiflis, Trebizond and Badrapur, Persia and Malaya was a triumph of imaginative bravura. Years later, lunching with EM Forster in Cambridge, Prokosch was delighted with the Master's judgement: 'Your book is much too poetic to have been based on vulgar tourism.'

Do not, I prithee, treat Herodotus as a vulgar tourist. Do not for an instant wonder how Herodotus could say that all the Egyptians were black-skinned and fuzzy-haired, or whether he actually saw heaps of the bones of flying snakes. These pleasing details are put in to please. And a great deal of pleasure Herodotus must have had himself if he can hear the comments of some of the gravy-stained greybeards of this University.

I have sung enough for my supper. I omit discussion of why so rarely do women raise their comely heads in Thucydides. There is, of course, one joke rarely noticed. Of the 400 left in Plataea to maintain the siege there were 110 women breadmakers, the idea being that they had made their bread and had to lie on it. But in general Thucydides was not keen on women. He didn't even mention Aspasia, a fairly noticeable girl, who must have very much enjoyed that bit in the Funeral Oration telling women to avoid being talked about; she was the Talk of the Town. I suspect Thucydides was in the class of those who 'will never want a wife', and the awful truth is that the young Alcibiades had told him to push off and it was this that upset Thucydides and his history. But Thucydides, it can be said, will do you no harm ...

This has all gone on long enough. If my message is not now clear to you, I'm not surprised. I conclude as one must at a college Classical Society. *Carthago delenda est*: Sybaris must be sacked, and so must all the dons.

Second retirement speech

[Delivered on 3 June 1995 to mark his ceasing to be a Tutorial Fellow of Univ.]

(It is very pleasing to have flattering things said of one by a man as celebrated for his sincerity as the Principal of St Hugh's. I know what perhaps Cicero did not. Flattery does you no harm as long as you don't inhale.)

It is well known that the late Canon Jenkins of Christ Church was given a dinner in his honour on his eightieth birthday by the History Faculty. They had the quiet expectation, indeed the hope, that he would announce his retirement. Jenkins made effective answer by beginning,

'Being as I am of a modest but not retiring disposition…' I might be held to be the opposite case – a man who so much enjoys retiring that like Mrs Thatcher he intends to go on and on. Lady Bracknell remarked that to lose one parent might be a misfortune, to lose two is carelessness. You might remark that to have to farewell someone once may be sad but to have to repeat the business eight years later provokes the cynical question, 'Will he be coming back for more?'

So I beg leave to explain that having ceased to be a Tutorial Fellow in 1987 I took up tutoring Univ Greek Historians again in 1989 because I found that I was forgetting far too much too quickly. So there began a very happy afterlife when to the great blessing of the retired condition, I mean having one's books at one's home, was added the unexpected pleasure of having a stream of young men and women coming to the house. We enjoyed that greatly and now greatly miss it.

I succeeded George Hope Stevenson in 1949 and am still amazed at my ignorance and my nerve. I inherited some pupils who would daunt anyone. Indeed one, Ernst Badian, who is now a *magnum nomen* in Ancient History, frightened the life out of Steve and made retirement sweet indeed. There was another very clever man, Raphael Sealey. He had got a First in Modern History and had gone off to do his military service. In the course of it he worked up his Greek and returned to Univ having read all of Herodotus, Thucydides, and 'The Republic'. It certainly put me on my mettle ('which was brass') to have this man coming each week with some entirely original view. To have a world premiere every Friday at 9 is quite exhausting.

Some of you will recall a famous speech of AE Housman, newly elected Professor of Latin in the University of Cambridge. In one version (not the correct, but as Plutarch would say let's not spoil it), in one version he was speaking in the Hall of Trinity College, Cambridge and began, 'Here I stand, a better scholar than Wordsworth and a better poet than Porson in a hall which never saw the one drunk or the other sober.' (Porson was not only the greatest Greek scholar of this age. He was also a great sot and Byron said of him, 'Porson could hiccup Greek like a Helot.') Well one day in my first term Giles Alington who had taken Sealey on the eighteenth century and knew what he was encountered him on his way to a tutorial with me and nicely said of me, 'He's a very much better Rugger player than you will ever be.' I don't know what Sealey said, but Giles had in effect revealed the answer to the baffling question, 'How on earth did Univ come to elect Cawkwell?' The list of candidates had included some illustrious names. Either the Fellows had been, as I found out they frequently were, quite dotty or some special explanation was needed. Giles's comment perhaps revealed all. The College had just won Rugger Cuppers. Was I elected to be a Rugger coach? If that was the Fellows' intention, they certainly got what they wanted. We did win Rugger Cuppers for the second time after I had been a Fellow for only thirty years.

Anyhow they got me and I have tried to live up to any academic expectation they may have had of me. I've written only one book, 'Shame,' but I've written a fair number of articles. Again, 'Shame'? I can tell you that if you are ever depressed you will be greatly comforted by reading what you have written. I am, in general, not outstandingly vain, but, when it comes to one's own writings, I yield to no one in the satisfaction I get from mine. Maybe I am not always right, but you would have a hard time persuading me of it. I am aided in that stubborn complacency by a general conviction that Cicero was unassailably on the right lines when he said *Ne plurimum plurimi valeant*, 'Let not the greatest number have the greatest power.' I have never been impressed by any view simply because it is held by the majority. In Ancient History I do not object to being in a minority of one. I approve of the motto I saw in a French château. *Sic omnes ego non*. As a professional scholar one will make no progress unless one suspects that everyone before you has got things a bit wrong. I beg leave to quote the blessed Enoch [Powell].

> As a Tory I have great respect for authority, but intellectually speaking there is no such thing as authority. Someone may have the right to tell me to do something, but there cannot be authority for a view. You cannot have anyone else's ideas but your own – at least I can't.

So I treat my heap of *opuscula* with piety they may not deserve and by no means identify myself with that African explorer of whom it was said, 'He made no startling discoveries and added little to the sum of human knowledge.' Those who disagree, today pray be silent.

I have certainly had most admirable colleagues. Frederick Wells was a superb Latinist, with a deep feeling for Horace. I know it's old hat but I cannot refrain from reminding you of his translation of two lines of Horace *Satires* II.2 for the benefit of the Head Porter, Douglas Millin, a man of military usage.

Quocirca vivite fortes
Fortiaque adversis opponite pectora rebus.

Frederick's crisp version was 'Bash on regardless'. No doubt many of you can recall other felicities. Frederick was succeeded by Martin West, a professional of the Premier League, incidentally the best picker of academic horseflesh I have known. Then came Christopher Pelling. He has had me rather at a disadvantage. He had attended my lectures and even a tutorial or two, and he has the superior look of a detective sergeant who has taken down everything you said and means to use it in evidence against you. He has been a wondrously congenial colleague and a wondrously good tutor. I can only hope he won't be like the cook in Saki who 'was good as cooks go and as good cooks go she went'. Quite simply, I trust he will see out his time in Univ.

As to Philosophy, I daresay we have had 'the best team in the University'; that was the phrase the late Freddy Ayer used of them. Of course, the subject remains dark to most of us. I remember a question in the Schools, which some of you may still be pondering. The question was: '"I feel a pain in your leg." Discuss.' George Paul said it was a textbook question. As Namier said to Isaiah Berlin, philosophers must be very clever to understand what they write. (*Si monumentum requiras, circumspice*. There is Peter Strawson himself, not a mere star but a constellation of the Philosophical Firmament.) Anyhow, our Philosophers have been superb. Although three have died in post, five have moved on to chairs, and important chairs at that.

You may say, 'Why have you, Cawkwell, not moved on?' The famous Bairnsfather cartoon advised, 'If you know of a better 'ole, go to it,' but I didn't know of a better 'ole than Univ. Like the lotus-eaters, I forgot to go home. But you may ask, 'How the devil could you go on prating of Herodotus and Thucydides all those years?' You may well ask, but in fact in Greek History it's just what dark old Heraclitus said, πάντα ῥεῖ – 'All is flux.' Recently a pupil of the late 50s, none other than that judge of the European Court, our Honorary Fellow, David Edward, was staying with us and I invited him to sit in on a tutorial on the Causes of the Peloponnesian War, with, of course, the consent of the young woman who had her essay to read out (and I may remark for the benefit of those who remain shocked at the presence of women in men's colleges, she acquitted herself impressively both on paper and in discussion). David's comment was that it was all very different from his day. Even if I have stood still, the subject hasn't. Scepticism. Of course, most of you did not believe everything you read in Herodotus. As Mark Twain said of him, 'Many things do not happen as they might, and the best things do not happen at all. It is the duty of the conscientious historian to correct those defects.' Herodotus was a conscientious historian and dullards like me just have to keep scepticism under control. I am not yet in the condition of that Irish bishop who declared of 'Gulliver's Travels', 'Frankly I don't believe a word of it.' But with Thucydides things were different. I was brought up, like thousands of others, including most of you – I mean those of you who got all of him read – to regard Thucydides as Holy Writ. Alas, it is no longer so. His Holiness is much under attack from various quarters including by another Honorary Fellow of this College, my first pupil, Ernst Badian. Badian's views are, I hope, all bunkum, but they certainly make for lively discussion. Things do not stand still. As to Xenophon and Demosthenes, if you are silly enough to believe me, you won't believe them. The subject moves on, and so I have been able to go on *in omne volubilis aevum* (just like the Master).

I have referred to two pupils who are Honorary Fellows, and there is another, that golden-haired Apollo Robin Butler, whom we are proud to own, and I especially so. [At the time of the speech Butler was Cabinet Secretary and Head of the Home Civil Service.] 'And some there be that have no memorial' or rather title, or eminent position, but in my book they are worthy of it. At my age one has precious little to preen oneself on, and one seizes on the success of pupils. 'The early disadvantage of my tuition has not prevented them.' Of course not all of you would have qualified for the Queen's Award for Industry. Occasionally one comes across abandoned texts of Thucydides with only part of Volume I bearing traces of what is termed 'close study'. But by and large you have turned out well. I continue to swank about you.

I return to that pleasing topic, myself. My origins were, you may think, inauspicious. Plutarch had quite false expectations of the Antipodes or at least of New Zealand. He opined, 'If there are Antipodean peoples, as some say, who dwell on the underside of the world, I imagine that even they have heard of Themistocles and the Themistoclean plan.' Knowledge of Themistocles was not, in fact, widespread. Study of Greek and Latin was not ardently pursued. A more practical attitude prevailed. I remember a schoolfriend registering his opposition by remarking, 'You don't talk to the cows in Latin.' (As a matter of fact, the same argument could have been applied to the learning of the Queen's English.) More physical attainments were esteemed and as the poet Cowper remarked, 'A very robust athletic habit seems inconsistent with much sensitivity.' But somehow I got out and have been treated as a prime example of the New Zealander 'more English than the English' – an accusation not susceptible of proof owing to the great dearth of Englishmen. When people go on to describe me as 'a perfect gentleman in the worst sense of that word', I know what they mean. Indeed when I read what my old fiend de Ste Croix says about the anonymous author of the Xenophontic 'Athenaion Politeia', the so-called Old Oligarch, calling him 'this unpleasant person', I wonder whether I am not myself the answer to the authorship problem. But I hope I may be pardoned for thinking I could write a better treatise than that. The truth is rather that I am an optimate, not the true-blue thing of course, but an optimate hanger-on of provincial origin, a Stoic of course. I do apologise.

Thank God, you may say, it's coming to an end! I half thank God myself. I'm heartily sick of hearing my voice. Anyhow, as Sam Weller says, 'It's over and can't be helped and that's one consolation as they always say in Turkey ven they cuts the wrong man's head off.' Retirement is certainly more enjoyable than one's funeral. For one thing, one can actually see who's come and those who couldn't come have been very polite. Nobody has resorted to the Mark Twain device. He said of a dead politician, 'I did not attend his funeral but I sent a letter saying I approved of it.'

I assure you that this is positively my last appearance. There'll be no more retirements. But I'm grateful to have had retirement in two stages. For dons, there is formal retirement when you cease to receive pay, and there is real retirement when your centre of gravity is no longer the College. I have found it hard to withdraw from the College psychologically speaking. I don't suppose I ever will completely. But now I am home, daily reciting you might think the one bit of Horace you must be expecting from me.

Eheu, fugaces, Postume, Postume
    Labuntur anni nec pietas moram
        Rugis et instanti senectae
            Adferet indomitaeque morti.

('Alas, good Postumus, the fleeting years slip by, nor will a faithful heart check wrinkles and the onset of old age and indomitable death.')

You may think my condition is hopeless, now that Screaming Lord Sutch and his Monster Raving Loony Party is likely no longer to offer the great hope contained in his last election manifesto, *viz.* for pensioners only, free heated lavatory seats. But not so. I have Greek History to keep me warm. In my diary I keep those lines of Tennyson's 'Ulysses':

    Old age hath yet his honour and his toil;
    Death closes all; but something near the end,
    Some work of noble note may yet be done.

I fear it may not be a work of noble note, but there will continue to be *opuscula.* I will not be unemployed, and I am not utterly done with the College or the College with me. That will require the flag at half-mast.

One Old Member who could not come quoted Virgil. *O mihi praeteritos referat si Iuppiter annos.* That is how I feel today. Thank you all for coming and reviving memories of forty-six years.

[Postscript

In sending me a copy of this speech, George wrote:
'You asked for the text of my speech on 3 June. Here it is – save that it is not exactly as I delivered it.' He added: 'In days past, when I was trying, I used to write a text, work on it so that it assumed speakable rather than readable form, and then learn the darned thing by heart, an awful sweat. That is, of course, what Demosthenes did ... However, he being human could not refrain from touching up the published version to remove bits where Aeschines had shown he was talking trash. In this case I am not able to do as he did. I simply wrote the speech, and made notes of it for delivery, and so this version is not exactly what I said, but it has not been "improved".

'I do not expect to make another speech in this life, voluble as I may be when in the furnaces of Hell.'

But in yet another note to me, he wrote: 'Since two or three asked for the text of my speech on 3 June, I have photocopied it – though the version I delivered was different and touched up by various insertions of *merum sal*, as my friend Tully would say – and now in the interests of truth (= self-esteem) I send it to you.']

'Thucydides'

[In 1998 he received the Runciman Prize for his book on Thucydides. This is the address he gave to the Anglo-Hellenic League on 25 May 1998.]

When I saw the name of Roger Tomkys on this society's letterhead, I did, I confess, slightly shudder, but as it turns out this is a much more agreeable delivery than the one I received from him forty-odd years ago on Balliol Cricket Ground. I warmly thank the society and the judges and, of course, the donor of this generous prize.

I am sure that most practising academics in this audience are well used to labouring on without any reward in the way of generous praise. One writes articles which one distributes and generally one has not the faintest notion whether the recipients approve or disapprove. Of course in Greek History one could be pretty confident that X would set out at length his inevitable disagreement and one learned not to answer him lest a *verbosa et grandis epistula* return, and the knowledge that X disagreed always gave one hope that one wasn't utterly wrong. Also it is just to remark that that great lover of Greece, the late Tony Andrewes, was ever most generous and encouraging. But generally one has little idea what impression one is making. For that reason I cherish one small academic memory. In 1971 at the University of Otago in my native land of New Zealand, I delivered a course of lectures in which Thucydides featured largely. There were two girls who had attended assiduously and just before my last lecture I received a bunch of flowers with a note on a page roughly torn out of an exercise book. It said, 'Thanks for the lectures. Sorry we can't come to the last. Thucydides lives. Love, Kerry and Tracy.' I was very pleased. They had got the point: Thucydides matters.

In a sense, there are too many books about Thucydides, but any book that sends us back to the Master cannot be wholly bad. Let us be frank. He is not easy. I was much comforted when a well-known Greek scholar said to me, 'The truth is that often we don't really know what he means.' It is hard labour, and indeed those who now begin Greek at university find the speeches almost impossibly hard. But the effort is infinitely worthwhile. It is hardly necessary before this audience to dwell on his remarkable qualities – his conciseness, his narrative skill by which e.g. he always makes me hope when I read VI and VII that the Athenians will get away, the lack of mush ('the Athenians put all male adult Melians to death and enslaved the children and the women.' Full stop). He will not let us be deceived. History is no laughing matter, nor is 'The History'.

But one thing in particular makes me hope that Thucydides will always live. Indeed if I had my way I would enforce the study of him on all our politicians and statesmen. His main message is that states that do not pursue their own interests will, short or long, suffer for it. This is not very difficult. Many have arrived at that view for themselves. But Thucydides works it out so consistently that it is indelibly impressed on the minds of his readers. It impressed Hobbes. It should have the opportunity to impress us. Anyone, Thucydides insists, who would 'play the good man', ἀνδραγαθίζεσθαι, 'pursue an ethical foreign policy' will in the end cause us all tears. (Of course, those who are so loud on this matter *may* do it only to deceive the masses. I can only hope so.)

I am proud to have the label Runciman fixed on me; though Sir Steven does not know it, he is a special inspiration to me, a bit like that stag in Virgil transfixed by a casual shot from the hunter unaware he had made a hit. When I was staying in the British Embassy in Athens some years ago, Sir Steven was there. Admittedly he was younger then, being only in his ninetieth year. But I thought, if he can keep going, I can try. I am very grateful to be provided with the means to carry on going to Greece, not just to Athens, the παίδευσις Ἑλλάδος, but all over Greece, the education of us all.

7   RULES OF THE GAME

[A card with five points written thereon was pinned to the door of his College rooms for the instruction of his pupils:]

1   Answer invitations promptly.

2   Wear a gown to tutorials.

3   Avoid the use of 'Sir' more than once a term at the most.

4   Neither seek nor expect deferment of tutorials.

5   Observe the ἀγραφοι νομοι [the 'unwritten laws'].

8   INTERLUDE

Letters and cards

[George had a high regard for the art of the epistle, an art that in the age first of the fax, then of the email, the text message and the WhatsApp moment, *seems* irremediably outdated, even if that same art can fruitfully be applied to digital messages. However their natural state is to disappear into the ether, whereas a good epistle has a better chance of being physically preserved. He admired Professor Hugh Trevor-Roper on various grounds, but none more so than for his epistolary brilliance and was pleased that it had been preserved in his many surviving letters. He developed his own style of which the following selection of cards gives some indication.]

letter re fishing in Scotland, 2 September 1970
My dear Tim,
I wish I had had you by my side for the last twenty-four hours, then might Doubting Timso believe. Down on Arienas last night three beautiful finnock, to be modest, or two beautiful finnock and one glorious sea-trout, to be truthful. The loch was very low and, my goodness, I was able to wade just that extra distance out into the loch, and then the beautiful monsters rose. Mum came to watch and encourage, as my morale had sunk rather low, but after that I am as Cocky as a Bondu can be. Then today with Jean Banister on the March loch, just on the seaward side of the Kingairloch Road (coming from Inversanda), my Stoat's Tail did perform most gloriously. First it raised a big 'un, then it caught a ¾ lb finnock and a nice trout, then it caught a 2 lb sea trout, and finally a 1 lb sea trout – all very beautiful. But why did I bring home only the trout and the 1 lb sea trout? First, the ¾ lb finnock. I was fishing for that from the shore and had to lean over a fence to net the creature which was rather too far away from the net, and while I was coping with all this caper it jumped off – a black mark to me. Second, the 2lber. I brought it into the boat in the net. It was admired. Capt Bannister removed the hook. He whacked its head twice on the gunwale. He put it down, for dead. Then he picked it up to give it one more convincing clonk, and let

it slip out of his hands into the loch. Gone, oh gone. Would it float? No. It was not dead. It was sped. The Captain was greatly dismayed. I said I didn't mind, but the family would never believe me. So could he let me have a sworn statement? I hope to come armed with an affidavit. Will you dare to accuse me of forgery?

Anyhow we, we missed your wise observation. We bought a bottle of whisky, and it seems so much more suited to the Highland climate than beer. We've got the Banisters to dinner tomorrow, and have some wine – we're rising in Morvern society, d'ye ken. . .

I mean next week to sample the loch above the bridge, on the way to Crosben. Also another day on Arienas. I'd love to get a real big sea-trout to land. I've sent for three more Stoat's Tails most urgently.

By the bye, the estate are going to plant trees all up behind the house! How sad. But I find that going up the water burn I can get much more easily to the Middle Loch. So the planting won't spoil that route too much.

Wish you were here.

love,

Dad.

postcard (showing the lion-hunt mosaic from Pella in Greece) to Tim and Maggie, 16 May 1976

Greece is the place for you two, especially Kavalla where we are today, having spent the day on Thasos where we walked the circuit of the 412/411 walls. . . On Sunday we went to Philippi, which was quite an eye -opener – the αγορα is about the size of a rugger pitch. The communal lavatory (of the Roman period) has 42 holes. How news must have travelled! Kavalla is the ancient Neapolis, which you will recall was a colony of Thasos? Anyhow it is one of our favourite places in the world. Φρεσκα Ψαρια ('fresh fish'), and all that.

letter to Sarah, 5 December 1976

. . . Also there is the Pompeii exhibition that we must see, and life is full of sweetness save for my Narcissus life. I mean my book ['Philip of Macedon'] which I gaze at with wonderful admiration but utter boredom, and I want to hand it over by Christmas but the plates are still a problem. Eight glossy photos and so far I have about four crummy ones.

Also there's the bleeding maps and all in all I long to be on with other things. I'm so glad I took Tim's advice to get the first draft done by September because I needed all this time to muck about with it all. It will be a great flop. Still I hope they accept it so that I can accept myself.

. . . Tony Stokes [the Russian Fellow of Univ] was pleased to receive a letter addressed to the Tudor for Admissions. So I promptly deflated him by saying that we have a Stuart of Common Room. I should have added that we also have King George. Still you can see how wet one becomes. There is a story about AL Rowse which goes that just after he published his book on Tudor Cornwall, someone said, 'Well Leslie, after Tudor Cornwall what next?' and a voice was heard from the rear to say 'Stuart Hampshire' (who was then a young Fellow of All Souls).

. . . There has been a nice storm on the Lit. Hum. Board this week. Peter Cuff of Pembroke wrote a quite frenetic letter complaining that de Ste Croix had 'railroaded through' a piece of business, and if that is true, it must be the Mukden to Moscow railway of 1890. We started discussing this matter in Michaelmas 1973 and got to a decision by twelve votes to eight in November 1976. So it was all very enjoyable, because Peter Brunt goes quite crazy at meetings and explodes at some unexpected moment about something that hasn't very much to do with the case. There's nothing so enjoyable as ruffled feathers – on other people. Brunt = 'Brusque' + 'Blunt'. Now we have a new hybrid Brunt + Cuff = Bruff, not to be coarse.

What a boring epistle, Yours a gimlet, Dad.

card to Tim and Maggie, 25 October 1977

Thank you very much for your note and also thank you in anticipation for Verbatim [the language quarterly started in 1974], a nice idea in the non-sense of nice. (I hope it's really nice about the Eng. Lang. In academic life the well-known principle, 'Niceness is not enough', touches non-sensical niceness, for true niceness is what we're all at and is more than enough. I can be as nice at Nice as the nastiest of 'em.) Love, Dad.

postcard (of the main doors to the Abbey of St-Pierre at Moissac in France), 14 April 1979

Have been carting this card around to send you since last Monday. We are entranced of course, but what chiefly strikes me is the magnitude of the Rivers. How did Caesar get across 'em? e.g. the Loire is immense or was t'other day. Also there is some really high ground in the Auvergne as everyone has always known *sauf moi*. Yesterday we drove up from Aurillac to the snows at Le Livran. / The best moments have been Notre Dame at Poitiers and the abbey at Conques. (What unhappy twist of character makes me such a sucker for the Romanesque? Suits Eliot's 'The Rock' better than Gothic but why are TSE and I such close buddies (so far at a distance)?) Another big moment was the Toulouse-Lautrec exhibition at Albi. He was born in 1864 and by 1880 was painting and drawing superbly. 'Tis by no means all *La Goulue et tout cela*. A sad talented little man. / We read a paper daily, and I was pleased to be reminded of (I think, Voltaire's last words) *Retirez le rideau, la farce est terminée*. But what news of Ougande! / Love, Georges

postcard to grandchildren Katy and Thomas, 21 July 1983
Dear Kate and Thomas
Your Pater sent me a copy of your school reports and I am delighted to see you are both doing so well and we are very proud of you.

It is 2.30 p.m., and here I am dressed in a dinner suit and in a sweat, just about to catch the train from London to go to a Jewish wedding. Think of me in a skull-cap. I'm glad it's going to have something to cling onto. How does a wholly bald pate keep its lid on? Uhu, says you? Or a blight of Araldite? Anyhow 5 p.m. will see me hatted and 7 p.m. tucking into my blinis (which are not bikinis) and 8.30 I guess 'tis tango time for me, or the blues, or the Paddington shuffle. Maybe I'll just shuffle off to Buffal -- o.

Love,
Your delirious Grand Paw

letter of 5 August 1983 to his son-in-law Sylvester Stein whose aunt Sarah Gertrude Millin wrote a biography of Cecil Rhodes published in 1933, revised 1952.
Dear Sylvester,

Thank you for your letter. I'm afraid I can't recall what I said. Are you referring to the bit in Time? (Where I am quoted as saying 'Many scholars are brilliant. Most are not. But the world is not run by brilliant people. It is run by good, sound individuals.') I was there referring to academic brilliance, but he [the journalist] omitted what I also said which was to this effect, viz. that the Rhodes Scholarships have produced scores of battalion commanders, barely a general, for the qualities of generalship are freakish, unpredictable, not to be recognised by Selection Committees, all of which does seem to accord with what your aunt said. . . . Silly people who can't see [Rhodes] in his age and the values of his age nowadays sniff at him. They might at least give him the credit for occupying the ground and preventing others getting it and making worse use of it. I am myself an imperialist in the Thucydidean sense, viz. that men always have sought and always will seek power over each other, that empire succeeds empire inevitably, that one empire destroyed is another empire begun, that empire in itself being inevitable is neither good nor bad but some empires are better than others. I recommend the June, July (and to come August) issues of Encounter with the articles about the origins of the Cold War. Gloomy but true. So, having such black thoughts, I'm not too ungrateful a beneficiary of the Founder's bounty . . .

Yours ever, George

letter from Stockholm to grandchildren Katy and Thomas, 25 August 1985, written on a 'photo letter' from the Wasa Museum that housed Gustavus Adolphus' sailing ship, the 'Wasa', which foundered on her maiden voyage in 1628, and was raised and restored over 300 years later.

Dear Cheerful Childie,

It seems irreverent to write on the Wasa's poop. The Admiral might be looking out. This was not like the famous case of Captain Brown – 'The captain's name was Captain Brown / And he played the ukelele as the ship went down.' Here the Admiral had just remarked that he'd polish off the Polish after he'd polished off his grub, when the whole ship rolled over, and he had salt water only . . . Anyhow, the Wasa's warlike Admiral went to his watery bier, and the Wasa wasn't seen for 333 years, but now it is worth a trip to Stockholm to see what the navy was like in the days of warlike Gustavus Adolphus. We have been to the Army Museum, and the Maritime Museum, and the great Stockholm Flea Market. To-morrow by boat to Drottningsholm and by train to Oslo, and then by heck to bed. Your silly Grandcorks./

card to Tim and Maggie to acknowledge receipt of a cassette tape enti-tled 'Silly Songs' sent to relieve a bout of shingles, 2 April 1988
Shingles are merely a disorder of the nerves, but with your Silly Songs you expose the roots of my being. (How much of it is American too!) I'm out on parole and go back for the Final Solution (cf. drug in saline) at 2 p.m. today – after which I hope to hear no more of this scabby busi-ness. (But I am an unsightly mess . . .) Love, yours to the last Drip, George.

card (showing the Great Theatre at Eles in Turkey) to Katy and Thomas, 4 October 1989
Greetings, oh toiling scholars, from the land of the Sultans, divans, bashi bozauks [*sic*], shish kebabs, and swart Musulmen, muscle men indeed . . . Here we have the place where St Paul preached to the Artemis-besotted Ephesians. (At least, I think it was here that he got chased out of town. Maybe I'm wrong. So don't take one of my Epistles as Gospel.) Nearby, we stayed in the Tusan Motel, which was not too san. In fact we got chased out of town by the smell of the drains. / Our visit to Troy was no disappointment, but we were surprised, nay delighted by Bergama – i.e. Pergamum, once capital of the Attalid kingdom, where first they made 'parchment' (same word). Rolls of papyrus ('paper') were light, but cum-brous. So the poor Anatolian sheep copped it, and gave us 'vellum'. (All very complicated...) Dearest love, Grandpa and ma.

postcard (showing the Arcadian Gate at Ancient Messene / Ithome), 23 September 1990
You may think this is pretty unexciting but since Diodorus says (I think) that these walls, 5½ m long, were built in eighty-five days and since the bottom course is about 4 ft deep, you may wonder how they did it. But, I ask, how did the Revolting Helots hold out on Mount Ithome for ten years (465-455?)? How did they feed themselves and how keep out Spar-

tans and Athenians? Did they build walls then and so make it easy for the rebuilding of walls in 369? Love to you all. George and P. There's no place like Ithome, sweet Ithome.

card from Rome, 8 April 1993

'Tis urgent that I win the Pools and make you all visit Rome. Today we went to Ostia Antica, the port of ancient Rome, and have snapped snappily, which snaps we will to your *snobbisme* submit. For lunch we went to a *ristorante* up in the village. I had a delicious fish lunch, quite delightful until I got a bone, *una spina*, stuck in my throat. 'All the crew were in despair / some ran here and some ran there / but the Captain's name was Captain Brown, and he played the ukelele till the bone went down.' On Saturday we travel to Napoli, quite happily, for we'll have a feast in Paest(um) and call out the Pompa in Pompeii, and by Heck, by Hercules, in Herculaneum we'll scratch the cranium. (Oh tish, my Muse, cry tush. Silence your poetry.) If all of this makes sense, you're a better man than I am, Gunga Din. Love to you all.

postcard from Prague in Czechoslovakia, 27 June 1993

In their less friendly moments Czechs go in for Defenestration, i.e. biffing chaps out of windows, and it's not wise to loiter, like these ignorant chums [the photograph had an aerial view of tourists in a public square]. The Commies did it to Jan Masaryk in 1948 to show the people how much they cared, and they sure made a filthy mess of things. / . . .

Prague is truly beautiful, one of the loveliest of cities. But what a history! We may be boring but we've been comfy as you might say. (Indeed the charlady said of A Hitler, 'What a fidget.')

scattergun letter to Tim, 14 August 1993

I derived, as Cicero would say, an incredible pleasure from your letter, or rather we both did. (I have an Italian ex-pupil who writes similarly enchanting letters. Indeed after the last one I was moved to enquire whether she was related to M. Tullius [Cicero], and I also complained about letters to the USA which almost universally evoke no response at all. I expect if you fax 'em, you get 'em back, but there's no refinement of style in a fax.) I do not dare to send this to Tavernelle [where we were on holiday], for where the helle is Tavernelle? So here it is in homely Hingham [in Norfolk, where we lived].

Yea, England lost the Test. They got two Australian wickets (Slater and Taylor) but Boon and Mark Waugh saw them through – but I swear Waugh was wrongly given not out and I believe that all commentators thought the same as it was replayed and replayed, though this is an *argumentum e silentio* (but a very marked Silence it was).

But, by sheer reckless folly, I have bought two Red Michelins of France 1995. May I give you one? I recall a sample of fearful schoolboy wit. Mike did not reappear from the loo. Pat broke in and found him in a faint with a note on his breast,

'Here I lie faint and downhearted

Paid my penny and only farted.'

(Imagine the youthful glee at that one!) Would you consent to condescend to accept it? If not, I'll faint.

We leave for La Belle France on 10 Sept. On 22 August we go to Arnold Goodman's eightieth birthday party at Lincoln's Inn, and as the result of an indiscreet conversation by your mother we will be coming home by hired car (half of). I sure was faint and downhearted until this morning along with your *verbosa et grandis epistula* (it wasn't but you must let me air my Juvenal) there came a cheque from British Airways for £72.00, compensation for our Lost Weekend in Paris. (Yea, the Lord God is good Hallelujah!) On the 28th we go to 'Separate Tables'. On the 7th we saw 'Oleanna' about Political Correctness, a compelling play as they say. You see, I have this awful malady of being utterly besotted with the Theatre.

Enough. Have a Red Mich, or expect to hook my carcass from the Seine."

On 26 October 1996, the day after his birthday, he sent a card cut from a Calvados box with a piece of Calvados marketing printed on it: 'Ses reflets ambres, son parfum puissant et délicat, sa saveur irremplaçable, ont contribué à faire sa renommée et celle de sa region d'origine: La Normandie.'

I'm always touched by the poetry of these expressions of French local puffing. Therefore I try my own: 'His ill shaven jowl, his overpowering and noisome smell, his unbeatable lack of taste have all helped to make infamous his person and his native land: New Zealand.'

On learning that Tim was participating in the Norfolk Churches Bike Ride in September 1997, he sent him these deeply moving verses (gamma plus):

Be like those dabbling ducks,
Heads down tails up,
As you pant from spire to spire.
Pull on your lycras, overtake the trucks,
Decline a vicar's kindly offered cup,
And no foul language when flattened is your tyre.

On 6 November 1998, he sent a card telling about an accident he had had.

I rejoice that the moral training I gave you in youth has rubbed off on myself. On Tuesday I missed my footing as I stepped out of the train at Reading and fell flat upon the platform, unable to rise unaided. My right knee and my right shoulder unfit [*sic*] me for the while as goal-kicker and fast bowler. I was helped up by a great cloud of witnesses and a good sensible body, who could have been a nurse, counselled that I sit awhile. Then came a clear trumpet-call echoing from your youth: 'Hurrah for Bobby Bumble / He never minds a tumble / But up he jumps / And rubs his bumps / And never seems to grumble.' So, to the silent applause and wonder of the concourse, I hobbled off to the Gatwick train . . . Laying aside a lot of my habitual modesty, I tell you this.
Love, George

letter to Maggie of 24 July 2000, attaching a copy of Newbolt's 'Vitaï Lampada' ('There's a breathless hush in the Close tonight . . .' and ending up 'Play up! play up! and play the game.')
Lampada is, I presume, the accusative of the Latin word *lampas, lampados*, a straight borrowing from λαμπας. *Vitaï* is the old genitive you will find in Lucretius. I always thought 'the Close' was the famous Close at Rugby, but Newbolt went to Clifton and for all I know there is a Close

there . . . The brave product of the system worked at home in the Easter vacation and had to be called to other pleasures by his father, who was one of the landed gentry at least, with the family church of glorious antiquity and around it the family graves etc. Clearly one of England's *jeunesse dorée*, from a stately home to a Public School to an Oxford College and out to the Indian army on the north west frontier. He carried the *lampada vitai* indeed.

Pray rally the ranks of your colleagues with 'Play up, play up' leaving it unclear which game you have in mind. It could be the noble game of cricket, it could be the Great Game in Afghanistan, it could be the Pyjama Game (either one-day cricket in blues or yellows or greens, anything save cream flannels, or larking in the night) or it could be the Game which, it seems, so many are 'on'. Don't therefore specify. Or take up fast bowling and castle each in turn.

After Enoch Powell had died in 1998 he became intrigued by his biography. On 20 July 2000 he sent this card:
He had himself called by his second name when he discovered that there was another Classical scholar, John Y Powell. I'm slowly getting through Simon Heffer's 'Like the Roman' [a biography of Powell published in 1998]. I feel very great sympathy and admiration for him. Maurice S[hock] always says he was the Second Founder of the NHS. He advocated privatisation and the floating exchange rate long before it became Tory doctrine. He belaboured Heath over the Prices and Incomes Policy and also the EU. His 'rivers of blood' speech has been much misunderstood, I believe. He was a very great man but I disagree with those of his Classical writings I have read.

In October 2000 Tim and Maggie had a holiday in Rome to which he sent this card on 24 October
We look at the weather charts and wonder how you are faring. Rome is to me indeed the eternal city – though Lydia Carrass, who makes documentaries, threatens to waylay and quiz me on the Acropolis on Thursday about how I react to the news that the Greek Government plan to create a basin for aquatic events at Marathon – 'may none those marks efface, for they appeal from tyranny to God' (Byron on Chillon Castle but not inept in the situation I face). But your mother says, 'Don't

worry, dear, these things tend not to happen.' Oh the Foolish Virgin, the lily of the field.

a thankyou letter on 11 June 2003 after a visit to Norwich
Gosford Park [directed by Robert Altman 2001] was an attack on the society of class differences, debasing both those who serve and those who are served. Except for those two maids (Lady Trentham's, and the one who forgot herself and exclaimed 'That's not fair') there wasn't a decent person in the whole piece. I wish to make clear that I am an anti-egalitarian person, that I almost like class distinctions. Class is essentially money, and unless some of us are a great deal richer than the rest of us there'll be no money to stimulate and reward artists, furniture-makers, cheese-providers, wine-producers etc. etc. I don't want a world in which everyone (save the Party Enforcers) rides round in a Trabant. Finally equality is the enemy of freedom to choose. So there. . . . Cherish Class Distinction, in which matter I remind you of that song 'Edie was a lady, Edie had Class with a capital K.'

Postcard from Rome, 15 May 2005. The card showed part of the mosaic of a hunting scene held in the National Archaeological Museum in Palestrina.
No, we have done and seen practically nothing, but we did go to Praeneste (as [Palestrina] was called in the days of C. Marius) and we did see the famous mosaic of which this is part, a second-century BC scene of life on the Nile. I cried out with glee when I saw it, and it made our whole week.

We had a very agreeable return to Ostia Antica and had a lunch at the very *ristorante* where we lunched in 1991 (or thereabouts) but this time I did not get a fierce fish-bone stuck in my gullet [see page 111]. For the rest we've had a lot of pasta without disaster. Today we went to the Palatine and then down to the Via Sacra, but did not meet Q. Horatius Flaccus having a saunter, nor M. Tullius on his way to do a Blair on the Rostrum, but there was a seething mass of the *profanum vulgus* [common crowd] which I myself also *odi* [hate]. Alas I can't quite recall Horace's words about *Graecia capta Romam cepit* [conquered Greece has conquered Rome], but if Graecia is the car, you can say that again. . .

Paternal Brio

By 1960, George and Pat were very well settled in Oxford, and now had three children: Simon, born in 1946, Tim, born in 1948, and Sarah, born in 1950. Here are two items that illustrate his character at the time, the first in trying to help Tim to participate in a Balloon Debate at school, and second a note dated 15 March 1962 and delivered to Sarah's bedroom across the landing.

[I was at the Dragon School in March 1961, aged twelve, and had volunteered, or was coerced, to take part in a 'Balloon Debate'. Five people are in a balloon over the sea, which is losing air – to save the balloon and its occupants, one passenger must be ejected. Each had therefore to make the case for being kept on board and once the five cases had been heard, there was a debate and then a vote by the whole class as to whom to eject. The five people in the balloon were Danny Blanchflower, President Kennedy, Agatha Christie, Pablo Picasso and Adam Faith. Since I had a great enthusiasm for football – and indeed for Tottenham Hotspur – I was obliged to speak up for the merits of Blanchflower, the Northern Ireland international footballer who, as captain of Tottenham Hotspur in the 1960-61 season, led them to 'do the Double', i.e. win the Football League First Division and the FA Cup. I struggled to compose any sort of speech and George, perhaps almost wishing that he was taking part in the debate himself, gave me a set of arguments to use in addition to what I had written already. They emerged from among his papers after his death, which is an indication of his attachment to them.]

1   (As you have written it.)

2   a) The sufferings of the Irish in history at the bloody hands of the English. Do not add yet another wrong.

b) The needs of Ireland. It does not care if it loses its place in the arms race or its temper, but it hates to lose a match against England. Do not be unsporting and deprive your rivals of their best player.

c) The needs of Spurs. How can they win the Double without Danny? I don't mean by the Double the first scholarships at Eton and Winchester. No, a far finer thing – Top of the League and the FA Cup. A free Cup-

final ticket will be given to every boy who doesn't vote against Danny –
60,000 angry fans will deal with the rest of you.

d) Only Danny was man enough not to appear on television, only he
deserves to be left in peace. Let others make a big splash.

e) And, little men, Danny eats Shredded Wheat. Do not make liars of a
million packets of cereal.

3   Of course, Danny is modest, and would not want to stay in the
balloon if there was anyone worth saving. But what a crew!

President Kennedy: Why is he in a balloon? He is wanted for the work
of Peace. He should keep out of 4th-class space travel. This is worse than
Ike and golf. Let us return him to serious affairs. Do not fear for his
death. American know-how will know how to save him. Anyway he
could swim in the shark-infested waters of the Pacific Ocean. So it will
be all right if he has to swim within range of Agatha Christie. You'll be
all right, Jack.

Agatha Christie! Do not save her from the shark-infested waters. She will
quickly get to the bottom of things and join Hans and Lottie Hass in
investigating the Mystery of the Ocean's Bed.

Picasso must go. He has painted his last picture and married his model.
Let him die before he is reduced to painting covers for Agatha Christie's
books.

Adam Faith is the real problem! His beautiful voice and his beautiful face
are at their very best and millions of merry milkmaids milk cows that
rock to the music of their own idol – far, far more lovely than the sound
of any milking machine. His songs will be played as long as mankind
endures. Dare we throw him out? Danny will only consent if you have a
recording made of his death screams. For sounds of such unique beauty
he resigns his place in the queue. I wish to deny rumours that this will
be the first meeting of Adam with the water. He always uses a bit on his
hair – being careful of course to keep it off his face.

But I appeal again for Danny. Think of Ireland, and Spurs. If you
deprive these great sides of their favourite boy, there'll be no kissing
each other when they score a goal; only sorrow. Not so, the fans. They
will be near Revolution, and are already storing up orange peel just in
case. Think of the ref and save Danny.

[History does not record how much of this text I used, but memory records that I did not avoid being ejected.]

a handwritten note to Sarah
HOW TO SPILL SAND AND SPELL SANDWICHES AND WITCHES
1   He eats the sand which was on the beach.
2   We went to the beach and rested for a while on the sandwich Daddy brought.
3   Dad found ham in the sand which he ate. Which sand which ham? This sandwich ham, you ham.
4   I do not care for sand witches and sand which is found in sandwiches and witches. And which is the sand witches make into sandwiches?
Your foolish pater.
BEFORE YOU EAT A SANDWICH, FIND OUT WHOSE AND WHICH.

The pull of Scotland

[In the late 1950s, George and Pat were thinking of finding a regular holiday cottage, and were very much drawn to Scotland as the place to look. This led to a family holiday at Killunaig Farm on the Ross of Mull in August 1960, for which George kept a diary. The entry for Saturday 20 August reads as follows:]

In the morning I sat writing notes and reading and doing nothing much, but in the afternoon I went off by myself leaving by herself my blister-footed spouse and drove into the hills by the back road to Salen. It was a narrow road with grass growing down the middle and I could hardly spare much of a glance to each side but I could see enough to know that it was most beautiful solitary country. The road ran along a typical highland stream [the River Lussa] as I dropped down towards Loch Spelve, and I turned across it and drove a couple of miles over a headline to the loch again. Here I left the car and began to walk – uneasily at first by reason of the presence of cattle from which I expected a bull to emerge any minute, but as I got on the walk turned into a Walk Through Paradise Garden (where a sharp shower is not excluded) and I reached Loch Uisg, to which I have given my heart. It is fresh water, quite small, say, a mile and a half long, surrounded by hills and almost utterly deserted. I was so delighted that I walked further than I should have, and got to a little tongue of land where I built myself a small cottage in which I will live at Easter and in August from now on, warm and comfortable. In furtherance of this design, when I return to Oxford, I will try the Oracle (i.e. paddle in the Pools [Littlewoods']).

During this walk I had reason to bless the rubber soles of my boots for with the wind in my face my progress was so silent that a small rabbit came along the road to within three yards of me and stood gazing respectfully at two vast (but not trunkless) legs of stone. This admiration of one for the other continued quite a minute, and then His Fluffy Lowness circled round His High and Mateyness (keeping an eye on each other) and when it attained a down-wind position bolted, don't you know.

Lord, please keep far from Loch Uisg
the evils of Mixamatosis [*sic*].
(Signed) Moses.

I had to scamper back to the car, and it was only by reason of my progress at a mile in thirteen and a half minutes as I timed it that I could get back to Killunaig. Even then I drove like fury over the bumpy road, scattered the rabbits and the sheep and got back at 6.05 PM for tea.

(Note: When visiting me in future at Loch Uisg, pronounce my habitat Ooshk.)

[On this 1960 holiday George and Pat had been enchanted by driving through Morvern to reach Lochaline in order to catch the ferry to Mull. The search for a cottage in Scotland led to the renting of Uileann (Ullin) in the White Glen in Morvern from 1962 for the next decade whither the family repaired regularly in the summer and often at Easter too.]

9 RELIGION

[George's interest in philosophy is not unconnected with his engagement with the matter of religion, and whether he should believe in God or not.]

Upbringing

[from NZRSOHP]

GC: I should say one thing that I expect makes me different from some New Zealanders is that I had a very Anglican upbringing. My father was, not uncharacteristically, an agnostic, and my mother was a Scottish Presbyterian . . . We all went to St Mark's, and that had a very large effect on me. I sang, I was in the choir, and you could almost classify people into the religious and irreligious in terms of whether they sing or not, because singing sacred music has a tremendous effect on the soul, I think, and you never get out of it. I can quote Anglican hymns now: words slip out to match the situation all the time, quoting from Anglican hymns. But King's College was religious in theory, and I was 'pi' beyond belief. It had a very great effect on me, and on the whole, I am grateful for it.

HM: Is that still important to you, the religion?

GC: No, not really. I go to the College Chapel, I feel that it's part of the society, and I don't think you can have a society without a religion. I feel like Cicero. It's good for us, it's good for them, I'll go along. At this moment I am without religious belief, though I go to the Chapel, and most people would say of course I am a pillar of the Chapel, but I am not.

HM: Have you taken your father's type of agnosticism then?

GC: Yes. I think things are somewhat different now, aren't they? I think that since Freud and the study of psychology etcetera, people can no longer think of the soul as a separate entity. In the seventeenth century, in the days of Bishop Butler, conscience was almost a faculty of the human being, there was mind, body and conscience. But of course conscience is gone. If people say 'I've got a bad conscience', they mean 'I think I should not have done that'. That's not saying there's a sort of bad register in my conscience. Well, conscience is gone, but the soul has gone too, because when one dies, does the soul remain? What about all these complexes? All these vicious things derived from things burned into one's psyche by experiences? Do they die too? One doesn't actually believe in the survival of the soul. I think that is a presumption you have to make with religion that the soul survives, and there is no such thing as soul. The other thing is of course, I think, that there is no reason to think that there is divine intervention in the world. I would say that the interventions of God have to be believed to be seen. Because they can't be seen without belief, I believe. Against that, of course, is the hard fact that it's very much easier to live with religion than without it. And I'm not clear that I will always maintain my present attitude. It varies a great deal in life. At some stage I thought that Christianity was true even if religion wasn't. Now nothing is true.

So there's a total change, and it happened in an interesting way really. Conversion is a very curious thing. It isn't actually a matter of argument. When Plato is trying to argue that the just life is the good life, he doesn't beat Thrasymachus, save by saying, 'Well now look, I paint the picture of the good life. When I paint the picture of the bad life, choose. You will see the bad life is 729 times more profitable and advantageous than the good life. Which do you prefer?' [Plato 'The Republic', Book 9, 587c--e.] And one chooses the good life, because the good life is attractive, and one is attracted by a way of living. If you look at that remark, 'Who seeing a Communist does not feel small?' – a silly thing, one would think on the face of it – but it's absolutely true. It was the image, the vision of the Communist good man, that attracted people. Total devotion, selflessness and so on. That's how conversions happen. And unconversions happen in a similar way, if you look at the history of the church. What broke the hold of religion in the Middle Ages was the corruption of the church, the corruption of the clergy, and people seeing that, they think this is a bad thing, it's lost its appeal for me.

I think that's what happened with the Reformation. The corruption of the clergy was enough to put people off. Of course any good man, any sensible man knows that human beings are human beings and people will do things, they will go in for paedophilia and all this stuff now, that'll happen, but when you come up against it, you are still very shocked. So that's the history of my religious opinions, which are not very interesting.

HM: I was just thinking of your saying there is no soul, and in a sense there isn't that permanence and guarantee of our continuity, yet you're surrounded by all these books and knowledge that you have of ideas. Is there some link between soul and idea in any way?

GC: My mind can have the ideas, the books are there, someone else's mind can have them. But I think they don't persist in me. I mean, when I am laid in the turf I will be laid in the turf, goodbye. And I think that's a general state of mind now, but of course whenever there's a great crisis people in weakness turn to the idea of religion and of course you are better to endure awful sufferings I think with religion. I hope I don't come to those terrible sufferings, but I wouldn't think I was strong enough to stand on my own. I don't think so. May I ask, are you religious?

HM: I would say I'm agnostic.

GC: Agnostic, yes. Well of course, I used to think that agnosticism wasn't really a viable position because in effect, in fact, one didn't remain agnostic in one's decisions, one was either for or against. You either thought God has an interest in this or he doesn't, you don't say, 'I don't know whether he hasn't,' you're actually, in fact, in your choosing, you are atheist. But in general, most of one's actions are conditioned by upbringing and social influences. But there are crucial moments, morally speaking, when you don't actually rely on background or upbringing. You've got to decide. I don't know whether you remember that hymn, that it is the brave man chooses while the coward stands aside.

HM: How does the tune go in that one?

GC: 'Once to every man and nation / comes the moment to decide, / in the strife of truth with falsehood, / for the ill or better side, / then it is the brave man chooses / while the coward stands aside, etcetera.'

There are these crucial moments, as you see when Emilia is dressing Desdemona for what is to prove her deathbed, Emilia says to Desdemona, 'Wouldst thou not do such a deed, to gain the whole world?' And Desdemona says, 'Not I, by this heavenly light,' and Emilia says, 'Nor I by this heavenly light. 'Twere as well done in the dark.' But there are crucial moments, which maybe have to be done in the dark, but you have to choose. And I think in those moments your religious attitude does affect you. I don't mean political moments, political morality, political decisions are not moral decisions.

HM: They're not?

GC: No. Moral decisions are what one does with regard to oneself. Political decisions always involve a choice between courses that have ill consequences. You just have to choose which has the least ill consequences. But it's always, in terms of conscience, it's a utilitarian decision, it's not a moral decision at all. Don't you think so?

HM: But wouldn't you say that that choice at base could have a moral choice to be decided?

GC: Not politically. I'm just reading that wonderful book of Sebald, 'Rings of Saturn', have you read it?

HM: No.

GC: It's a work of absolute genius, you know. This German, he was living over in East Anglia, and he wrote this book about it, and there's a chapter there about Roger Casement, I expect a villain in my parents' eyes. But of course Casement was a good man, a great and good man, and his decisions were moral but the politicians he came up against were entirely 'Don't rock the boat, don't let's say anything that will upset the Belgians.' Political decisions are always like that. I mean, you can see them at the moment with Blair, wobbling between thises and thats. That's what politics is. But morals is not like that. You know, come what may, I would rather die than do that. And that's a moral decision. Well, every so often you have a great moral decision and if you are religious I think the choice is easier than if you are not religious. You might say to yourself, 'Don't be a bloody fool. Why do this? Why lose the whole world over this? You're not all that important.' But religiously of course, this moment is eternally important, you mustn't miss it. So I think religion does affect moral behaviour in that way.

HM: Yes. But just one more thing on that political-moral question, for example the bombing of [cities in the War] and the knowledge of, [to] just take an individual, the prime minister of the time, through the Ultra process, all the background to it. In the end was that not a moral decision that he had to make?

GC: No, it wasn't himself, it was the country, what was best for the cause. I mean, with politicians they have causes, but they don't have individual moral decisions whereby you have a clear 'I must do that. Let the skies fall, I will do that.' Well, you don't have that as politicians. There seems to be a very great difference between political and moral action. Anyhow, that's what it seems to me.

HM: Fascinating.

GC: So religion I think does actually make a great difference to people in those times. I wish it was more clearly true. It seems to me to be a falsehood.

HM: With the present day situation of the Church's constituencies falling away and people going to church for weddings and funerals and things, is that just holding on in case, do you think?

GC: I think it's just sort of a hangover and that's the way to do it. We need forms. I mean, we are developing new forms. It used to be the case that there was always a memorial service in Chapel here when Fellows died, but now when people who are known to be unbelieving, they don't have that. They have a sort of concourse when speeches are made and a bit of music played, etcetera. You develop new forms. I went to the burial of that great man, one of the heroes of my life, Herbert Hart, HLA Hart, the great Jurisprudence man, and no religion there at all, absolutely not. He was Jewish, but he had no religion. And what they did was that the coffin was simply taken to the graveside, lowered, a piece of Schubert was played on a tape recorder, the children each said something about their father, and that was that. And it was very convincing. It wasn't gauche and embarrassing. I think we will develop a new set of rituals, but we haven't got that, so that's why people like to go to church.

HM: And is that the kind of ceremony that you yourself would like for yourself?

GC: Oh no. I don't want my family to know what I think. I couldn't afford to tell the truth to my family. They must be themselves and not – they must have nothing to do with me. I would just be a conventional man, I wouldn't have any different – the Anglican order of service would be read, absolutely without a word of intrusion.

Catholicism and Father Allerton

GC: There was a strong social division in Auckland between Catholics and non-Catholics. It's partly that the Catholics in Auckland had come out as lower-class people, refugees from Irish poverty very often, and there were clusters of them down in Southland and so on. In Auckland they owned the pubs. The Labour party was Catholic, we had nothing to do with the Labour party. And it had quite an influence on New Zealand politics, because they may have been Labour but they weren't radical, they weren't trying to turn the world upside down, they just wanted a just and decent society, and Catholicism as it were kept the Labour party steady, I think. But no, one didn't know them. One felt they were just different socially. They were different socially. We didn't mix. There were one or two Catholics at school, but not many. And Catholicism was never discussed.

HM: You mentioned this important influence, Father Allerton.

GC: He was a High Church priest.

HM: What was his influence?

GC: He was the vicar of St Thomas's Parish, down in Freeman's Bay, where I went. High Church Anglicanism, at its very best. And he had a very great influence on me indeed. I was a High Churchman when I was young, and he had quite an influence on a number of people.

HM: What was that influence specifically?

GC: Basically holiness and devotion. He was really a very devoted priest, and also he was very interested in the theatre, there was culture and books and so on. I had quite a lot to do with him, I thought he was a wonderful man. When I saw him in his last days, he was by then blind, led up to the altar. [pause] It was very moving. Well, I greatly admired him. He was a socialist, he came from humble circumstances in Liverpool. [pause]

HM: One of these models of people, in a sense.

GC: Yes, he was a great influence on my life. You can see I'm a very emotional man. I can recreate situations in my imagination. I had an elderly colleague called Carritt [Tutor in Philosophy at Univ, 1898-1945] and we were talking at High Table one night, and I said, 'The trouble with utilitarianism is that it makes a calculus of pleasures and pains on a false basis, because the curious thing about pleasure is that it reproduces itself in the mind, whereas one cannot remember pains, so that the balance is always going to be in favour of pleasure.' And he said, 'Yes, that is true, but every so often, that is not true of, as it were, spiritual pains. Every so often, I remember the death of my son in the Spanish Civil War, and it strikes me with the impact undiminished of the first time.' And I have that, I can remember situations, and, I think, experience them emotionally. With age you become more emotional, don't you?

HM: I suppose so.

GC: I'm very moved by things. But also, the world has changed. In Cicero's time, people wept freely. They wept in court. It was not shaming. The notion that weeping was bad came in with the public schools in the nineteenth century. When Nelson left the fleet, they all wept. Just as when Teleutias left the Spartan fleet in 388 BC, they all wept. But this stiff upper lip business came in with I think the public schools in the Victorian period. And you see it in the poetry of Kipling and so on. And I expect that continues a bit, but people are much more emotional now. You see them on the box, hugging each other after scoring a goal, in the sort of way that boys would have been caned at school for behaving in a public place when I was at school. But now they're all over each other all the time.

HM: Every goal.

'The Unknown God: St Paul before the Areopagus'

[This address was given on 26 May 1968, probably in Univ Chapel.]

Acts 17:23

For as I passed by, and beheld your devotions, I found an altar with this inscription, TO THE UNKNOWN GOD. Whom therefore ye ignorantly worship, him declare I unto you.

It is said, and for all I know rightly, that this verse prompted TH Huxley to the name Agnosticism and is thus a suitable text for a consideration of Agnosticism in all its guises, ancient and modern. I mean by Agnosticism the belief that we do not and cannot know whether God exists and must therefore proceed to disregard religion until God's devotees provide satisfactory evidence of His existence. Not that the Areopagites whom St Paul addressed were agnostics in the modern sense, but, in so far as many of them were Stoics and Epicureans, no matter what St Paul might say about Athenian superstition, he was addressing men who were not all that different from their modern counterparts, Humanists and Hedonists of various sceptical hues. It is these latter that I am particularly consider-ing, but the case is not basically different from age to age, and perhaps St Paul's argument is not so slight as it might at first sight seem.

I should make it clear that what I say, I say on my own authority and the Church should in no way be blamed for my folly or my errors.

The first point I have to make is so obvious that I scruple to make it – but it is this. All religion is in large measure Agnosticism. When young men tell me that they are 'agnostic', they seem to think that they have annihilated the question of religion. This seems to me a fundamen-tal error. I presume in what I say, as 'agnostics' seem to presume in what they say, that arguments for or against the existence of God are indecisive. So neither do atheists know that there is not a God nor do we religious know that there is. Believing is not knowing. When I say that 'I believe in God', I mean in part 'I do not know that God exists'. If I knew that I would not talk about 'believing'. Of course, the case of the mystic is different. I believe that mystical knowledge is possible and I judge by external criteria that it is sometimes attained but, in so far as the mystic knows, he does not merely believe. For the rest of us, in so far as we believe, we do not know.

This is simple and obvious enough, but much religious talk conceals it. Statements like 'I know that my Redeemer liveth' refer to a state of conviction *akin* to knowledge, but essentially different. If some-one says, sensibly enough, 'Faith is a process of cumulative certainty', this is not certainty in the sense that I am certain that port is sweeter than claret, and those zealots who seek to obscure this aspect of religious utterances do religion a great disservice. Let the truth be constantly told. *'I believe' implies in part 'I do not know'.* All religious people are agnos-tics, and sensible ones know themselves to be so.

The second point is more difficult to state – not that it is less easi-ly comprehended, but because it runs counter to the conventional opin-ions of our time. Perhaps it will be best if I put it in personal terms. Throughout many waverings of opinion I have always found that it is not possible to be neutral. If one does not believe that God exists, one believes in practice that God does not exist – that is, that one swings between religion and atheism. Notice that I add 'in practice'. Of course one may assert that one does not know that God exists or that He does not exist, but when it comes to action one always acts as if one does know. But am I unusual in this? Can others be neutral? Can they be agnostics in action as well as in opinion? Clearly many think they can – to judge at any rate by what they say about bringing up their children. They are of the opinion that they can bring up their children in a state of neutrality so that they can let the children choose what will be inscribed on their own *tabulae rasae*. This is, to my mind and in my experience, pernicious nonsense. Had I not been most fearsomely warned that this address may not exceed ten minutes, I would enlarge on this matter, but I must simply assert what seems clear to me that *children cannot be brought up in a state of neutrality about God, because human beings are not made that way.* Children depend on their parents, even in their most independent moments, and will reflect parental attitudes. In the vast majority of cases belief begets belief, and unbelief begets unbelief – fortunately so, for otherwise society would be most unstable – and neutral upbringing is a twentieth-century myth. But perhaps there are *adults who, through reason, attain neutrality*? I hardly dare assert that there are not, but I must say that I have yet to meet them. For either men act as if God has an interest in their actions or they act as if God is wholly irrelevant, and whatever they say of their opinions, this seems to amount to atheism in practice. This is, I imagine, what Jesus was pointing to when he said, 'He who is not for me is against me.'

Thus there is a dilemma. *We must be agnostic in theory, but we can't be agnostic in practice.* We will inevitably be atheist or religious. Which should we be? And let me remind you that I am here presuming that there are no convincing arguments either way. One must therefore always be as much interested in why atheists are atheist as they are in why theists are theist. For we are in a *vacuum of arguments*.

If, like Plato, when he posed side by side the two lives of the just man and the tyrannical man, we inspect the two lives of the theist and the atheist, our choice is not so simple as Plato's – for, even if we were minded to choose the better, it is not immediately apparent which is better, and, if we do decide that the one looks better, must one necessarily choose that? One would in that case seem to believe what it suited one to believe – a feeling that should give comfort to neither theist nor atheist.

The only way of deciding which to choose would seem to be the pragmatic test of which works. From this point of view even our keenest foes would concede that religion does work for the religious, or at any rate does not work notably badly. So it is pointless to enlarge on this theme. I merely remark that every period of one's life has its problems, and one continues to find that religion answers them. Nothing, for instance, in one's life may have been more potent than the temptation to despair that may assail one in middle age, and only religion seems to be equal to the task of mastering it. But this is not enough. Many an atheist feels comfortable enough in his atheism and thinks that it works. Now if atheism really does work, then there seems to me to be no potent argument against it. The only question is whether it really does and really will continue to do so. For the present it can draw on an ample credit from Christianity – Christian morals without Christian theology – but as things are going now it won't continue to do so. For there will be fewer and fewer with Christian belief, and atheism will stand uncluttered by the past. Now there are plenty who would assure you that in fifty years this cathedral will be a museum. Time will show, but it begins to look as if the great abandonment of religion is not faring very well. At any rate increasing atheism is accompanied by increasing violence, chaos and empty despair. Humanity may come to feel that there is a necessary connection between those things and that atheism does not work – a great opportunity for modern earthly creeds in little red books.

But I speak of 'choosing' the one life or the other – but for most of us that is quite false. What converts men to another way of life does not permit him choice. The truth of the matter seems to me well summed up in the famous line 'Who seeing a Communist does not feel small?' Not that too many of us have that particular feeling, but the presupposition of the line is right, that primarily we do not choose the good life but are attracted by something that is apart from choice. That is why the life of Christ and the lives of the saints have worked so powerfully on men.

This must seem a lame conclusion, but it is the best I can do. If God exists, he did not make belief a matter of intellect. It depends on forces outside ourselves. All we can do is not deceive ourselves by thinking we are neutral or ever can be. A lame conclusion indeed – but it seems to be the way St Paul answered his Humanists and Sceptics, who could themselves have nothing better to persuade. Nor, to my mind, have ours. Their certitude is false and time will prove it so.

Address on Remembrance Sunday

[Delivered at Oriel College, undated but presumably 1970, twenty-five years after the end of World War Two]

When the War ended twenty-five years ago a great number of men including the honourable quota of Oriel and, I expect, relatives of at least some people in this Chapel tonight, had died, as they believed, in defence of the liberty of this country, and I expect the first thing to do on Remembrance Sunday is to thank God that their deaths were not in vain. It is true that there is a generation gap between those who know of Nazi Germany as a matter of history, and those who contemplated it more directly, and the latter feel more sharply than the former the benefits of not having had to endure the blessings of a *pax Hitlerica*. But all sensible men would agree that we have a great deal more liberty than we would have had if the men whose deaths we remember today had not done their utmost for what they believed was a good cause.

Secondly, we should thank God that despite changes of fashion and feeling the will to defend liberty is strong in the young men of this generation and that in this sense too the men who died have been victorious.

Thirdly, Remembrance Sunday should be an occasion for remembering the sufferings of all men, friend and foe, in the great conflicts of the twentieth century and for strengthening our resolve to act rightly in regard to other peoples and to avoid, if any of us attain power in high places, the spiritual wickedness of pursuing narrow national interests.

It is hard to know what else to say and I hope I may be forgiven if I proceed to talk about what may seem to be only loosely related to Remembrance Sunday. Memories of the War do however prompt one to consider what effect the experience of war had upon oneself and the progress of one's opinions.

I must make clear at the outset that I had very little experience of the War. There were moments of danger and I could modestly claim to have been in the War and not just near it, but my share was so small compared to that of no doubt many of the fathers of the present generation of Oriel men that what I say may seem not only ludicrously presumptuous but also quite untypical of the experience of men who were constantly in danger. Still one can only speak of one's own experience in such a matter, and I therefore presume to speak of myself.

I remember during the War reading the remark of an American Army Chaplain to the effect that there are no atheists in foxholes – foxholes being the American equivalent of what we would have spoken of as slit trenches. The remark sounded very well but I venture to think that it was by no means true. Not that I was an atheist in a foxhole but the experience of danger and fear can make one feel more like a rat than a child of God. No doubt people do have certain experiences of danger, especially prolonged experiences which set them praying to God for their release. But if the Church depended for converts solely on men's reactions to danger, I do not think there would be a great prospect for religion. I expect one did say prayers in foxholes, but I don't particularly remember doing so and to judge by the conduct of one's companions in danger, when danger was past, one could hardly think that they had been through some sort of religious experience. I do remember a moment when I did feel greatly thankful to God but it is not a moment that I feel particularly proud about. There was an evening when the battalion in which I was serving was seeking to withdraw from a beach in the Solomon Islands and it did look for a while as if the Japanese might break through and simply destroy us all on the landing-craft before we got free of the beach. We did get free and in the dark of the evening the machine guns fired into the shore a spectacular and indeed beautiful hail of tracer bullets and I remember feeling an overwhelming gratitude to God. It was partly simple relief at escape, but also I think relief that the enemy were receiving what we might have been receiving ourselves – not a particularly godly thought. So much for my religious experience in battle. I think the truth is that armies are not holy places. The atmosphere is much more that of what one might describe as a moral holiday. One might at moments squeal to God, but basically one became, or was in danger of becoming, something less than a man, let alone a person in communion with God.

However, in reflecting on the War afterwards two things did stick out in the mind and help me, through the scepticism of undergraduate life of post-war Oxford, to feel more firmly settled in religious belief. The first is of course the experience of walking so near to death. It is not that one is not constantly in danger as one drives along the road any day of the week but one's life is so full that one can easily not notice. But the prospect of imminent death concentrates the mind wonderfully and it is a great help in thinking about religion to realise that one is in that sense very close to God and while no man needs a war to make him so aware yet the recollection in tranquillity of that experience had the effect of making one feel that the question of God is urgent. One might face Him at any minute, and one had better not treat Him as a matter that could be deferred.

The second aspect of my experience was purely a matter of analogy. When you walk through the jungle having only what you carry, cut off as it seems from all hope of other things, one seems as one looks back to have been in a position in which intellectually speaking all men seem to be. Many young men of honest mind and good intention are reluctant to decide for religious belief and practice because they think that time and reflection will arm them with more conclusive arguments one way or the other. And it is not always the devil who prompts, 'Sometime maybe but not yet.' This attitude I hold to be understandable but wholly wrongheaded. We will be in no better position in twenty years or in 1984 [presumably a reference to George Orwell's book] to decide these matters than we are today, and will walk through life like a man walking through the jungle with no more resources than we carry on our backs at this very moment, and it is a great mistake to think otherwise. This might prompt men to think that we must therefore all be agnostic and that that is the end of the matter.

To me that is the start of the matter. All religion is agnostic – in so far as one believes, one does not know and we should never be blinded by the way in which religious people are prone to talk about religious experience. Such sentences as 'I know that my Redeemer liveth' or 'faith is a process of cumulative certainty' obscure the fact that religious knowledge is not quite like or not at all like the sort of knowledge we have about the world in which we live. In so far as we believe we do not know.

But there is an important further consideration. There is to my mind no genuine position to be described as agnosticism as opposed to belief. Psychologically speaking we are all either theist or atheist. We may pretend to have attained neutrality, and sit on the fence between believing God exists and believing He does not, but critical moments in our lives always show that we have in fact come down on one side or the other of the fence. For whether God exists or not makes the greatest difference to us when we come to bear suffering or to divorce our wives or to instruct our children. Either we *act* on the presumption that God exists, or on the presumption that He does not. Of course most of our acts are governed by ethos and upbringing and manifest no more than our conformity to convention. But there are decisive moments in which in calculating our interests we must either take God into account, or so leave Him out of account as to show us clearly that whatever we say, we do in fact believe that there is no God. On the other hand, like the man walking through the jungle we are equipped with no conclusive arguments and it is by some positive act of belief or unbelief that we take up our attitude. This is the human dilemma. We seem to have no means of resolving the question of God's existence but we inevitably do resolve it. I fear it may not be orthodox and I apologise if it is misleading, but it seems to me that the only way in which men decide for or against religion is by the criterion of whether religion or irreligion works better. Nor do I suppose that this blunt instrument will necessarily lead all men to the same conclusion. But it is the only instrument that one has in one's haversack and to my mind it is religion that takes one best through the jungle of life, protecting one most effectively from despair and selfishness and hatred and acquisitiveness and all those states of mind that one might judge to be somehow a distortion of humanity.

This however is a large matter and may awaken as much scepticism as assent, and is perhaps too large for a sermon or indeed for my wits. But I might remark that when people change from religion to irreligion or from irreligion to religion they generally seem to do so for no other reason than that the one offers the spectacle of a more blessed way of life. One sees the exponents of this or that view possessed like Michael Cassio of 'a daily beauty which makes all else seem ugly'. Some of you will remember the line the author of which I think but cannot be sure was Stephen Spender, 'Who seeing a Communist does not feel small?', and this line is less absurd than it might seem for it reflects the fact that men are attracted to a way of life rather than persuaded by a set of arguments. Against the compelling power of the devoted Communist or the enthralling assurance of a Casanova, one sets the spectacle of

Christ and the saints and of lesser holy men, and the one seems to work better than the other. It is indeed a blunt instrument but is all we have and there is no reason to think that by walking further through the jungle we will acquire a better.

If therefore these reflections pinned onto Remembrance Sunday have a moral, it is contained in the words 'Remember now thy Creator in the days of thy youth.' Life is too precious to misuse and we may as well decide now how we are going to use it. So we should look around a sort of Platonic portrait gallery of lives and choose the most appealing – realising that that is the only method and ever will be available to us. If we choose well, we will fare well and not lose our way.

At least we have liberty to do so, and as I remarked at the beginning it is principally why we should keep this Remembrance Day with gratitude.

10 THE LOVELINESS OF LIFE:
Greece 1990

[From the late 1970s, whenever George and Pat went on holiday, George kept a diary of their travels, their meetings, and their pleasures. As an example, and in order to give an idea of their lively style, this edited extract draws on the diary kept of a visit to Greece from 18 September to 2 October 1990.]

Tuesday 18 September
Off on a Heathrow bus at 9.30 and arrived 10.40. In the air on Olympic Airways by 12.50. After a long wait an excellent lunch arrived with smoked fishes and a veal dish. Landed at 6 p.m. (Greek time) and met by Imelda [Miers, wife of David Miers, Ambassador to Greece 1989 to 1993. David had been at Univ as an undergraduate]. In white Jaguar to the Embassy which is a very palace, most excellently redecorated and refurnished under Imelda's direction.

Wednesday 19 September
Breakfast in our own sitting room! Served by a Filipino maid (there are two, Pasita and Lucy). Rang Christiane [Sourvinou-Inwood] at 9 and arranged for them to come to tea at 4. Then tentative booking for flight to Thera on 29 September, returning 30th – but at present Olympic Airways are on strike! Then walkabout along Ermou and up to the Plaka and back and up to Panepistimiou and wiggled through to Kolonaki and so back to a 'light' lunch! Sleep and the Inwoods to tea at 4 with Christiane at her engaging best on Robert Graves' 'White Goddess' or whatever the book is. Arranged to meet for dinner 28 September. Merrily we live.
 Disaster as we returned before lunch. The security man pushed the door to let us in and toppled a decorator off his ladder which broke the glass of the door which fell and socked Pat on the head, and bruised her nose and cut her wrist! 'Twas not my fault, but I felt guilty. By 5.30 p.m. 'twas all repaired! Oh to be an ambassador.

Thursday 20 September

Breakfast is in one's room, which is very pleasing, for one doesn't have to suppress oneself. The Ambassador visits one!

[Epidauros]

At 9 the car arrived, and we set off at 9.45 along Vasilissis Sofias and Panepistimiou, round Omónoia and out. All very easily done, despite gloomy prognostications. Left the motorway in Isthmia and drove along the coast. First Cenchreai, and coffee in a little nameless place. Stopped at a monastery (Μονη Αγνουνδας?) with a charming little church and yard with the living quarters around it. Pat took a number of photos. Then on to Epidauros Palea where we walked around and surveyed the enchanting little bay, and had a fish lunch of mixed fry, which was most delicious and with the σαλάτα χωριατικά was very filling. We set off for the Asclepeion at about 2, and after a sleep began on a reasonably thorough tour which was much improved by tagging along with a party in the museum, for a girl guide gave an admirable account of the Tholos and theories thereon. Then up to the theatre where various guides clapped hands from the centre of the orchestra and went clapping back and fro. Again very uplifting. So we sat down awhile, and Pat took some snaps of it all.

[Nauplion]

Then we drove cosily to Nauplion, and parked on the seafront, while we looked for a hotel. We picked on Hotel Otto which was full (chiz, chiz), but were directed up the hill to Hotel Leto which took us in for 4,500 drachmae (about £16 bed and breakfast). Pretty plain, with a shared loo and shower but an excellent view over the bay. Then we walked around Nauplion which is a delightful place. No doubt it was in 1951 [when he and Pat had holidayed in Greece], but we had no sense of it then. I think one was shocked by the poverty of the Greeks, whereas now they seem reasonably well off. We reconnoitred a taverna, and did well, for we were invited to inspect the kitchen and see all the dishes cooking away. We chose άρνάκι with rice and again salad (again onions and so on). All very tasty and filling. And so to bed.

Friday 21 September

(Despite the roar of traffic, and a bit from some Unnamed Laconian Dragon in the night, we bless the name of Sparta.) In the morning we drove along the shore of the Bay of Nauplion and then inland and over by a very good road and down to Tripoli. Having picked up a young man, we drove him into the centre, but the place was quite unrecognisable. Either it or we have changed so much, or both. Southwards, and into Ancient Tegea where we walked in the temple of Alea, all very peaceful. Then back south again with coffee in a roadside place, run by a Greek who had been in, and learnt his English in Australia! A coachload of people in a coach marked H. arrived – which we took to be Hungary – and reflecting on the astonishing change in life for all those people we went on to Sparta, where we parked the car and reconnoitred. Coming to the Tourist Information Office, we were referred to the B-class Hotel Menaleion, which suited us wondrously, what with bath and bidet, and view of Taygetus which one could touch outside the window.

[Mistras]

After picnic lunch in our room and a sleep, we set off for Mistras with heavy clouds above, and by the time we got there it was raining quite heavily, and we saw our Hungarians returning awash with capitalist rain. So we waited and then went up to the deserted city which we had almost to ourselves, well, nearly almost. We began with the Metropolis church where Pat had a bad attack of Snaps, and expended seven films before you could say Georgios Palaeologus. A lovely little courtyard at the entrance, then another with a gallery around it where there was a museum and also signs of someone living. The church itself was beautiful, imposing, holy. The views from the gallery sublime; the whole place a vision of a peaceful life. Then on to St Theodore and to the Aphendiko (both relics out of use), but we pried around. Then up to the Palace of the Despots, being restored, where we sheltered under a fir tree while it really rained, and a black cat came and made up to Pat, who had to be bullied into not indulging her mad passion for cats. I pointed out the danger of fleas, but pussy was most persistent, clearly being used to being fondled by tourists. Then on and up to the Pantanassa (or Panagia) where six nuns cling on to religion and solitude. Again, the peace of

Orthodox monasteries overflowed onto one. Then down to the car, and back to Sparta. Mistra, *je t'adore*. ('Tis called Mistra because that is the Frankish version of 'mistress', but the name is a corruption of I forget what.)

For supper, we sought the advice of that same Information Office, where we found this time a good-looking Greek girl who had grown up in Montreal, paid a visit to Greece before going to university, and met and married a Greek, who now runs a shoe shop! That's ζωή for you (*zoe* ['life'] to the Greekless). She told us about the sort of place we wanted and so on. So in due course we went there, and saw the dishes on the stove, and chose what we wanted, which all tasted most tasty especially with retsina. In the middle there was a power cut – due to a strike which 'goes on and on'. So lighting of Bottagas lamps and the like, and for us home to nothing but bed.

For the night, see start of entry.

Saturday 22 September

We rose to view Taygetus' majestic beauty in a clear sky, and after breakfast a visit to the museum, a pleasing little fellow. Then off and up Taygetus, a dream world of trees and solitude. (How the devil did the Spartans get to Messenia, I'd like to know.) Had coffee at a small restaurant-hotel at the top called Canada, in the sun on the verandah. Blissful peace. Then we glided down to Kalamata, and found Hotel Philoxenia, not without trouble, right at the eastern end of the bay. Splendid swimming pool, and not many people.

[Pylos]

Lunch and sleep, and forth to Pylos and Nestor's palace, to which I drove and drove through Messini, 'good to plant, good to plough', but oppressively humid. First sight of the bay of Navarino very startling. Sphacteria looks enormous, and so too Pylos. Did the Athenians camp on the high ground or the low? I took a photo, which probably won't come out. After some cartographical havering, we finally reached the hill called Epano Anglianos at about 4.20 p.m. to find that it closed at 3 p.m. By the dust of Nestor we sat down and wept, I can tell yer. So we buzzed back to Pylos town which is a nice enough little sea place, and then hastened back to Kalamata encountering some pretty rotten driving on the way. But I was in time for a swim, which was jolly d. (In the pool there is one bit with underwater stools where you can sit and have drinks served! (Did you ever? How do they keep the drachmas dry?)) Back for a whisky, and then out to look for a very Greek supper. We got one verily. First, on the direction of the girl at reception we walked up and along the Mani road for several thousand miles, but the promised land was not sighted. There had been a power cut, and of course no Greek on a Saturday night sits down to sup until 2330 hours. So we trudged back, got into the car and went along the seafront, finally in despair fixing on any place, and sat on the pavement where we had an indifferent meal to the roar of 25,000 bloody Vespas. 'Twas hell on earth. So we gobbled up and flew back to the Philoxenia to enjoy a power cut. So into bed again, Nancy, and heigh ho for the jolly Electricians' Union. Μπυγε them say I. And all night long the sound of battle rolled with cars on the road behind us and a snoring gent beside.

<u>Sunday 23 September</u>
Breakfast is distinctly good at the Philoxenia. One helps oneself, hurrah, and we did and so had enough coffee and too much else.

[Ithome]
Then off for Ithome. We got to Mavromati, and on the advice of an old man turned up a side road to Merigala allegedly, and this brought us to the Laconian Gate, which we reached on foot (having parked after turning a twenty-point turn with a huge hiatus beneath my field of vision and my faithful mate looking for cyclamen, ect.). Amazing spectacle, of huge blocks neatly squared and put together. (Diodorus says, the Guide Bleu says, that they did it in eighty-five days which I do not believe in view of my theories about walls in Asia. Search into this matter, boy.) Then back, and to the Arcadian Gate, even more amazing with stretches of wall to a considerable height here and there (average 15 feet high, according to Guide Bleu), and a great circular entry. (Read all about it.) (I have many dark thoughts about all this that I keep to myself for the moment.) Then down to the Roman Agora, past a theatre and a temple and so on. Then up to a shady taverna where we had salad bread, retsina, and café ellenico, sheer bliss in every detail and way. Back to Kalamata without incident. All very successful.

Monday 24 September

Off early after a shirty discovery that the Philoxenia cost nearly twice what we had expected. So I tried to black the eyes of the boy behind the desk, but he wouldn't take 'Bugger you' for an answer. So I paid and buggered off. Bugger. I felt like making off to Mac's for a big Ham Bugger, but pushed on for Megalopolis, fine, but we took what we thought was the road for Andritsaina and ended up on a mud road being made and having been waved across a muddy flood by a worker, who gave us the stark choice of Megalopolis or Kalamata, we went on and came to a village where no one had heard of Andritsaina! So we pushed on and found a sporty Greek with a shotgun who carefully directed us back to Megalopolis, where we finally arrived after 15 extra kilometres, distinctly feta feta (meaning local chiz chiz, silly).

[Bassae]

So we stopped in Megalopolis for the second time and bought our lunch (beautiful bread as it turned out) and then hastened on for Andritsaina which we reached after a hundred hours of drive, and on up on the road to Bassae, which was very disheartening to the driver who felt quite dizzy by now. *But* we got there, and there it was in its tent, very marvellous. Fancy those guys taking all that trouble for Apollon Epikourios [Apollo the Helper], who wasn't the slightest bloody use! Then we had lunch in the sun, which was delicious indeed, only interrupted by a fat Frenchman leaping down from the Holy Heights and tearing his *pantalons* and grazing his leg. I offered plasters. His woman says, 'I have alcohol.' Says I, 'One usually applies that internally.' Then he pushed off in his Jag, and I finished my lunch.

Then off and on to Créstena, and up and over to Olympia, where, rebuffed at Hotel Neda, we fixed ourselves at Hotel Poseidon and off to see the museum, which was jolly decent. Oh, those Greeks!

Olives and retsina on the pavement, then a sleep and σαλατα χωριατική, and σουβλάκια at a real Greek taverna. All very delish. And so to bed.

[Olympia]

'And sang within the Sacred Wood', but not quite sang, and not Agamemnon. Up early from our clean C-class hotel for a perfectly nice cup of coffee and so on (but, ah, we think us of the amplitude of the Philoxenia – and then we should think of the amplitude of the accursed bill), bought stamps for our postcards in the ταχυδρομεῖον and our lunch, and up to the Site of Sites.

'Twas no disappointment as we sorted out the various buildings, but most of all the temple of Zeus, what a whopper, what a monster. And if Phidias' boy had stood up, he'd have gone through the roof. (Not inept. Zeus was always hitting the roof. But what did pious viewers think when they saw it? 'Tis beyond my imagining.) We walked the length of the *stadion*. (Some tourists ran it up and back; that is, the *dolichos* so-called.) Past the judge box. (One thought of *Trial by Jury*, 30,000–35,000 spectators hissing and booing and cheering. (Did they have any hooliganism?)) All very satisfying indeed.

So on to Langadia, up wooded valleys, all quite different, with a pleasant coffee somewhere, and on towards Vitina (Βιτήνα) lunching high up beyond trees and so on in a pretty rocky bit. We nosed off the road onto a bit of the old road and had our bread and feta and tomato and olives in the sun, then our melon and some grapes. Plenitude of contentment. (Will one recall it, or will it all be lost in the fog of time?) On to Vitena, a pleasing town, and on a good road to Nemea, the dimmest town indeed. Only one hotel, a D-class, and it sure looked it. The police said that was all ye know in Nemea and all you need to know. So we cheesed off to Corinth, and turned in to Old Corinth to find the Xenia Hotel [presumably a reference to their 1951 visit]! Well, we found the relic thereof. It had closed in 1982 and no one had mourned or even noticed the passing. So we set off for Corinth, and after a kilometre or three we thought we must be going in the wrong direction. So we swung round, and, Pat having said she saw a sign for Tourist Information, we went in search of it, and saw a place called Rooms Zimmer and the word, mysteriously, Information. So I asked, and we got shown to a very very very decent room with bathroom and so on. On the up-stairs balcony, a family of Australianized Greeks with Anastasía aged 21 and her almost identical sister Georgía, and simple well-cooked food and good retsina and local Greeks. What luck!

Wednesday 26 September
[Corinth]

Off and up to the site, where we wandered to and fro and took a number of photos of the Temple of Apollo (seventh century), a very frustrating affair with too many people crawling all over it and being photographed. Then to the Bema where St Paul gave the besotted, licentious Corinthians a good ticking off and on to the Spring Peirene, back to the museum and then out along the Lechaeum road and back to our Zimmer where we had café ellenico. Then off to Nemea and so on.

[Nemea]

Cleonae turned out to be an invisible presence, so we pressed on, after lunch under an olive tree, a very delicious one as usual (bread, feta and tomato) but shared with a goodly company of flies which fair chizzed *me*. On to Nemea, an enchanting solitary site, where we sat in the shade of a column of the sixth century and read. Much snapping by Pat of temple and grove, the Sacred Grove *redivivum* (τὸ ἄλσος), then into the enchanting little museum, which (closing time 3 p.m.) we barely had time to digest (but we snapped it thrice).

On then, through modern Nemea which did not show us one single signpost. And so thoughts of Phleious vanished, but we drove up through Koutsi and Stamenga (?) and down to the plain through delightful vineyards, about as cultivated a part of Greece as I have encountered. Again a total lack of signposts, and so we abandoned the quest for Sicyon and floated along home to shower and so on. Then beer for me and tea for her, and sleep as we awaited dinner, or rather the coming of the Greeks for their dinner.

But dinner turned into a solitary orgy. Yes, we would try taramasalata, yes, and the aubergine mix. Then I would have Mumma's 'canolloniee' and keftedes, and Pat would have a small lamb chop or maybe two. Gee, what a marathon of guzzling, and then on top of it the boss, Chris Marinis, brought us four chunks of kid to taste. We had to eat it and stuffed it down.

In the night Nemesis? My insides turned to liquid mud and I went to the loo a hundred times. (And all paper had to be put in the basket!) By the morn I was wan.

Thursday 27 September

We rose slowly and breakfasted gingerly, said farewells to Anastasía and off. First to the Isthmia Museum which we found with difficulty, and looked at cursorily, then out to the site but I had no stomach, literally, for the task. So we drove across and saw the Diolkos, right beside the western end of the canal. Then having rung the embassy and announced our return, we flew along the Scironian Way and all went merry as a marriage bell, until we got to what we thought was Omóneia (and wasn't), and so set off in quite the wrong direction, from which error we had to and just did extricate ourselves with the temperature at 33 degrees. Then when we got into Stadion we were swept left into Akademia, and only by the grace of God and much waiting did we get into Ranaris and Kolonaki and so home. Phew! By that time I was ready to drop.

A special salad lunch prepared for us of which I could not partake. So Pat virtuously stuffed it all in. Then sleep, and sleep. Then supper and bed. Thank God for our being in the Embassy and not in Pension Poseidon at Olympia!

. . .

Sunday 30 September
[Athens]

We walked pleasantly to the National Museum, and looked mainly at the Attic vases, but also saw the frescoes from Thera. Then went down and had coffee and regarded the 'fakes' for sale, not very expensive and most of them quite nice, and if we had the car we might be tempted. Walked back for lunch, slept, and then David [Miers] drove us to the Acropolis; closed! So we walked quietly back reconnoitring where we were due for dinner, which we duly had with the Inwoods, Christiane very voluble and tense and clever and learned, Michael very intelligent and right on the point all the time. Restaurant abominably set up for tourists, and food not great, though very expensive. They walked with us to the bottom of Loukianou and there we parted.

Monday 1 October

We walked up Ploutarchou to the funicular and so got to the top of Lykavittos, whence we regarded the immense spread of Athens bathed in smog, a most discouraging spectacle. I would not want to live in it, egad. Then on the terrace we had the most expensive and the worst cup of coffee ever to pass my lips, but it was pleasant just sitting in the sun.

Tuesday 2 October

To the Acropolis with 50,000 others by way of the Zappion, where we chanced upon the lions' cage, a noble pair. Ye Gods, what bulk, what power, what terror on the loose! A longish walk, and then a climb, but beautiful and moving unto this last. Into the Acropolis Museum, which is a miniature history of Attic sculpture.

Then down to the Agora and the Stoa of Attalos, all engaging and delightful, but tiredness came on us and we limped back – for a shower, and a whisky, and a lovely lunch and all very amiable.

A taxi at 3.30, and a last view of the Acropolis, and it's Athens goodbye for ever probably, and one felt and feels a bit melancholy.

Bus at 10.50, and home by midnight. Mixed emotions.

11 REFLECTIONS AT THE END OF LIFE

Thinking about New Zealand, the view from 2002

[from NZRSOHP]

HM: Is New Zealand fading into the distance for you?
GC: Oh yes, you see, I have no close relatives there. I would be too uncomfortable sitting in the plane, and I think now dangerous – my left leg needs to be stretched and so on, so I wouldn't go. But more than that, I felt that things were very different the last time I was there, with the Māori problem, and there was a lot of violence, and it wasn't quite what I had grown up with. It was just a different atmosphere. I admire New Zealanders. I always say to people, quoting that hymn of New Zealand, 'Every prospect pleases, but only man is vile.' But actually New Zealand men are bloody good, and I admire them greatly. But at a distance, I couldn't live there. I had a dream once that I had resigned my Fellowship and gone back to New Zealand, and then I thought, 'Oh God, I've lost the secret of eternal life.' And then I thought, 'Ah, but the college doesn't meet till next Tuesday. I'll get back and withdraw my resignation.' [laughs]
HM: Well, in spite of all that, does it matter to you to be a New Zealander?
GC: Oh, I'm proud of New Zealand, and I am proud of my origins, yes. In a sense it is God's own country. When one talks about the Jews feeling themselves the chosen people, I regard New Zealand as the chosen people. They're jolly good, these chaps. I would like to be worthy of them. Remember that moment in the Cretan campaign, there was some terrible situation, the village was held by the enemy, and a chap got up and said, 'Come on for New Zealand!' and they all dashed in, suffered casualties, and took the place. I admire the guts of New Zealanders. I remember during the War one had to censor mail. And one little chap called Jackie Stevens, he wrote in his letter, 'We'll be going up north soon, but I guess the Pig Islanders will come out on top' [laughs]. There

was a confidence about us and determination. I'm proud of my origins, of course I am. Complicated as they were.

There is one story that sticks in my mind that is worthy of our native land. During the Napier earthquake in I think 1930 or something like that, terrible disaster there, half the roof of the Cathedral had fallen in and the walls were shaking. The Hawkes Bay Infantry Regiment was said to be on parade, and the Colonel called for volunteers to go in and rescue the regimental colours. And he said, 'Volunteers, take a step forward,' for he had memory of that moment in British military history when the whole unit as one stepped forward. But on this occasion not a man moved. And the Colonel said, 'Oh well, we'll just have to leave them' [laughs]. Those chaps went and did their stuff in the desert within not so long a time.

HM: And from here, the perception of New Zealand amongst your colleagues?

GC: They do think it's a pretty good place. Not just athletically but in general, there's a lot of good come out of New Zealand. In Oxford there's able people who have come here, and New Zealanders have done things. They tend to come out on top very often.

HM: You'd be classed as one of the successful New Zealanders.

GC: Maybe, yes. Not by me.

HM: You got what you aimed for.

GC: Well, my aim was Oxford – Shangri-La. I'm here, and I've never gone away, or like the lotus-eaters, I forgot to go home: I have eaten of the lotus flower in Oxford. It suited me from the beginning, and will till the end.

HM: It still tastes sweet?

GC: It does taste sweet, though sometimes bittersweet. I do think the situation of Oxford now is very serious. I long to get rid of this government. By saying that we can't raise our fees, they're saying, 'The long slow death for you.' I hate them because I love Oxford so much.

Quotations shored against his ruin

[In George's annual desk diary he used to note particular quotations which were in his mind, many of them classical Latin or Greek, but also from English poetry. This selection gives some indication of his cast of mind in the last three decades of his life. Those marked with an asterisk were regular favourites from year to year, carefully re-entered not in all but in a number of subsequent years. They were a consolation of a kind, but also, I believe, a memory test: could he recite them to himself or to visitors?]

1992
Old age hath yet his honour, and his toil;
death closes all; but something near the end,
some work of noble note may yet be done.
– Tennyson, 'Ulysses' * [This may be a pledge to himself to write 'The Greek Wars' finally published in 2005]

ὸστις δ'άπ' άλλης πολεος οίκησῃ πολιν,
ἀρμος πονηρος ὡσπερ ἐν ξυλῳ παγεις,
λογῳ πολιτης ἐστι, τοις δ'ἐργοισιν οὐ.
– Euripides, 'Erechtheus' quoted in Lycurgus, 'Against Leocrates' 100
[He who adopts a city, having left
some other town, resembles a bad peg
fixed into wood of better quality,
a citizen in name but not in fact.]

σχετλιε, τιπτ' ἐθελεις ἐρεθιζεμεν άγριον άνδρα;
– Homer, 'Odyssey' IX.494
[You rash man, why do you want to provoke a savage?]

1993
οὐ γαρ τουτ' ἠν εὐδαιμονια, ὡς ἐοικε, κακου ἀπαλλαγη άλλα ἀρχην μηδε κτησις.
- Plato, 'Gorgias' 478c
[So absence from pain isn't happiness, it seems, but not getting it in the first place.]

Quocirca vivite fortes / Fortiaque adversis opposite pectora rebus
– Horace, 'Satires' II.2.135*
[Therefore be strong, and face adversity with a brave heart. (See also page 98.)]

The smaller the pit, the fiercer the rats.
– Goldwin Smith (British historian 1823-1910) [This would get repeated until 2004 when it is dropped.]

O mihi praeteritos referat si Jupiter annos.
– Virgil, 'Aeneid' VIII.560*
[If only Jupiter would give me back the years that have gone.]

But what avails the Classic bent
and what the polished word
against the undoctored incident
that actually occurred?
– Kipling, 'The Benefactors'*

1994
ἔστι γαρ, ὥσπερ και σωματος, και διανοιας γηρας.
– Aristotle, 'Politics' 1270b 40
[Just as there is of the body, so there is also a senescence of mind.]

το τε καταμεμπτον ἐπιλελογχε
πυματον ἀκρατες ἀπροσομιλον
γηρας ἀφιλον, ἱνα προπαντα
κακα κακων ξυνοικει.
– Sophocles, 'Oedipus at Colonus' 1235 sq.
[Last of all comes old age, blamed, weak, unsociable, friendless, wherein dwells every misery among miseries.]

Senescence begins
and middle age ends
the day your descendants
outnumber your friends.
– Ogden Nash

1995
Eheu fugaces, Postume, Postume,
     labuntur anni nec pietas moram
          rugis et instanti senectae
               adferet indomitaeque morti

– Horace, 'Odes' II.14*

[Alas, Postumus, the fleeting years slip by; love (*pietas*) brings no delay to wrinkles, to looming old age, and to ineluctable death.]

Nil habet infelix paupertas durius in se
quam quod ridiculos homines facit.

– Juvenal, 'Satires' III.152-3

[Miserable poverty holds nothing more injurious than that it makes men ridiculous.]

το έργον του καλου δικαιωματος υποπτευοντες.

– Thucydides, 'Histories' VI.79.2

[. . . while suspecting the truth behind the fair plea . . .]

ἡ ἐν δημοκρατιῃ πενιη τῆς παρα ταις δυναστῃσι καλεομενης εὐδαιμονιης τοσουτον ἐστι αἱρωτερη, ὁκοσον ἐλευθεριη δουλειης.

– Democritus, fragment 251 (VS 68)

[Poverty in a democracy is preferable to what is called happiness among autocrats as much as freedom is from slavery.]

Rusticus expectat dum diffluit amnis; at ille
labitur et labetur in omne volubilis aevum.

– Horace, Epistles I.2.42-3*

[The countryman waits while the river flows on – and it keeps flowing, and will flow rolling for ever.]

Shelley's 'Ozymandias' is given complete with a note appended: 'Diodorus I.47-9' (which is a description of the tomb of Ozymandias). Whenever he quotes the sonnet, which is frequently in these diaries, he always appends the Diodorus reference.

1997

Inane studium supervacua discendi

– Seneca, 'De Brevitate Vitae' X

[An empty passion for learning the superfluous.]

2000

You should have caught us in better times. We were purists then.

– Player king in Stoppard, 'Rosencrantz and Guildenstern Are Dead'*
Cur, inquit, me putas hos tantos dolores tam diu sustinere? ut scilicet isti
latroni vel uno die supersim.
– Pliny, 'Epistles' I.12.8   [quoting Corellius Rufus on the Emperor
Domitian as the gangster (*latro*)]
[Why, he said, do you think I carry so great a grief for so long? Of
course! It's to outlive that gangster by even one day.]

Better a dinner of herbs where love is, than a stalled ox and hatred there-
with.
– Proverb

2001
I am a very foolish, fond old man,
fourscore and upward, not an hour more, nor less:
and to deal plainly,
I fear I am not in my perfect mind.
– Shakespeare, 'King Lear' IV.7

2002
ὡ ξειν' ἀγγελλειν Λακεδαιμονιοις ὁτι τῃδε κειμεθα τοις κεινων ῥημασι
πειθομενοι.
– anonymous but perhaps Simonides, quoted in Herodotus, 'Histories'
VII.228.2*
[Stranger, go tell the Spartans that obedient to their laws here we lie.]

For right and not for rights
– Kipling, 'The Holy War'

La vie doit avoir un courant, l'eau qui ne coule pas se corrompt
– Lamartine epigram
[Life should have a current; water that does not flow stagnates.]

2005
Now the Rome of slaves hath perished and the Rome of free men holds
her place
I from out the Northern Island sundered once from all the human race,

I salute thee Mantovano, I that loved thee since my day began,
wielder of the stateliest measure ever moulded by the lips of man.
– Tennyson, written for the nineteenth centenary of Virgil's death
[repeated in later diaries but towards the end he only wrote out line 2:
was he thinking really of his New Zealand origins?] *

Three things come not back: the spent arrow, the spoken word, the lost
opportunity.
– Proverb

Let nothing trouble you. All is fleeting. God alone is unchanging.
Patience . . . He who possesses God wants for nothing. God alone
suffices.
– St Teresa of Avila

'Has she no faults then (Envy says), Sir?'
'Yes she has one, I must aver:
when all the world conspires to praise her,
the woman's deaf, and does not hear.'
– Pope, 'On a Certain Lady at Court' [I believe he felt this applied very
aptly to Pat.]

2006
Ille vir haud magna cum re sed plenus fidei
– Cicero, 'De Senectute' I.11
[The man was rich not by virtue of lots of money but by probity.]

Tatenarm und gedankenvoll
– Hölderlin
[Short on action and long on thought]

And my ending is despair
unless I be relieved by prayer.
– Shakespeare, 'Tempest' V.1.333-4

2007
Sic omnes, ego non

– Catherine de Clermont (seen at Château de la Ferté St Aubin) [See introduction page xi]
The Gatling's jammed and the Colonel's dead
– Newbolt, 'Vitaï Lampada'

I am for other than for dancing measures
– Shakespeare, 'As You Like It' V.4.192-3

Last scene of all,
that ends this strange, eventful history,
is second childishness and mere oblivion,
sans teeth, sans eyes, sans taste, sans everything.
– Shakespeare, 'As You Like It' II.7.162-5

Studiorum omnium satietas vitae facit satietatem
– Cicero, 'De Senectute' 76
[To feel you've had enough of studying means you've had enough of life.]

Et quasi cursores vitaï lampada tradunt
– Lucretius, 'De Rerum Natura' II.79
[Like runners they pass on the torch of life.]

Amicus certus in re incerta cernitur
– Ennius
[A true friend is revealed in moments of anxiety.]

2008
What is this life, if full of care,
we have no time to stand and stare?
– WH Davies

2010
entry for 2 February (the second anniversary of Pat's death): +7 a.m. The End – I will say no word that a man might say.
– Swinburne

2011

He left a name at which the world grew pale
to point a moral or adorn a tale.
– Johnson, 'The Vanity of Human Wishes'

Wretched, rash, intruding fool, farewell
– Shakespeare, 'Hamlet' III.4

Naturam expellas furca, tamen usque recurret.
– Horace, 'Epistles' I.10.24
[You may erase nature with your fork, but it'll keep coming back.]

Into my heart an air that kills
from yon far country blows:
what are those blue remembered hills,
what spires, what farms are those?
That is the land of lost content,
I see it shining plain,
the happy highways where I went
and cannot come again.
– Housman, 'A Shropshire Lad' XL

Three new quotes in entry for 2 Feb. [see 2010]:
1   Many waters cannot quench love neither can the floods drown it.
2   Walk on through the rain / though your dreams be tossed and blown / walk on, walk on with a hope in your heart / and you'll never walk alone, you'll never walk alone.
– Rodgers & Hammerstein
3   He whom we love and lose / is no longer where he was before. / He is now wherever we are.
– St John Chrysostom

2012

Oh yet we trust that somehow good
will be the final goal of ill.
– Tennyson, 'In Memoriam' canto 54

2013

Pulvis et umbra sumus
– Horace, 'Odes' IV.7.16
[We are but dust and shadow.]

Last, loneliest, loveliest, exquisite, apart
on us, on us the unswerving season smiles.
– Kipling, 'The Song of the Cities: Auckland'

entry for 2 February: As 1 and 2 in 2011, plus:
Long as I can be with you, it's a lovely day
– Irving Berlin ['Isn't it a lovely day to be caught in the rain?' sung by
Fred Astaire in *Top Hat*]

entry for 5 February: 'A soul from sin set free – NOT YET'

2014

Laugh in my great loneliness
– Rupert Brooke, 'Paralysis'

Solve senescentem mature sanus equum
– Horace, 'Epistles' I.1.8
[If you are sensible, in good time loose the ageing horse.]

Parturient montes, nascetur ridiculus mus
– Horace, 'Ars Poetica' 139
[The mountains shall give birth – a silly mouse be born.]

Fame is a food that dead men eat.
I have no stomach for such meat.
– Austin Dobson

2015

O Hamlet, what a falling off was there
– Shakespeare, 'Hamlet' I.5

Vae, puto deus fio

– Suetonius quoting Vespasian on his deathbed, 'Life of Vespasian' 23.4)
[Alas, I think I am becoming a god.]

2017
We are Fred Karno's army
what bloody use are we
we cannot fight
we cannot shoot
so we joined the infantry.
But when we get to Berlin
the Kaiser he will say
"Hoch! hoch! mein Gott
what a jolly fine lot
are the ragtime infantry."

All of G.M. Hopkins' 'The world is charged with the grandeur of God'

2018
[This was the last year he kept a diary. The six quotations recorded here may have the privilege of being special to George.]

We are Fred Karno's army . . . [see 2017]

The world is charged . . . [see 2017]

O mihi praeteritos . . . [see 1993]

Ω ξειν' ἀγγελλειν . . . [see 2002]

All of Psalm 15: Lord who shall dwell in thy tabernacle . . . [a new entry, but see p.13]

All of 'Ozymandias' [see 1995]

PART TWO

LETTERS TO GORGO

Letters from George Cawkwell to George Engle

2013 to 2016

INTRODUCTORY NOTE

In the 2010s George's pen did not drop. When his old friend George Engle, nickname Gorgo, suffered a stroke with the result that, while he was mentally fully capable, he was physically incapacitated, in an endeavour to keep him entertained George resolved to write to him regularly. In the end there were some seventy-six letters between November 2012 and August 2016. They are full of anecdotes and reflections vividly told, and amount to a moving reflection on Oxford life and what it means to be old. George Engle did not reply (except once or twice) since he could not. He died in September 2016.

The letters to Gorgo were read to him by his wife Irene, doing her best to decipher the minuscule handwriting (see photograph), a point that Cawkwell regularly refers to pseudo-apologetically. It should be mentioned too that while George Engle was in a miserable position, he was able to get up, get dressed and move about. In effect he was speechless but not witless, and it was the deprivation of speech – and the ability to write – that was his real affliction.

These letters have been edited to a certain degree, principally to cut out repeats of stories he had already told (or which have appeared earlier in this book), private family references, and some of his references to current politics, in order to focus on the archive of vivid Oxford stories he held in his head. In the last decade of his life, an innate tendency to pessimism began to come more to the surface, which included a feeling of uselessness. Along with others, I had urged him to write down his fund of stories, both because he liked writing, and secondly because otherwise they were in danger of being lost. It was only after his death and the emergence of this cache of letters that I realised he had used them as an opportunity to record those stories in the knowledge that Gorgo would make an appreciative audience. There is one caveat which George himself mentions (see the letter of 13 June 2013): "People say to me that I ought to write all this talk about Oxford in my time down for the record. I would fear to do so. The best stories exist in different versions and, if I wrote one account, I would be critically reviewed as a bogus retailer of inaccurate versions." I took the view that while inaccuracy

13 June 2013

Dear George,

(This is meant to be a treat, not just for you but for your letter or rather letters. I'm using a different pen. Say you: Why use a different pen for your indifferent letters?")

There was a scene in Common Room last Tuesday that gave me remembrance of things past. There is a Fellow who, though wanting from Ellerton, wants to do his 'best' by Oxford. He had forgotten to bring his gown from his room. So he got a gown from the coatrack & put it on. He is rather short of stature and the gown was trailing on the carpet and this reminded me of an apt quotation from Tennyson which I had deployed at a Degree Ceremony. Those graduating as Doctors make a splendid entry in their new habit. On one occasion a group of doctors advanced in a body up the Sheldonian to the applause of the assembled company but at about six yards interval came a straggler. He no ste had obviously been looking for a Doctor's gown in the heap provided by his/her college but, being short, had finally had to make do with a gown that trailed the ground. The congregation warmly applauded his/her late entry as I, yea snap I, said

"Not in entire forgetfulness, nor yet in utter nakedness
But trailing clouds of glory do we come . . ."

So the scene + other evening was déjà vu, and gives me a chance to repeat myself; which is never to be desired by those unlike myself. (Do you recall the story of Oscar Wilde saying, generously, to James Whistler "I wish I had said that" to which he, J.W., replied "You will, Oscar, you will"? However, if Oscar's wit could be second-hand (of which I am unaware), I am not beyond such dealing myself. In my last letter, or my penultimate letter, I used a remark made by Giles Alington describing a point made by one of my colleagues about one of the candidates for the vacant Mastership; several times repeated by that same colleague as "an idea that had taken sole possession of that *mighty* ~~mighty~~ mind." But here more pleasingly I am quoting myself.)

Compared is a favourite of Ronald Syme my quotation from Alf. is crude. The Principal of Brasenose in the early Fifties was Sonners Stally brass (He was called 'Sonners' because he had changed his name from Sonnenschein.) He was may vitiate the perfection of these stories, imperfection does not mean they are without value.

We have these letters because Engle's family, notably his wife Irene and daughter Eleanor (Nell), ensured that the letters were kept. As a result of Eleanor's close friendship with George Cawkwell's daughter Sarah, the letters came back to the Cawkwell family. Why include so many letters at such length? The answer is that they have their own epistolary merits, but there is another important reason. If the materials assembled in Part One of this book were considered in architectural terms, they comprise a set of columns, some complete, some unfinished, and some missing. The great merit of the Letters to Gorgo is that they provide a pediment to this edifice: the building may be incomplete but these letters add a distinguished façade.

One formal point: nearly all the letters were written by hand on notepaper 23 cm by 18 cm, and George set himself the task of covering both sides down to the bottom. As a result the length of each one is unexpectedly regular, and this formal constraint is only broken by the last eight letters written on A4, presumably because he had run out of his special notepaper.

George Engle may seem silent in this correspondence, but his presence and their friendship are invoked so much by George Cawkwell that he is far from absent. In order to flesh him out, it is worth giving some details of his distinguished career as a Parliamentary draughtsman, drawing for this purpose on his entry in Wikipedia:

Before going up to Christ Church, Oxford to read Mods and Greats, Engle completed his National Service in the Royal Artillery. He took a double-First degree. Although he considered becoming an academic philosopher, he opted for the law, being called to the Bar in 1953 from Lincoln's Inn and taking a post with the Office of the Parliamentary Counsel in 1957, drafting government bills. He was seconded to Nigeria to draft legislation in 1965 until 1967. Engle was appointed CB in 1976, and KCB in 1983 having become First Parliamentary Counsel in 1981. Engle was also appointed Queen's Counsel in 1983, and Bencher of Lincoln's Inn in 1984. Retiring in 1986, he retained an interest in legislation as a member of the Hansard Society's commission on the legislative process. Engle was a founder of the Commonwealth Association of Legislative Counsel.

He was noted for a vast library, containing, alongside major works, very obscure books. He was president of the Kipling Society from 2001 to 2008. He died 14 September 2016 aged 90, survived by his wife of sixty years, Irene (née Lachmann), three daughters, and grandchildren.

Tim Cawkwell / Norwich / April 2022

2013

Dear Gorgo,

Here are my paltry thoughts writ large.

I don't want you to think as you lie low that I have no prospects in that regard. There seems to be something amiss in my inner parts & I am waiting for the Hospital to call me for MRI (= Magnetic Resonance Imaging – I'm a modest chap but I'm bound to swank a bit), maybe followed by Endoscopy, followed by the dusty road to D. After all, when one is in one's 94th year, one is bound not to be allowed to stay around. So that's me.

I really don't do much now. I've just read William Dalrymple, 'Delhi: City of Djinns'. Did you ever do so? Kipling (your old pal) was right when he said, "East is East and West is West and never the twain shall meet." They're an impenetrably complex lot. The Raj was only 300 years and they're immovably ancient. What did they get from us? Cricket, a common language, the English judicial system, & that's about it. We got from them curry and chutney and a good lesson. Of course, I am an Imperialist (of the academic sort), as all wise men are; i.e. I hold the view that history is just one bloody empire after another. And the victims of empire are finally the half-castes, not really accepted by either side (and there are some touching pages in Dalrymple on this subject). Did you long ago read Paul Scott's 'Raj Quartet'? The sequela was 'Staying On', about a woman left behind after Partition. She could perhaps have got out, for she was English, but just didn't and the longer she stayed the more impossible it would have been for her to leave. But say she had been half Indian, half English. She would have been unwanted by both sides, like the Cape-Coloured and half-castes everywhere, a real victim of Empire.

I know not whether this waffle is tolerable to you. Anyhow Irene and Nell [Eleanor] will readily consign me to the bin. I would like to visit you (briefly, never fear) but I expect snow soon & then I shall shut down, if not shut up. O bugger human frailty! I'll write again when I have something unimportant to report.

Loving thoughts, George

26 January 2013

Dear Gorgo,

Please don't think you are the only one in the firing line. There is something amiss with my innards judging by the unusual emissions of my excretion. So I am in the hands of the doctors and on Thursday last I went to the Churchill Hospital for a CT Scan, the results of which will be sent to my doctor in the next ten days (in theory, but I'll be surprised if they arrive before that same doctor goes off on holiday on 11 Feb.). My sister developed bowel cancer when she was about 85. It was cut out only to reappear four or so years later in her kidney, at which she said, "Satis casuum, satis eventuum" (on Tiberius' withdrawal from Germania, as Tacitus has it) and died of a heart attack after a period in a hospital bed. So I expect it will be the same, *vel sim.*, for me. I don't care at all about dying but the process is emotional for such a wet-eyed creature as myself.

Nonetheless the scanning had points of interest, in particular the radiographer. He was a big, black-bearded fellow and I presumed to ask him, 'Whence?' He said, 'Guess.' I said, 'Russia?' thinking he could well be a descendant of Rasputin. 'No. I'm a Palestinian from Nazareth.' I shook his hand & we parted. One was required to attend 45 minutes before the bell invited, and one was given a huge jug to drink, with a solution in water of Gastrograf, the meaning of which you can guess. So merrily we live for the moment.

Satis indeed. My dearest wishes,

Your poor old Corky, George

4 February 2013

Dear Gorgo,

. . . I went into College for dinner last night, the first time since December 4th & quite enjoyed it. The Master (Ivor Crewe), whose special patch is Elections & Electoral Systems, was talking of US 'gerrymandering'. I said, 'Was there once a Mr. Gerald Mander?' He thought not; there was a constituency the long slithery shape of a salamander & a guy called Jerry went in for gerrymandering (which seems to me a pretty lousy aspect of what Raymond Seitz, the American Ambassador [to the UK] beside whom I once sat at dinner, described as 'an ideal constitution' – at which I had the impertinence to demur). Political theory fascinates & disgusts me.

I'm sorry you can't strike back at me. Still, I hope it will bring mild comfort if you know I think of you often, with affection & happy memories of better years.

Love, George

9 February 2013 (postcard)

Dear Gorgo,

"A soul from Sin set free." This is Captain Cawkwell announcing to all the ship's company that his bowel has been pronounced 'pristine'. (I fancy that is rather a misuse of 'pristine', though was there not a Pristine Keeler?) Anyhow 'tis enough for a nonagenarian to swank about, despite hints of coming Verticulitis. Now all attention is concentrated upon the prostate. A doctor told me that practically all male nonagenarians develop Prostate Cancer, but that it grows so slowly that one dies before the worst. He might have added, 'Don't live beyond 130 or you may die of it.' I know your situation is bloody and you may not want to hear about our bloody winter. But I rejoice I do not live in Boston, USA. where there has been a huge snowstorm. Do you remember 'There ain't no sense in sniffing snow', with which sullen truth I tend to agree, radical as I may sound.

Love, Captain Cawkwell RN

17 February 2013

Dear Gorgo,

One aspect of old age for me is that one becomes distressingly slow at reading. I have now completed the rereading of Anthony Powell's 'Dance [to the Music of Time]' (12 vols, but averaging a mere 220 pages each) and his Memoirs (4 vols), but it upsets me that I am so slow about it. But it's done and I haven't time to repeat my labours. But, my goodness, I do admire him partly for his wit, partly for his style, the paragraphs garnished with a multitude of ablative absolutes, but especially for his wondrous knowledge of English literature. Evocative phrases keep evoking one's memories. All the titles of the four volumes of Memoirs ('Infants of the Spring', 'Messengers of Day', 'Faces in my Time', & 'The Strangers All Are gone') are to be found in Shakespeare. But the wit! e.g. when he was in Saigon: 'I asked why there were so many police about the streets. It was almost as if they were lining the way for a procession.' The reply came: 'Tomorrow is the first of May. The results of the university examinations will be published. If there is a single failure there will be student riots.' . . . 'When I set off for Saigon Airport the following morning the town was fuller than ever of police. No violence was to be seen, so presumably all students had passed their exams.' Elsewhere when a Japanese escort was 'anxious that I should try a bottle of Japanese wine . . . The wine turned out to be of claret type. I can unhesitatingly confirm that Japanese red wine is better than Guatemalan (to be sampled on a visit to Central America some years later), beyond that I should not be prepared to make a considered judgment on a single bottle. That particular bottle might have been said to glory in its own lack of pretension. Since then many years have passed, and I don't doubt that Japanese claret has made great strides.' That is true Socratic irony (= English understatement) not practised in New Zealand you may think.

My thoughts are rather messy. But as you lie in your bed of weary boredom are you aware of the ghastly distress & confusion in English diet. We have all been in recent times eating horse! Of course, in Paris in 1946 I ate horse with ne'er a whinny, but now we're all very prissy. I saw a headline in a penny paper the other day: "Horses in dinners at schools" (*vel sim.*). Can you think what it is like having your lunch between an old nag and a skittish pony? It's not as if a taste of red rum helps one along the racetrack of life. Think of the dung. I hope the State is providing free Wellies for our young ones.

No, my pen is a flop today. I must yield as they say in the House of Commons. But despite my floppy pen, I send you my dearest sympathy.

Love from Korky (the cat, not the pony), George.

1 March 2013

Irene, I accept that this is nigh illegible. You'll have to pore over it for hours.

Dear Gorgo,

I hope you are fulfilling your God-given duty this day – which is to be as mad as a march-hare. For my part I am on the lookout for April 1st, on which day Simon is prone to some foolery.

But I write with the news that the death of Ronald M. Dworkin, once part-time Professor of Jurisprudence in the University of Oxford and Fellow (unfortunately) of Univ has left many of us griefless. At any rate a man who treated the College with maximal contumely has left us untouched. Indeed my feelings about him make me think of Ernie Bevin's reply to the statement that 'X was his own worst enemy'. Ernie replied, 'Not while I am alive.' At one stage he (Dworkin) was much concerned with Civil Disobedience and I have to concede that although he entirely suited himself, his disobedience was pretty civil. He did nothing for Univ save that he persuaded the Fellows to elect, as Master, Kingman Brewster, once President of Yale, and that was undoubtedly the silliest election in Oxford of my time. (Admittedly KB had had a stroke between election & taking up office, but I was pretty sceptical about his intellect anyhow.) Dworkin did not learn & continued to fancy himself as Kingmaker, for after Robin Butler had been elected he (Robin) met some liberal peer who said that Ronnie had just told him he was going to the USA hoping to find a new Master for Univ – a good reflection of Dworkin's utter ignorance about the College. A man he was who professed the most profoundly held liberal principles but who held a job in Oxford and another in New York thus depriving a young man/woman of a job somewhere. He never attended a College occasion save that once he came to a College Meeting or a Feast & he knew nothing about us. Even Herbert Hart whom he claimed so much to admire (& whom I near adored) told me that he really didn't like him. Dworkin was the typical American academic . . . but I say no more. He & I had rooms in the same building and on the same floor, but we had nothing in common. Enough, no more. A great mind indeed, but despite having been a Rhodes Scholar at Magdalen he cared nought about Oxford, only for his friends.

A minor compensation for your miseries is that you do not know about the wrangle between China & Japan about some bloody rocks in the East China sea; the Senkakus the Japanese call 'em, the Chinese name is unpronounceable by a heathen Brit. But it's all quite serious, & I hope I get out of the world before the worst begins. A Japanese who had been at Univ and had been indeed a member of a dining club I ran, called Shinichi Nishimiya, had had an illustrious career in the Japanese Foreign Office & had just been appointed Japanese Ambassador to Beijing (the top of the diplomatic mountain) and had been on the point of going to Beijing, suddenly dropped dead, perhaps luckily. As the Chinese Empire grows & more & more Africans are 'enslaved', the Chinese will be ever more & more 'difficult'.

There's a line in Marlowe's 'Faust' which I use whenever I should be rising to my feet. 'O, I'll leap up to my God. Who holds me down?' Which you may think of about your own situation which is, as Peggy Ashcroft in her 90s said in answer to a query 'How are you?', a bugger. My remote & distant best wishes.

George, who first encountered you at the Twenty Club

egad, George

10 March 2013

Dear Gorgo,

This is the way the term ends, not with a whimper but a bang. No doubt any climatic horror you would prefer to lying 'struck' on a bed, and your friends should be, you would say, grateful for large mercies. In my school English language book (Nuffield, the basis of my usages) there was an example of some figure of speech "She lay all night on a bed of sorrow" which, changing 'night' to 'nights & days', suits your condition about which I am indeed sad and, I prithee, never think I do not think of you.

But the end of term bangs on. Last night we had St. Cuthbert's Feast which was decent enough, but it began at 7 p.m. & I got into my taxi at 11! The servants are very kind to me and cut up my meat into suitable bits but I await some magician giving me a new set of teeth, which I need most dreadfully. I was in bed by midnight, and today at 12.20 I am being collected by a car taking me to an 80th birthday lunch at Al Shami's Restaurant just opposite the Synagogue in Jericho but expect to settle into my armchair by 4 p.m. (But sunset is now at 6 p.m. even if the temperature is expected to be Siberian.) So it goes on to the last syllable of recorded term. I will be guest or host every day until the 18th [March] lunch or dinner, here there or somewhere and if anyone tells you that I am a vapid twit you may believe him/her.

However 'tis not all eating and drinking. On Thursday I went to a German film *Lore* about the children of Nazi parents who being high enough to be punished by the invading armies of 1945 solve their problem by committing suicide having told the children to go under the leadership of their daughter Lore to join grandmother, which proves difficult, since the trains have all been commandeered by the Allies and the children must get across north Germany on foot. They get there but in the course of their journey Lore slowly realises that she has been lied to. It's good & makes one think and go away sadly. It's all in German, subtitled in English, and I commend it to Irene. (How boring you are, Corky.)

Not only am I boring, but heavily laden, for I have begun to read William Dalrymple's 'Return of a King', a history of Afghanistan. What a bloody lot! It makes one think of the Parthians in Tacitus.

George

14 March 2013

Dear Gorgo,

Lying on your bed of woe you may not greatly care but I have to say that March, which is supposed to 'come in like a lion and go out like a lamb', has come in like a polar bear and for all I know will refuse to go out. When I was a little boy, we all in chorus sang, 'I say, bluff March, ye prophesy a singing wide afield / and a crop of verdure that is springing to feed wild herds / when your wavy shadow passes, / over wavy wavy grasses, / Very soon, very soon, I say bluff March.' That was for nice little boys, but here one is a cussing old gent, maybe wetting one's pants in chagrin. These things were sent to try us and by heck the sentence is harsh.

But while I'm on the subject I have to say, for purely party political purposes, that so many of the things we did at school in the 1920s have enriched our lives. Not just this choral singing (and I recall there was one song which went 'See our oars with feathered spray / sparkle at the break of day') but also all the poetry we had to learn. I have no poetry in my soul, but all those bits like 'Earth has not anything to show more fair' or 'If I should die, think only this of me' or 'She should have died hereafter . . .' have stuck in my mind like bits of pie in an incompletely washed pie-dish, and I pick at 'em & they refresh my spirits. They come out perchance and seem to express perfectly one's present position and, like bits of Homer in Virgil, they seem to enrich it.

Incidentally, I have been looking at Horace for comfort ('The snows have fled away, the grasses return to the fields') and I have been reflecting on what a glorious Latinist Freddie Wells was. He never wrote a word and had I fancy no original ideas but Latin was in his soul, especially Lucretius and Horace, and perhaps under their influence he was wise and humane, and, so, a wonderful tutor and I treasure his memory. How sad that he should have died in his late forties (I guess). But, of course, he smoked a great many, too many cigarettes.

I say he 'had (I fancy) no original ideas', not ideas of a large sort, only little bits of emendations of texts, but there are perhaps still alive people who owe their lives to him. Working in Naval Intelligence he had to vet plans for naval operations and on one occasion he was startled to find that there were plans to bomb the sewage works of some Italian city and the sewage works were supposed to be in the middle of the sea-front of this city (maybe Bari). He thought Italian taste & style made that unlikely. So he looked it up on the map & found they were planning to bomb a convent entitled 'I Suori della Purificazione' and so some little old nuns were saved from death & destruction. Just as a fancy flourish he would add that the Madre Superiore was called Lavatina!

. . . 'Bash on, regardless.' No basher-on I, but I beg you to bash on regardless, for what else can you do.

My dearest wishes, George

22 March 2013

Dear Gorgo,

I went last night to a small dinner-party in Vincent's Club, of which possibly the name and almost certainly the interior is not familiar to you. The dining room is on the third floor of that building on the corner of King Edward Street & the High and the climb was demanding of an old gentleman (who is none other than your feeble Corky). As I rose ever higher, I could not stop thinking of that hymn with the couplet: "They (i.e. the saints) climbed the steep ascent of heaven with sorrow, toil, & pain. / O God to us may grace be given to follow in their train." At every step I had to contend with the thought *facilis descensus Averno.* 'What if I lose my footing in the descent?'

Had I fallen, I would have had only my vapid mind to blame. I was elected to Vincent's before I had even heard of the place. I was playing Rugger for the University and so many of that sort had been killed in the War that they filled up with any Colonial Rubbish they could find. Little did I know of the great felicity on which I was entering. For, as a member, I would be able to wear the Vincent's tie, that splendid creature covered with crowns. I wear it often and you may all these years have been thinking 'Corky is a very loyal monarchist', as indeed I am but you should have been thinking, 'What a tremendous Rugger bugger is Cork!' The Club was about 90% athletic heroes (i.e. brutes) with an ample sprinkling of Trinity, i.e. largely Etonians, if not athletes. The reason for this favouritism was that the Senior Treasurer of the Club was Philip London, Trinity's Law Fellow, who, coming from uncertain origins about which 'twas not wise to speculate, had a tremendous obsession with Etonians. His fellow Fellow of Trinity, Ronald Syme wrote a verse or two about Philip, who liked to have dinner in the Club, which ran

'When dining in Vincent's with abandon
Friends surround me, Philip London.
With this grace my meat I savour' –

Oh hell, I've forgotten. The loss of memory is very distressing as no doubt you know full well. I've rung various Trinitarians to try & get the full version. But the last line, i.e. the Grace, was

'Eat, and if you can, be Eton.'

This letter is a chatty *farrago* (if you remember that word in Juvenal). I wish I could quiz you about your and my Oxford in 1946-9, but alas no more. Herewith, however, my love and best wishes (but ain't your bloody stroke a bugger, as you might not say).

                Yours, George

P.S. I was talking to David Raeburn on the phone and he told me that his wife died early this year, not an enviable position. *Credas experto.*

On the envelope:
The proper version is:
When dining in Vincent's with abandon
Friends surround me, Philip London.
With this grace my meat I sweeten
"Eat and, if you can, be Eton."

How the heck, could I forget?

27 March 2013

Dear Gorgo,

    Here is your Easter egg.

    Irene sent me a bookmark depicting Dr. Syntax having a dinner on the halfway landing of the stairs up to Hall. Which raises a serious question. Was Dr. Syntax a Christ-Church man? I've rung the Archivist to get her answer to this pressing problem. But alas she is not at her desk. She has disregarded that important principle enshrined in a hymn in the English Hymnal, 'Ye servants of the Lord, each in his office waits.' Over the last sixty-five years I must have on many occasions drawn your attention to the wisdom of that book. (My favourite hymn is Kipling's 'Lord God of battles, known of old / Lord of the far-flung battle line . . . The tumult & the shouting dies, the captains and the kings depart . . .' Wonderful bad stuff, nothing to do with Christianity.)

    God bless you, my dear old horse, Porky Corky.

5 April 2013

Dear Gorgo,

Tomorrow night there is a Gaudy in Univ to which I am bidden & indeed feel myself beholden, but in any case I enjoy the company of the young. Those invited on this occasion are those who matriculated between '80 and '84, which presents a special challenge; these are they who joined in the great Boring Postcard Contest which I began for my pupils but which spread in the College. One of those whom I mildly fear to meet is a girl who read English & lived on my staircase. She sent me a superbly boring card & added, 'I defy you this time.' I had to submit and concede her victory, which was all very well until a few years ago, say 12 or 15, when I saw an advertisement for a National Boring Card Competition, the prize for victory was a weekend for two in Wigan. Hurrah, cried I. At last I am in the honey if not the money. I wrote to her announcing my great expectations & bidding her pack her bag. But that was the end of it. No weekend, no joyous acceptance from her, no card returned to me. She is coming to have coffee here on Sunday, maybe in contentious mood. She, like me, must have been confident that her card would triumph. 'Has Cawkwell done the dirt on me & taken off to Wigan some latter-day floozy?' and similar posers. She must now be 50+. She was ever a powerful gal. Will there be vigorous fisticuffs? You see the miserable uncertainty of my condition.

The question of what Ronald Syme wrote about Philip London of Trinity, which I raised in an earlier letter has had a by-product. Peter Brown, recently retired Classics Fellow of that College, says that some attribute the rhyme to Trevor-Roper! Could it so have been? I think not, flatly. Of course T-R when quizzed who was the author of the 'Letters of Mercurius Oxoniensis'* said it was not his but he suspected Dacre Balsdon who was not capable of such wit but who, feeling flattered that anyone could think such a thing, beamed his denial in a rather suggestive manner. But truth is to be found by reading T-R's review of a book about 'D', our own RH Dundas [see pages 48-9]. The review was in the same style as the 'Letters'. T-R was plainly their author despite his denial and it is conceivable that, having denied that he had written the Letters (when one knows he was the author), T-R could well claim authorship of Ronald's immortal words. But I don't entertain the thought for a second, and will write to reprove Peter Brown. Such are the inner workings of Oxford scholarship! It does strike me that you may instruct Irene, if ever there is a Boring Letter Contest, to submit this letter & expect a week-end in Wigan or Blackpool. I beg your pardon & send you my love & sympathy.

George

[* 'The Letters of Mercurius' (1970) is a collection of letters from Mercurius Oxonensis to Mercurius Londiniensis in a pastiche seventeenth-century style reporting on Oxford goings-on in the University in the late 60s, notably student agitation. Trevor-Roper wrote them for publication in The Spectator under the pseudonym Mercurius. When they appeared in book form he had the pleasure of writing a review for The Spectator in which he speculated on who the author might be.]

15 April 2013

Dear Gorgo,

I like to be in a cheerful mood when I write to you & have delayed hoping for relief from my feelings of, well, mixed emotions about Margaret Thatcher [who had died on 8 April]. I seem to remember Irene being sour about her and, if she has to read this to you, she may not restrain herself. Papers and magazines are full of her, and likewise radio. I shall watch the Funeral on Wednesday, probably with tears. I looked at the DVD of *The Iron Lady* yesterday. Long ago I saw the film twice but the more I see the more there is to see, a wonderful film. On the Andrew Marr programme yesterday there were Cecil Parkinson and (Baroness) Helena Kennedy (for whom I have a high regard). Parkinson represented the millions for whom Mrs T. was the saviour of her country, & Helena K. the millions who think that all would have been set to rights by dear Labour. There seems no point in discussing these different views. I am governed by the strong feelings I had, & still have, that the indiscipline of the unions would ruin us, and it is crystallised by my memories of 1971. We were going on sabbatical, to New Zealand, & I wanted to order a new car which would await us on our return. Up till then I was the complete chauvinist. I would never have bought a non-

British car; one had to stand by *our* workers. But just as I was trying to decide which British car would suit us best, the motor unions (do you remember Red Robbo?) went on strike yet again for some petty point (as it seemed to me) and I thought, 'They don't give a damn about England, & won't mind ruining us all,' and I ordered a Renault, a revolutionary move for me. For I thought England is done for. If I were younger I would have got out of the country. Come 1979 all was transformed, and I will be eternally beholden to the Blessed Margaret.

I met her twice. First in Downing Street in 1987. She said, 'What do you do?' 'I teach Greek History.' 'Ah, Thucydides, I read him two or three years ago. It's all there, isn't it?' Which won my heart indeed. I've never known whether it was a put-up job, but on balance I decided her remark was spontaneous. The other meeting was over drinks before dinner in the Common Room, when she talked to me but more or less disregarded Pat, an aspect of her character often remarked. But at dinner I sat beside Denis who was a worthy, conventional chap full stop. But earlier I had been seated at a table at Vincent's Dinner where he was the guest speaker. He told a memorable story which I hope I haven't told you before. (I apologise if I have. One has a very limited store of stories. When I began on one which Pat thought I had told before, she would scratch her nose and warn me off. Alas, no more!) It concerned a man who in the next Honours list was to be raised to the Peerage but who had a day or two before the publication of the list been arrested in St. James's Park at 2 a.m. having sex with a young 'lady'. The Civil Servant responsible thought the report ought to go to the PM (then, Churchill). Churchill sent it back having written in the margin: 'Considering X is 75 & the girl 19 and the temperature was 5 below zero, it makes you proud to be British.'

Love & best wishes, George

23 April 2013

Dear Gorgo,

I would, if I could, write a cheerful letter, but I have been trying to arrange for registering for meals 'online'. That bloody word has caused the greatest misery to me as to many an oldie. Sarah advised me to avoid banking online. But one can't escape. To get a University card which is a necessary part of the process one has to pay '£10 online'. 'Christ Jesus,' cry I, 'the hounds of hell are at my guts.' I pay no one online. If I try, I will shortly be deluged in a tsunami of scams. But now I must. 'Sweet Jesus, I'd rather be a pagan & suckled in a creed outworn etc. than pay online.' 'O.K., oldie, no goodies for you.' Such shocks always cause me to (near) wet myself.

But 'online' is just part of it. When I was Senior Tutor in the 1970s, the College had a Secretary & an assistant Secretary who sat in the College Office & did all. Now in the so-titled 'Academic Office' there are an 'Academic Support Administrator', a 'Schools Liaison/Access Officer', an 'Academic Services Manager' & an 'Admissions Manager'. Pooh Bah had nothing on us, I can tell you.

O for the good old days! The College Secretary knew all, both persons & secrets. E.g. when a Freshman walked across the quad in full view of the College Office, someone said, 'X. seems to be very much at home here,' to which the College Secretary replied, 'He should be. He was conceived on Staircase 11.' Now I expect she would be prosecuted & dismissed for failure to protect a student's privacy.

Did I tell you I had in December (swank, swank) a CT scan. I had to go yesterday to the Colorectal Department of the John Radcliffe for a further appointment. I expected to have mirrors, or such, pushed up me from the backside, to see what developments are in progress. But, no, I have a clean bill of health (if not a clean backside) and march on to my delayed doom.

I've finished Braithwaite's 'Afgantsy', & it is a marvellous & shocking book. I've come out of it with quite a lot of sympathy for the Russian people & a more sceptical view of the US and, yes, ourselves.

Boring, boring. 'Give us less,' they (or rather she) do cry. I'm planning to pay you a visit if it can be done. So brace up. Corky is coming.

Love, George

16 May 2013

Dear Gorgo,

This week's sermon is no laughing matter. It concerns our mutual friend, Merton Atkins [at Christ Church just after the war], that complex creature.

Merton's widow, Janet, gave me 'A Life in Secrets: the story of Vera Atkins and the lost agents of SOE'. What's she to him or he to Vera? Vera's grandfather was, I think, a brother of Merton's grandfather, family name Rosenberg. I always thought M's father must have been a plain Mr. Atkins, but not a bit of it. Sometime the name must have been changed. The Rosenbergs went out to South Africa as many European Jews did to get away from European anti-Semitism. Vera's part of the family came back to Romania, were successful and rich, but with the menace of the Nazis in the early Thirties got out & Vera & her mother came to England. Merton's branch remained in South Africa.

All along, there was the effort to blend into the society they had joined, wherever it was. So they became 'English' in tastes & sympathy, were educated at English type schools, sometimes going to the extreme of adopting Catholicism, as did Merton. The interesting thing was that, though I was friendly with him for 54 years and we saw a lot of him, he never said he was Jewish &, I think, never explained the position to Janet. So he like Vera led a life of secrets indeed, and I have been thinking of him a great deal as I read this book. (Vera was the officer responsible for dispatch of SOE agents to France and control of them when they got there. So she 'handled' Odette, who survived, and Violette Szabo, who was tortured and shot, etc.)

It all reflects the ambiguous position of Jews in Europe. One of the books I was impressed by was de Waal, 'The Hare with Amber Eyes'. This concerned a Jewish family which began a bank in Odessa, moved to Vienna and felt themselves fully integrated in top Viennese society, but in a few days were swept away by a tsunami of Nazi anti-Semitism. When the war was over, 'Where were we to go?' as a professor in Haifa (?) said to me when I visited Israel in 1970. So to Israel they all went and on the whole I think it was the best solution, though of course now we have all the miseries of the Middle East to behold.

I apologise for this boring sermon. The whole problem seems reflected to some degree in the life of Merton. I sometimes think of all the people I know whom Adolf would have murdered if he could have got his hands on them, on you all.

I must add that New Zealand, at least in my youth, was not at all racist. There was a boy at school who was a much admired athlete, a runner and a member of the First Fifteen (God's holy Rugby, don't you know). His name was Moses. He was swarthy, & I thought he must be Maori & it never occurred to me that he must be Jewish. When I came across his grave in the NZ cemetery on Crete I wept.

Fortunately paper has run out. My dearest wishes to you. I have you very much in mind constantly.

Love, George

21 May 2013

Dear Gorgo,

I am besotted with love for the Goddess, Economy, & in hopes of encountering Irene at Sarah's on Friday I seize the opportunity to send this to you by hand. So here comes, as coming men say.

I am forgetting all my languages, Latin, Greek, French, German, Italian. (Only Bad Language remains.) But only partially. So I got down the 'Letters' of Seneca, which are a patch on mine, and I can read 'em. Hooray for Silver Latin!

I turned to Seneca, because the bit of Tacitus which describes his end reminds me of that infallible precept. "History repeats itself and when it does it generally turns out as comedy." Here was this Elderly Sage trying to commit suicide and his blood wouldn't flow and he had to have his slaves put him in a hot bath and what a bloody mess there must have been before he bled to death. As an imitation of Socrates, 'twas a bit of a joke.

When Pat and I visited the Pergamum Museum in Berlin, we observed a double head, Socrates in one direction, & Seneca in the reverse. Unfortunately, for my present letter I can't remember the expressions each of them had on their faces. Socrates inevitably looked his unhandsome self, but I just do not recall the look on the face of Seneca, whether he looked defiant or regretting the hot water he had got into. But 'twas a piece I would have liked to snitch. I could imagine that Seneca was advising against drinking one's bath water but solid evidence is lacking. (Problem: should one giggle when giving oneself a strigil?)

A crisis has intervened. So goodbye Seneca. Edward Grey said in 1914, 'The lights are going out all over Europe. We shall not see them lit again in my lifetime.' Not of quite such devastating effect, in the middle of the night the lights here went out. 'Pooh,' sez you. Sez I, 'twas practically in mid flow. I cried, 'Lighten our darkness we beseech thee, O lord,' but the darkness persisted and I was, as your old friend Algernon Swinburne declared, 'helmless in middle tides'. 'Tis now 10.30 a.m. on the 22nd and all is restored and the Toll *puddle* martyrs have been shipped to Aussie, but think of this old man paddling to bed and feel sorry for my sorry experience.

I have a Professor of Law from Edmonton, Alberta, staying and she is a cheerful gal, at least when she is in England. Edmonton has the worst climate in the world; hence the frost-bitten look of so many Canadians. She treats Oxford's as a little bit better which perhaps has *some* truth in it. She came to hear the Hart Lecture. As almost usual, it was about Animal Rights, an idea that has taken almost sole possession of these mighty minds. I wish I had been there so that I could pose the problem raised by the Rights of Silverfish. When I find one in my sink, I would try to save its life, but the slithery little bugger resists Salvation. I sit for hours with a minute fish-hook on a thread but the s. l. b. refuses it. I need advice on how to deal with this moral crisis. But the lecture is supposed to be about Jurisprudence and the law on Silverfish is elusive. Please get Irene to deliver to me any tips on how to catch 'em and what to do with 'em when caught. 'Tis plainly improbable, intolerable that one should try to bottle 'em and send 'em to the Animal Rights Issue Society. If they get 'em, I'm told they do not make of them a shining pâté, but what the heck do they do? (As you know, I am *tout simple* against Rights. Mostly against Natural Rights, even Unnatural Rights, both of which cheese me off.)

This fatuous blather must cease! My constant & dearest wishes, Giorgio.

3 June 2013

Dear Gorgo,

'Tis a misery of ageing that one forgets what one has said. I don't forget pupils and, being a boring chap, I am like the cat that walks alone. For all faces are alike to me, but unlike that cat I like 'em all. But there are those whom all others have forgotten and I engage in this laboured introduction so that I can tell you about one of them. He was, and possibly is, Willie H*** with the heavy Lancashire accent but of humble origins. Not, however, without wit. (Here I fear I have told you this before, for I don't remember what I've said to you & now wish I had kept photocopies. In a historian reprehensible indeed. 'Who other than yourself calls you a historian?' True, true, O sage.) Willie was in the Beer Cellar when he heard someone rather grandly say, 'My father's house in Leicestershire is being taken over by the Ministry.' Willie flashed back, 'Pooh, that's nothing. My father's house in Rochdale was condemned by the Council *twenty* years ago.'

Willie was a homosexual & lodged with one of the scouts on Osney. He amazed the man & his wife by 'cross-dressing' and liberally making up his face. The scout said to me, 'You don't know, sir, who does what to who.' A remark generally true for the gay kind. (Do you recall that song of the Thirties, 'When I pretend I'm gay, I never feel that way / I'm only painting the clouds with sunshine'? But I do resent that useful word 'gay' being taken over by the brethren.) Still, Willie having read some lines of Homer said to Frederic Wells, 'It's not at all bad,' which much pleased Freddie.

Did you know Guy Wilson & John Maitland Moir? They are both recorded in the latest Gazette as dead. I feel very much alone. I used to go & have dinner on High Table in the House once a year. I never asked you because you are not, were not ever, a dining type. But one by one they have 'dropped out'. Why are *we* still on parade, doing pack-drill?

I hear the clatter of mail coming through the letter-box. I rush to pick it up. Only six appeals for money. And a local advertising magazine on the back page of which is an advertisement for Hazlemere Windows & Doors. It says: 'Why move? Just improve.' *You* could say, 'Can't move, cheeky bugger,' but I feel it too. I have no expectation of improvement . . .

My dearest wishes, George

13 June 2013

Dear Gorgo,

(This is meant to be a treat, not for you but for your *lector* or rather *lectrix*. I'm using a different pen. Sez you: 'Why use a different pen for your indifferent letters?')

There was a scene in Common Room last Tuesday that gave me 'remembrance of things past'. There is a Fellow who, though coming from Elsewhere, wants to do his best by Oxford. He had forgotten to bring his gown from his room. So he got a gown from the coat-rack & put it on. He is rather short of stature and the gown was trailing on the carpet and this reminded me of an apt quotation from Tennyson which I had deployed at a Degree Ceremony. Those graduating as Doctors make a splendid entry in their new habit. On one occasion a group of doctors advanced in a body up the Sheldonian to the applause of the assembled company but at about six yards interval came a straggler. He or she had obviously been looking for a Doctor's gown in the heap provided by his/her college but, being short, had finally had to make do with a gown that trailed the ground. The congregation warmly applauded his/her late entry as I, yea smug I, said, "Not in entire forgetfulness, nor yet in utter nakedness / But trailing clouds of glory do we come ..."

So the scene t'other evening was déjà vu, and gives me a chance to repeat myself; which is ever be desired by dimwits like myself. (Do you recall the story of Oscar Wilde saying, generously, to James Whistler, 'I wish I had said that,' to which he, J.W., replied, 'You will, Oscar, you will'? However, if Oscar's wit could be second-hand (of which I am unaware), I am not beyond such dealing myself. In my last letter, or my penultimate letter, I used a remark made by Giles Alington describing a point made by one of my colleagues about one of the candidates for the vacant Mastership & several times repeated by that same colleague as 'an idea that has taken sole possession of that mighty mind'. But here more pleasingly I am quoting myself.)

Compared to a favourite of Ronald Syme my quotation from Alf. is crude. The Principal of Brasenose in the early Fifties was Sonners Stallybrass. (He was called 'Sonners' because he had changed his name from 'Sonnenschein'.) He was indeed popular with the undergraduates, with the Fellows less so, and after a stormy College Meeting he went off to London & during his return journey fell out of the train and was killed. (The cause of his fall was ever speculated about. Some said he had been thrown out by some disgruntled Fellow – and it is proof of the high reputation of Robert Shackleton, Bodley's Librarian, who was on that same train, that I have never heard anyone opine that 'twas RS who performed his act of service to BNC of which RS was a Professorial Fellow –

but perhaps when the train stopped outside Oxford Sonners thought he had arrived, leaned out and opened the door, and fell to his death. Anyhow, Ronald's version of this not displeasing event included this detail; the following morning the then young History Fellow, Eric Collieu, rang his wife about some trivial matter and she said, 'There's a strange note of elation in your voice. Has the Principal died?'

Thinking of Ronald Syme, I remind myself of a remark I wish I *had* made but missed my chance. We were entertaining to supper Ronald and a French historian called Vidal-Nacquet and he was recounting his part in *Les Événements* of 1968. He said he went out to observe these on-goings and 'that evening turned into a book of a thousand pages'. I should have said, 'A thousand pages in thy sight are like an evening gone,' but I failed to say it. (I don't elucidate or quote the opening of the Anglican hymn whence the line comes corruptedly. I expect a Carthusian who no doubt had to hear this hymn often enough even though as a Jew you were laughing not too inwardly about our Holy Hymnal.) (Of course, Carthusians were expected to keep their chuckles to themselves. Another Carthusian called H. Trevor-Roper said to me of a Fellow of Oriel, 'He's so coarse-grained that he laughs aloud over Punch.' [Punch was a humorous weekly, now defunct.])

I meant to give you my thoughts about the Class System stimulated by a book by Richard Davenport Hines about the Profumo affair (called 'An English Affair') but I'll have to reserve those for another week. People say to me that I ought to write all this talk about Oxford in my time down for the record. I would fear to do so. The best stories exist in different versions and, if I wrote one account, I would be critically reviewed as a bogus retailer of inaccurate versions. Trevor-Roper's 'The Wartime Journals' contains a salutary story on p. 273. The Steward of Christ Church in my time was 'Hooky' Hill, who had been a POW of the Japs, and I have long told how he was heard in Ch. Ch. Common Room to say, 'When I was a prisoner of the Japanese, I had time for reflection and after a great deal of serious reflection I came to the conclusion that claret is the best of wines.' But T-R says that in conversation with him Hooky said, 'If I were condemned to drink only one wine for the rest of my life, I would choose Burgundy.' T-R said, 'But come Hooky, there are some excellent clarets.' 'I thought of that too,' he answered, 'and I know my answer to that: there hasn't been a decent claret since 1892.' Think, my dear Gorgo, what would have been said, if I recounted my much inferior version! My silence may not be golden, but my utterances would be pronounced 'brazen'.

My dearest wishes, George

24 June 2013

Dear Gorgo,

Life has been dislocated by a new computer. The one it replaces had done seven years service and, like its owner, was getting slower and slower. 'Tis another Apple, which I hope is less vulnerable to hackers, but the filly has to be disciplined. The week has been wearing . . .

Let us turn to simpler matters. John Sparrow once told me this story about Joseph, the New College Philosopher. He was a man celebrated for his contorted language. A page of his writing contained not a word that a child of twelve could not understand, but the total effect was quite obfuscating. On one occasion, at a meeting of the Philosophical Society, Joseph said something which moved Prichard to say, 'Would you say that again, Joseph, and for God's sake don't say it in monosyllables.' (Herbert Hart told me that Joseph said in a lecture, 'If figs grew on thistles and grapes grew on thorns, that would be no more a breach of the Laws of Euclidean Space than if some wag had hung them there.')

I hope you don't know or remember the Spooner story which chimes well with the Oxford obsession with Aristotle. The story is this: at the end of a sermon in the University Church Spooner descended the pulpit steps but when he got to the bottom he turned back & went into the pulpit again and said, 'Whenever I said Aristotle I meant St. Paul.' Some of the celebrated Spoonerisms are perhaps invented. E.g. when a guest at New College High Table spilt some salt, Warden Spooner bade him pour red wine on it. Again he is said to have gone up to an Old Member in the Quad & said, 'I remember your name but not your face' . . . After all, Diodorus of Sicily was the great Inverter; whenever he said Tissaphernes he meant Pharnabazus; likewise Thrasyllus and Thrasybulus. Easy when you know his habits!

Gorgo, this is a poor, poor letter & I beg your pardon & promise to try & do better next time. But the fact that I do write is a sign that I think of you & your wretched plight a great deal.

My dearest wishes, George

6 July 2013

Dear Gorgo,

. . . I used to be a man of uncommon powers of memory, but 'tis all slipping away. In particular I do not recall what I have said in previous letters or only fitfully do I recall. This, of course, is the lot of lots of ageing dons. Thomas Parker, formerly Chaplain of Univ and much regarded as a learned divine, is a bad example. Even he had a limited stock of stories but his declining memory could not stop him deploying these stories as we affected to smile.

Aged dons are indeed prone to not recalling who has heard what, but we will NOT be stopped. Did I ever tell you Peter Bayley's story of a Canaletto painting? An American collector went to Italy in the 30s bent on buying a Canaletto. He found one in a shop in Rome but the attendant told him that it was forbidden to export a Canaletto. 'However, Sir,' he whispered *sotto voce*, 'there is a way round the problem. I can have a portrait of the Duce painted on top of it and, if you take it to this address in New York, the proprietor will have it cleaned off and lo, there is your Canaletto.' The deed was done, and the New York expert set to work. Alas, he cleaned off not only the Duce but also the Canaletto & there underneath it was another portrait of the Duce.

I am not to be stopped, egad! Knowing the style of Arnold Goodman you will appreciate this one, after which I will stop. Just see if I don't. Arnold had a florid style and after a particularly florid outburst at a College Meeting one of the Fellows (not I) said, 'That is colourful, Master, but barely informative.'

Corky, enough! So I will conclude by telling how it was that Univ elected the Duke of Edinburgh (*vivat Ille* and *vivat Regina*) to an Honorary Fellowship. Over lunch on the day of a Stated General Meeting CK Allen, *perhaps* playfully, suggested to the Master, Arthur Goodhart (a man whose memory I will always treasure and admire), that we should elect the Duke; Arthur, who was of some innocence in matters pertaining to Royalty, snatched the idea up and, within minutes of the meeting resuming, the Duke was elected and Arthur said, 'Good. I'll write & invite him to visit the College.' The Senior Fellow (Bowen, a chemist of renown) said, 'I hope he'll let us know when he's coming.' Bowen's simple mindedness became ever plainer when one of the Palace Stooges came down and reconnoitred the ground. He even timed the walk to the toilet which the Duke might make! (Arthur, a true Yank, was a bit put out by this!) I may add that only two Fellows voted against this Election, Herbert Hart & George Cawkwell. Herbert said he was against it 'on general Republican principles'. I, as you know, am an ardent Monarchist. I just thought it was not all *comme il faut.*

Love, George

11 July 2013

Dear Gorgo,

The practical consequence of your *lectrix* being in France now will be that you may hear my epistles in the wrong order. I think in my last one I talked about Tom Parker's 'telling me the old, old story' but I received a check from my Sarah; I presumed to give her over the phone the opening of Gunga Din and added, 'I think I used to recite it while driving.' I said to Sarah, 'Did I ever recite it to you?' & she replied, *humaniter* Cicero might add, 'Many times.' So I hope that letter is read to you before this.

I was rereading the other day Dryden's 'Alexander's Feast – An Ode for St Cecilia's Day' and it struck me that the medallion pictured on the cover of my Oxford Edition of Dryden showed him not the sort of poet who could be lined up beside those 'poetical treats' , Shelley & Keats (though I am always uneasy about Wordsworth being in that list). Having been much devoted to Keats when I was young, I am now a Pope & Dryden man. In Housman's lecture 'The Name & Nature of Poetry' he professed that the real thing made his hair stand on end as he shaved; at least that is what I vaguely remember, having read it about 70 years ago. I don't think Pope has that effect on one. I would like to define a 'poet' as one clever in the use of words, which is rather more suitable for various poets of antiquity. Indeed, if I had had to teach Ancient Literature, I would have begun my course with a reading of Gray's poem about the pussycat falling into the goldfish bowl. It is like an exquisitely wrought snuff-box; one admires the craft; as one does in 'Mr Eliot's Sunday Morning Service' (Polyphiloprogenitive / Superfetation of τὸ ἕν ... etc.) where very great skill is manifested in each of those short stanzas, just as it is in Horace who moves one to admiration for his great skill.

Stop, Cawkwell. Spare me further tosh. I am going out to lunch in the country to watch the Test Match [on television], the sort of watching I have never known you to desire. I have always loved cricket, a sign you may think of spiritual weakness. But before I go, I must go out into the garden & pick myself a sprig of rosemary for a button-hole. Plainly nothing to do with cricket, but you might wonder why I so constantly wear such a button-hole. I confess what Pat would not be pleased with me for confessing, for she kept her feelings to herself always. I confess that, as in that song of the war-years, 'And if you asked her why the hell she wore it / She wore it for a soldier who was far, far away.' *Mutatis mutandis*, I wear it for her, for never do I forget her. One of the books I most love is Hardy's *Woodlanders* and it ends up with Marty South, saying of the dead Giles Winterborne, '... whenever I get up I'll think of 'ee, and whenever I lie down I'll think of 'ee again. ... But no, no, my love, I never can forget 'ee, for you was a good man, and did good things!'

Pat would never have written such words, let alone said them, and I will try & redeem myself by begging your pardon. Let us think rather of Irene stifling in the Midi. Tennyson wrote in the Lotus Eaters, 'Into the land where it was always afternoon', not inappropriate when one speaks of your part of France. But, O George, I think with horror of your lying in the state you are in. You make me think of Thucydides' comment on the end of Nicias: 'He was least deserving of the Greeks of my time to come to such misfortune.' I myself am bashing on regardless, but you remain much in my mind.

Your loving friend, George

22 July 2013

Dear Gorgo,

Do you remember the summer of 1976? It has come again. The grass is quite browned off and so am I. I do not, I dare not, go out. I have had to cancel trips to visit family, and all because I have heeded dire warnings on the radio about the vulnerability of the old in very hot weather. I feel contemptibly feeble!

As Bob Dylan sang, a sentiment hardly original, 'times they are a-changing' & changes in Oxford come thickish and fast. My first grouse concerns the marking system. When we were lads, in our twenties, papers were marked in alphas, betas, etc. Now they are marked 'arithmetically', i.e. in percentages. I simply can't think of a pupil as a 75% man/woman, for numbers denote quantity not quality. One used to be able to think of a pupil 'an alpha' man or a 'pure beta' and two people of very different qualities could each be regarded as, say, 'alpha'. I don't know how these numerical distinctions are fixed on. And what is to be made of the celebrated rhyme:

> 'I spent all my time with a crammer
> And then only managed a gamma
> But the girl over there,
> With the flaming red hair,
> Got an alpha plus easily – damn her.'

(I've never known anyone getting an alpha plus, but Peter Brunt gave Elizabeth Rawson a pure alpha for her Ancient History paper in 1956.) I remember Herbert Hart telling how, when Harold Wilson told an audience of distinguished foreigners that he had got 'an alpha in every paper in PPE', some Spaniard got up & said, 'What are these alphas?' It was an Oxford secret, for I don't think Cambridge was still using alphas etc. after the War. But now all gone, alas. I give the man responsible 'Beta two minuses'.

Next change. Finals are still called 'Second Public Examination' but they are no longer 'Public' in the sense that the results are published in the Schools. I remember escorting friends to the Schools to see what Class they had been assigned. One was a Rhodes Scholar who privately hoped he would get a First. His eye went through the Classes until he found his name in the Fourths! Poor fellow! He was utterly despondent. At that stage I had not read 'Brideshead' where, very near the beginning, Jasper, Charles Ryder's cousin, called on him & said, 'And as to Greats, only a First or a Fourth will do.' (Alas, the Fourth Class was abolished in the 50s, just after I had done my first stint of Examining (1956-8). I remember two Fourths. Indeed I remember their names, which I here omit. But I do recall the nice distinction posed by Guy Chilver of Queen's: 'I do think that a man who gets a Fourth at Oxford should know at least as much about Greek History as the sort of man one meets in the train from Didcot.' We considered, & decided that the candidate we were considering would be in difficulties in conversation in such circumstances. So we ploughed him.) But gone are the days! *Nos numeri sumus*, as Horace didn't quite say (he said *numerus*). Privacy is the God of the Age. It must be very helpful to those who lie to prospective employers about their academic attainments.

Finally, Pornography! Like that character in Plato's 'Republic' who is at once attracted & horrified, I find pornography both enjoyable and abominable. I remember when we were in Vienna there was a pornography channel on TV in our hotel for which one was charged save for the first five minutes. I was amazed & shocked that such a programme could be seen at the merest press of a button. I looked but turned off before beginning to be charged. Pat said, 'We've got better things to spend our money on than that.' She didn't like it; I was fascinated. But I disapprove of such things being so readily available especially to the young, and I would try to prevent my family from watching them. So I sympathise with David Cameron who wants to prevent such ready access. This is not a party issue. No doubt MPs of all colours will express disapproval but like Pooh Bah they will think, 'It revolts me but I do it.' (Compare Maria Theresa who 'wept but took'. It was over a Partition of Poland.) But it is all very corrupting & I say 'Good luck' to our PM.

The temperature is to rise today to, I think, 29°. I try to keep cool and stay out of the sun, being neither a Mad Dog nor an Englishman. But I hate to think what it is like for you in a bed. Oh George this is a hateful condition in which you find yourself. It doesn't help but I do feel for you, be it hot or cold.

My dearest wishes, George

27 July 2013

Dear Gorgo,

Memory is fallible indeed. Which makes me think of that absurd hymn which you may have heard at Charterhouse (for I think you went to Chapel). 'Grant to life's day a clear unclouded ending / An eve untouched by shadows of decay'! I expect that the man who wrote it knew as well as Laurence Binyon what lies ahead of us aged. In 'To the

Fallen' he wrote, 'Age shall not weary them nor the years condemn.' But I cannot touch on the 'English Hymnal' without saying again that my favourite 'hymn' is your Rudyard's

> 'Kipling and the shouting dies
> The captains and the kings depart
> Still stands thy ancient sacrifice...'

I don't think they included that bit of his about, I think, Auckland, my native city, 'last, loneliest, loveliest, most beautiful gem of all the Pacific' [*sic*] (but, damn it, I've mislaid my Penguin Kipling and I may have messed this up [see page 154) but it would have done very well as a hymn as much as that hymn in *Babette's Feast* which treats Jerusalem similarly (but, pooh, what is Jerusalem compared to my native land, 'God's own country' at which *les bien pensants* sneered but as I see it in my old age). Let twaddling cease!

But, to return to memory, did you in your pre-stroke years ever look at YouTube? I had an undergraduate here for supper on Wednesday and he with effortless ease, a Univ man not a Balliolensis, he got up a dialogue between Peter Strawson and Gareth Evans (both of Univ), and another between David Pears (the House's Own: do you remember him) and Iris Murdoch with whom I was acquainted, both dialogues concerning Truth ('What is truth?, said jesting Pilate, and would not stay for an answer'). (I can't help swanking about Univ's philosophers, the sacred procession being Paul, Strawson, McIntyre, Mackie, MacDowell, Hart, Evans, Dworkin, Child... as pretty a lot as Dame Philosophy could attract.) On this same YouTube programme were Berlin & Ayer et al. I looked for a notable Classicist of my acquaintance, ML West, but he did not show up. I shall seek others but I fear 'twill be in vain. Anyhow the sight of all these philosophers stirred up my memories. On one occasion when Freddy Ayer was Chairman of the Lit. Hum.* Board, there was one of those situations where of two claimants to an award no means of discriminating between them could be found; Freddy got a coin out of his pocket, flipped and made the choice. I did the same when, as Vice-Master, I was chairing a College Meeting and one of my colleagues expressed grave displeasure; he thought that we should sit on seeking to disentangle the Gordian Knot. Freddy and Alexander the Great did not waste time.

As ever, my dearest wishes, George

[* Lit. Hum. is short for Literae Humaniores, known in the vernacular as 'Greats' covering Ancient History & Philosophy.]

2 August 2013

Dear Gorgo,

'"At the risk of repeating myself," he said, whereupon everyone braced themselves to endure yet another repetition.' Writing to you weekly makes repetition an ever more serious problem.

Now I dare to repeat to you a story I derived from the little Eng. Lit. book I used at school. When Tennyson went to Lyme Regis and was asked, 'Shall we show you where the Duke of Monmouth landed?' he said, 'Monmouth be damned. Show me where Louisa Musgrove fell.' I pray God I've not told you this before, but 'You did, Corky, you did'. (Still, while I am on the name of Alfred Lord T., I retell another favourite story. When Tennyson was staying with the Master of Balliol, one Jowett (wouldn't you know it?), Jowett said to him, 'Will you read us your latest poem, Tennyson?' Tennyson went upstairs & brought it. When he had read it to the assembled company, Jowett, not a very wordy man egad, said, 'I wouldn't publish that one Tennyson.' Tennyson flashed back, 'And the sherry you gave us before dinner was disgusting.') Pat & I went to Lyme Regis, in pious mood for she greatly admired Jane Austen & her favourite was 'Persuasion'. But I now hit back. The end of 'Enoch Arden' is a favourite couplet of mine.

'And when they buried him, the little port
Had seldom seen a costlier funeral.'

(The reason why it appeals to me is that it seemed a suitable comment on many a decision of the College.)

Enough of repetition and repetitions . . . So let me say that I am now on a new tack. You must as lawyer have been annoyed at the sentences passed in our courts, but nothing here can match the sentences passed in American courts. I have just heard of some miscreant being sentenced to 'life' and 'then one thousand years'. I guess that guy will serve at least five years! To my surprise I found myself recently admiring the line taken by the European Court of Human Rights in a case where the appellants claimed that a life sentence where 'life' meant life was a violation of their Human Rights. To me most talk of Human Rights is sickening but the comment could be rephrased & become valid. For to commit a man to a term of imprisonment which will only end with his death is to my mind most inhumane and also most unwise. For all sentences should allow something to hope for. That is humane but also wise, for those who have no hope and have nothing to lose are very difficult to manage.

Likewise I found myself sympathising with Kenneth Clarke, then Secretary for Justice, when he argued for prisoners having the right to vote in elections. 'Twould be impracticable, but outcasts should not feel utterly outcast. Human beings should not be dehumanised. Indeed one of the most disgusting aspects of Nazi murder of Jews was that the Nazis dehumanised people before they murdered them.

I hold it abominable to confine a man for ever with nothing to hope for. The USA has not come out of things lately very respectably. The poor, misguided young man, Bradley Manning, was actually held naked in confinement, until moral shock around the world shook the US military out of such barbarity. But such things are not the monopoly of the Americas. In the War I was posted to act as deputy for the Commandant of the camp where those sentenced by Court Martial to jail were kept. There was a wire cage where the most intractable of the prisoners were put 'to teach them a lesson' and there was one individual, Gunner Ritchie I think his name was, who was put into the cage for a day or two naked. Mosquitoes on that island were not malarial but in great numbers they did bite. The man, who was responsible, the Sergeant Major, heard Gunner R. screaming all night long, 'X you bastard, I'll get you.' I wonder if after the War he ever did. (While I was in charge of the camp Gunner R. was marched in before me on some charge of 'conduct to the prejudice of good order & military discipline'. I dealt with the case and afterwards the Sergeant-Major said, 'You handled that well. I was certain he would hit you.' I say this mildly to boast. The true Commandant who had been in the Palestine Police was said to have dealt with recalcitrance by taking the miscreant into the scrub and punching all the mischief out of him. Perhaps that had been expected of me.)

This is a shamefully muddled letter for which I apologise to you & to her who tries to read it to you.

My love to you both. George

Dear Gorgo,

Here's a howdydo(?). When you were a merry lad in your first term of Greats and were with a fresh, lively mind reading the first book of Herodotus, were you acquainted with the problems raised by his account of Babylon? Chief was why did he not mention the famous Hanging Gardens. Now it is true that Herodotus may never have gone to Babylon but what he says about the city must in that case have come from someone who had gone and so one still asks why didn't X mention the Gardens. The answer comes from Stephanie Dalley (daughter of our Denys Page [Classics lecturer at Christ Church 1931-9 and 1946-50] who may have tutored you) that the Gardens were not at Babylon but at Nineveh; she, an Assyriologist, produces archaeological evidence about gardens at Nineveh. However, later authors, in numbers, ascribe the Hanging Gardens to Babylon. So why, oh why, and when oh when and where? Tis a baffling business indeed. I know her and we have exchanged cards on the subject, and now she has produced a book on the subject. Alas, I am too damned old to do more than give it a casual perusal. Berossus wrote a history of Babylon in the days of Antiochus the Great, that fellow who fought the Romans, in the early Second Century BC and indeed describes the Hanging Gardens. As far as this slothful old man is concerned let them go hang. But 'tis a howdydo as I am sure you will agree. Like Don John of Austria I see across

'a weary land a straggling road in Spain,
Up which a lean & foolish knight for ever rides in vain,
And he smiles, but not as Sultans smile, and settles back the blade...
(But Don John of Austria rides home from the Crusade).'

So for a simple lad like me, 'tis goodbye Babylon, but 'twill never be goodbye G.K. Chesterton, though, alas, 'tis indeed goodbye to his *Weltanschauung*. When one has lived as long as we have, there is much intellectual baggage one has to abandon along the way.

Having expressed in an earlier letter my discontent with the European Court of Human Rights, I felt, as I tossed in the night, that I should not have said so little as to why I am agin' it. I am no jurisprude and I hesitate to express opinions on this department of the mind, but it seems to me that if laws are to be taken seriously by the people whom they affect, a law must express the attitude of a majority, a vast majority of the people. If the judgment of the European Court of Human Rights does not receive the assent of the British people, that judgment can excite only ridicule or contempt in this land. E.g. it may be, abstractly speaking, desirable that the British people accept that prisoners should be kept from feeling totally outcast and that prisoners should be allowed to vote in elections if that is practicable, but if the large majority of British people agree with the Prime Minister and not with Kenneth Clarke, rulings by the European Court of Human Rights should not be obligatory here. I am afraid that de Gaulle was right about us; we are not 'European' and we should not belong to a European system. So I think we should get out of this ECHR, though of course we may well have our own Bill of Rights which largely overlaps with the European. You may think 'true but trivial'. (I remember Gilbert Ryle, who was fond of Jane Austen, writing, to my mind, an admirable essay on her, which was pooh poohed by the Eng. Lit. people. 'How dare he pronounce on our holy speciality?' So you may wish to tell me to keep off, keep out of the Law.)

People occasionally ask me, 'Did you know Lord Beveridge?' I did but not as Master, only when he retired to a college house in the Woodstock Road. I heard quite a lot about him from senior Fellows. When he was elected Master of Univ, 'tis said that the LSE could not believe their good luck. He had a secretary, Mrs [Janet] Mair (?), whom he brought with him to the College. She had pained the necks of people in the LSE & she did even more so here. On one occasion, when there was a question of who should be Estates Bursar, William B. talking to GDH Cole said, 'There's only one way out. We'll have to make Janet Bursar.' Cole said, 'What a marvellous idea, Master. There's only one difficulty. Stevenson has always wanted the job. I'll have to square him.' So Cole went away to his room, rang Stevenson (my predecessor) and said, 'You must be Bursar. Otherwise it's that woman.' So began GH Stevenson's tenure of the office, marked more by Christian charity than hard economic sense.

Dearest wishes, George

25 August 2013

Dear Gorgo,

You were much in my mind last Friday, 23 August, when you completed a whole year of detention in 'durance vile'. 'Tis a lousy way to end up and I greatly feel for you. I think again on the death of Nicias, 'the least deserving of the Greeks of my time to come to such misery.' There is another sentence you might care to ponder. It is recorded in those deathless words,

'There ain't no justice in this land
Just got divorced from my old man
And did I laugh at the Court's decision
He got the kids and they ain't his'n.'

But I can only commiserate. Sorry! & love from your old pal.

It is one of the curious things about memory that one remembers the more clearly the farther back one delves. As Oscar Wilde lay dying, he thought of his crossing to Ireland on the ferry service he had used as a very young man. Of Drake 'twas sung, 'And he sees it all so clearly as he saw it long ago.' 'Tis a consolation for us aged gents. I hope you are so affected as you lie in your boring bed. Despite the fallibility of my memory I do remember much about the College and recall clearly events of my early days. As I probably said, GDH Cole used to come to dinner every Tuesday in term when he moved as Professor to All Souls and Attlee used to come to Feasts as did Harold Wilson, and I remember it all so clearly. Given the way dons delight in gossip, I am well supplied. Your Freddy Wells, the divinely inspired Latinist, was an ample source.

I dare say I have been myself quite a source of College stories, and it is satisfying to be able to answer queries. But there are damned few queries I welcome touching the Greeks!

One little story you may savour. In a conversation dredged up by YouTube one can see the shaggy, sharp young Gareth Evans of Univ conversing with, I think, Peter Strawson. He does look farouche, and Martin West told me t'other day that, once when he had Hugh Lloyd-Jones as a guest at lunch, Martin chanced to seat him by Gareth. After a lively exchange Hugh said to Martin, 'That's a loathsome fellow on my left.' Of course, Gareth was the Philosophical light of his age, and no respecter of persons. He famously shut up Freddy Ayer in a discussion, but I can't remember his exact words. I bet Freddy always could.

Yours, George

1 September 2013

Dear Gorgo,

German car ads, and the like, often appear with the motto *Vorsprung durch Technik*, and I have just had the idea of a Vorsprung for myself. Thought I: 'I'll look out the dictaphone I used to use when doing letters for the Master's Secretary to type out for me (when I was begging all & sundry to give, give, give). I will record the letters I do for Gorgo and I will be able to play them over every so often & so avoid repeating myself.' So I got it out. 'Tis only a quarter of a century since I stopped using it. Damn it. I can't make it work for I can't see where to insert new batteries. So much for my Technik! Similarly one of the pupils of the 80s sent, at my request, an email with Edith Piaf's 'La vie en rose'. Unfortunately it arrived upside down. I thought I could read it if I stood on my head but I failed in the attempt and had to consult the sender & get instruction on how to right it all. 'Tis now done but 'tis very humiliating not to be able to do it for myself. The young who come to the house sit down and 'with the greatest of ease' like the man on the Flying Trapeze (do you remember him?) fiddle with the keypad & extort all sorts of electronic mysteries. I do feel pretty stupid. Of course, I've never done a course. I had never, never typed a word until I could no longer get secretarial assistance in the College or in the Sub-Faculty Office. One can understand why one is in such a mess, but I fear I will always be a bit behindhand when Technik rules.

I went yesterday to a Memorial Assembly, in the Sheldonian. 'Twas for a former member of the College who died this year of a brain tumour, aged about 35 [Acer Nethercott]. Academically gifted but, more remarkable, he had coxed the British VIII at the Beijing Olympics [where he won a silver medal]. So there was quite a concourse. It made me think of the many Memorial Services I have attended. They have grown larger and longer as religion has declined. One used to go to some college's chapel in a gown and the whole thing was over in 45 minutes. That is what happened in the case of Frederick Wells, which I don't think you attended. It was in Univ Chapel. There was a hymn, a lesson, an address, some prayers and it was over. Nowadays some ampler space is found, generally the University Church, when it is available. Old Members turn up for a nostalgic afternoon, and if one hasn't lived too long a goodly host attends. The religious aspect is reduced as much as a College Chaplain will suffer, and the service goes on for a couple of hours, with not one address but as many as six. George Forrest had a do in New College Chapel, and anyone who wanted to say something was free to do so. By god, they did! And there is music. At Isaiah Berlin's Memorial, in a crowded Sheldonian, Brendel played. Perhaps not surprising, but at Tom Braun's in Merton Emma Kirkby sang, very beautifully but it was 'over the top'; after all, he had in his forty odd years written practically nothing about his subject, the ancient Greeks. The whole business is getting absurdly unwieldy.

Incidentally, Frederick's service included an address by a former Master, which was embarrassingly inept, for it compared AFW with AE Housman! Frederick was a sublime Latinist. He had, & communicated as you know, a wondrous enthusiasm & feeling for the language. But, if I, who must rate as a Fourth Division professional if I am rated at all, dare say it, Frederick was a gifted amateur, and to compare him with AEH was, to my mind, absurd. Still, it's nice to be able to hear tosh, compared with one Memorial Service this April, when from the three speakers I could hear nothing.

This is a scrappy letter of which I am much ashamed. I know the only thing to do with letters like this is not to post 'em. But, Engle my boy, I am off to Aldeburgh tomorrow for the annual jaunt, and I just haven't time. So, on the principle of better a bad 'un than none at all, I am just going to send it.

I must have told you, but cannot forbear now to tell you, that my favourite bit of the eighteenth Century is John Wilkes' reply to Lord Chesterfield saying, 'Sir, I am convinced you will die either of the pox or on the gallows.' He said, 'Sir, I must first embrace your mistress or your principles.' Shocking, ain't it?

Love, George

20 September 2013

Dear Gorgo,

At last I can settle down to humble life. I got back from my East Anglian excursion on Monday 9th. There was the usual lot of emails on my computer and then the inrush of visitors. This last week I have had, on successive nights, two dinners in College which I felt obliged to attend, and sundry people have, as usual in September, called on me. So with one thing and another I fill my days with 'the long littleness of life'.

I started at Aldeburgh to read George Eliot's 'Scenes of Clerical Life'. Did you ever read it? She has a very witty pen indeed. But the book that has most touched me is 'Stoner' by an American, John Williams. It was published in 1963 and is having a sort of revival. It's about a man of humble origins, who became a lecturer at the University of Missouri; he rose and fell, slowly, honorably, & not at all his fault. At the end he dies & I wept (a thing I am all too prone to do). If a book has such an effect, it must be the mark of a good writer. The whole book is an explication of that unfailingly true bit of the Bible – 'to him that hath shall be given and from him that hath not shall be taken away even that which he hath.' Stoner was a good man, of principle & honour, & he was gradually reduced by lesser men. (I hope you agree that that bit is 'unfailingly true'. It certainly is true of capitalism. Like Enoch Powell, I thank God for capitalism even though it raises the explosive problem of our time, viz. the rich becoming fantastically rich; literally so, when you think of the sums rich men extract for themselves from their businesses; why, that head of Barclays (I think) a man called Diamond (?) [Bob Diamond, employee and CEO of Barclays PLC 1996-2012] received a retirement bonus of £18 million, and if this sort of thing goes on, short or long there will be blood shed upon our streets. Death duties don't really work. They hit only those like you and me, who are comfortably off. The rich can make provision to keep their wealth in their families long before death. I rather sympathise with Margaret Thatcher's notion that the very rich should make very generous donations or bequests to benevolent institutions. A rich North American (I can't remember whether he is American or Canadian) has just given the Rhodes Trust $75 million, in such a way that it will not be given in full unless humble chums like me make their humble contributions. So I have just sent my modest £500, a lot for me but a packet of peanuts compared with what the donor wants us all to give in total – an American device which I admire. But it is doubtful whether such generosity by rich donors will ever succeed in checking the feelings of ordinary people that the vast fortunes we read of are a scandal. Where, oh where, will it all end? I hope I shall have gone before the bloodshed begins. End of vagrant excursus!)

2014 & 2015 are to be the years of mighty issues. The first is the Scottish referendum, about independence for Scotland. I feel myself a helpless interested party. My mother was very Scottish indeed. In the course of 41 years or so of living in New Zealand she never lost her Scottish speech and constantly longed to see it all again. (We were not rich enough for her to make a trip to the Old Country.) My father was of English descent, but had come over to Edinburgh to do his Medical Degree (lodging with my mother's family). So he was fond and admiring of Scots & Scotland . . . and for long I thought of myself as half Scot. If the Referendum should be in favour of Independence, I shall be torn in half, like myriads of Scots around the world, and I don't want to be. However, the feelings of those who do not live within the land of Scotland count for nothing with the Scottish National Party. So a crisis looms. The other crisis will be a referendum about our membership of the EU and I have the most mixed opinions. Of course, if the Liberal Democrats continue to form part of a Coalition Government, they will block any such vote, though in the long run the question will have to be settled one way or the other and I just don't know which view to take. Of course, if UKIP have the effect on the Election Result that I fear, & let Labour have a further term of mad government, they will have to face the Issue short or long. Anyway the crisis will not go away and will not for ever be swept under the carpet.

This boring letter must stop. I am not proud of it. I just haven't yet returned to my usual routine after East Anglia. Next time I'll try harder. Oxford is full of former Rhodes Scholars (& their wives, etc.) at the moment, for the 110th Anniversary of the foundation of the Rhodes Trust. A man I played Rugger with in 1946 rang me this morning from Trinity but neither could hear the other. I thought of the Mikado. 'And there he plays improbable ['extravagant' in original] matches on fitless finger stalls... etc. etc.' [WS Gilbert continues: "On a cloth untrue / With a twisted cue / And elliptical billiard balls."]

My dearest thoughts, George

4 October 2013

Dear Gorgo,

The world may be alive with the sound of music, but my little corner hears only the sounds of fund-raising. I used to think it was an American lark and in a sense it still is. America is a very rich country & people have large sums to give and they give 'em. Their tax system is suited to giving to charities but, quite apart from that, Americans are generous. They think big & they give big. When I began to interest myself in fundraising for the College, I found that if you explained the College's financial needs to an Englishman, he would say ('like patience on a monument smiling at grief'), 'How sad!' But an American would say, 'What can we do about it?' and would proceed to do. An American, unprompted, wrote to the College in 1979-80 asking if he could organise fund-raising in the US. The College did not leap into accepting, but it did accept and from that initiative grew our present large operation. Old Members contacted by phone have very generously responded, a good half-million or so being raised each year by this 'Telethon'. I for a period was wheeled in to address the junior members & give advice. I used to say, 'Some people will just be rude but don't worry about that. They're the sort of people who wouldn't give anything. Most of those rung up will enjoy talking to you about the College and will give.' Give they do indeed and it is a source of satisfaction to me to have had a part in establishing a system that has made Univ a leader in this regards.

Some people seem to think that millionaires knock on one's door every week seeking to buy a place for their sons. It is not so. No one has ever done such a thing at my door anyhow. If anyone had done so 'twould be such a rarity that I personally would have seriously considered the case; if a man would provide education for needy young people for eternity in return for our educating his son for three years, I would have been sorely tempted – not corruption but consideration of the College's long-term advantage. Like Agesilaus, I care more for people than for principle. Shocking ain't it? But the innocence of some of the

Fellows is wonderful. They seem to think that money will be found for them to continue writing little articles as they sit in their high-principled ivory towers. The world is not so! Money does not come easily.

But we are learning. When fifty years ago St. Cats [St Catherine's College] was turning itself from being a 'collegiate society' into a college, one of the Fellows, a man you may have encountered, John Simopoulos, discovered when he was in Athens that JP Getty, whose name had been found on St. Cat's books, was staying in a penthouse part of George V Hotel. So Simopoulos went to the lobby of the hotel & rang him up. He got through but pretended he could not hear Getty and asked whether he could come up & see him. He saw him & explained the College's financial needs. Getty said, 'I'll be staying in London at the Ritz. Come & see me there.' As it happened, the Master Alan Bullock was free to go himself. He repeated the account of the College's needs. Thereupon, Getty rose, went over to a desk, got out a cheque-book & wrote him out a cheque for £100. What did Alan Bullock do? Did he reject it saying he was giving more himself? I know not. But any fund-raiser worth his salt would have spurned so paltry a sum. The right course would have been for AB to say, 'Haven't you missed out three noughts? I wouldn't like it to be known that a person of your standing has offered such petty pence.' Now we know and Getty would not get away with it. . .

Love, George

15 October 2013

Dear Gorgo,

I don't forget 'ee, but I find I am getting slower & slower. Pat was very nippy and used to remark on my slow ways long ago. Now it's worse & worse. Thank God for Judy who has to do & does more & more for me. Anyhow here's my latest.

If you tutor in an Oxford College & then hang around after you have ceased to do so, you have the satisfaction of seeing former members rising to eminence. The latest is Josh Frydenberg who is in Tony Abbott's Cabinet. He was a member of my dining club, The Bentham. Of course Tony A. is a boo-name with *les bien pensants* and the Press has kept on at him. E.g. he made a speech in which he was said to have described someone as 'a suppository of wisdom', a slip due to nerves perhaps. Hosts of boos all round of course. Like John Howard, he did not want to open the floodgates for immigrants to Australia.

Founding the Bentham is one of the decent things I have done. When I became Dean of Graduates in the 60s, I was appalled to observe that, though the College was taking quite a lot of money off them, it was giving very, very little in return. So I resolved to establish a dining club for graduates in Law, Philosophy, & Politics. The SCR held, at a maximum, twenty diners, and this was sufficient. I had four Fellows, two notable guests whom the graduates would never have had a chance of meeting elsewhere, and fourteen doing graduate work. It all went merry as a marriage bell. My local stars were Herbert Hart, & Peter Strawson, also John Finnis and on rare occasions Ronald Dworkin; the notable guests included Isaiah Berlin, Iris Murdoch, a couple of Law Lords, William Waldegrave, Elizabeth Anscombe, Old Uncle Tom Cobley & all. At first we lacked a title. I had in 1955 begun a dining club for junior members at large and told the Butler that I would let him know what we would call ourselves when we had fixed on a title. But I never did and the Butler charged it on battels [an account for food and accommodation expenses] under the title 'G.L.C.', which title stuck (and it was that club to which the future President of the USA belonged). So I resolved to do better with the Graduates. We discussed it at a dinner. The title 'The Bentham' was suggested, Bentham being the subject which much engaged Herbert. Herbert said, 'Excellent! Maximising pleasure!' And so the Bentham it was and I dare to say that it was, as one Australian said to me, 'a lifeline' and as the present Master goes around the world meeting Old Members, he constantly hears praises of the club. So, for moments, I feel I have not lived utterly in vain . . .

I think & feel for you constantly.

Yours, George

29 October 2013

Dear Gorgo,

Now we are ninety-four [on 25 October] we mean to do better. (Irene sent me a card of Paul Klee from the pair of you for which I thank you. I find it hard to abandon cards which are often very beautiful and often evocative – e.g. an old pupil, whom I now know pretty well, sent me a card with a Top Hat on the front which says inside that in 1986 I introduced her to Fred Astaire, of which, if I did it, I am not ashamed. Perhaps it will make you think of the thoughtless hunter in Virgil who fires off an arrow into the wood and does not realise that he has hit the stag and 'lets the stricken hart go weep'. I have had many, & many of great interest, including a 1700 plan of Athens, a Cézanne whom I used to admire most of Impressionists, etc. etc. I can't keep 'em forever, but I try to cling on.)

'Do better'? It is now Oct. 30th. I don't like to say it to you who linger in durance vile for you must long for the busy life you have lost, but I do say that while loneliness is for many oldies a great limitation on happiness, I am a very, very busy old man. E.g. last night I went to a lecture by our Master, Ivor Crewe, on the question 'Why is Britain so badly governed?' which was very interesting & the discussion went on till 6.45 when I rushed forth to meet two Old Members & their daughter. Then to dinner, & home about 9.45. I am very busy, but it may all change tonight or tomorrow morning as you would feel you have to warn me. Much of the busy-ness, indeed nearly all, comes from being a Fellow of an Oxford College. E.g. the two Old Members I mention were both in Univ in the mid-1980s, he from the USA & she from South Africa. Her father was a South African Rhodes Scholar in Trinity in 1947 and I knew him. Their daughter is in the College for the moment, doing an M.Stud. Never a dull moment in this world of woe.

Oct. 30th 6.20 p.m. This letter is being frustratingly not completed. A woman we met at Delphi in 1992 was due for lunch at 12.30 but arrived at 11.55. So another hiatus. I talked in my last letter about the Bentham Dinner which I began in about 1970 and the Old Member I speak of in the last paragraph and with whom I had dinner last night actually spoke of it before we went into Hall in terms that satisfied my ego. (Easily done, thinks you?)

I was for ever a-dining, vapid fellow? Perhaps, but not for that reason. I found that people from ordinary backgrounds who had never been to a dinner before gained a great deal of social ease with a dinner or two in their experience. I knew well the Wildean dictum, 'A conservative is a man who has never thought, a radical a man who has never dined,' but, although you may think me a thoughtless conservative, I was not after converting radicals so much as trying to put those unused to such social occasions at their ease. It worked. Only in the last day or two I was minded of this. A 'noble lord' was talking in the House of Lords quite a lot; I remember that at his first dinner he upset a glass of sherry; 'twas sheer nerves on that occasion but he never did that again. I now only wish I had done more. I always closed things down at 10 p.m. so that members were not involved in greater expense than the minimum and did not have to join the late carousers. The wine, too, was quite plain. Occasionally some knowing lad would show that the wine was pretty ordinary, if not *vin ordinaire*; a simple little Beaujolais like Juliénas, for example. But I did not care. I was not teaching vinology. Many who came were grateful, and I have not lived utterly in vain.

Life in Oxford is, however, greatly changing. In our time one generally had a tutorial on one's own, certainly in the House, and I practically always taught pupils on their own. Now, whereas I tutored, say, for fourteen tutorials a week, Fellows (in Arts Subjects, that is – scientists give and get a mere four a week) take their pupils in pairs, perhaps no more than eight a week. This greatly changes Oxford life. Pupils don't mind making a fool of themselves before their tutor, but in pairs they clam up & try to escape inquisition. With singleton tutorials there is no escape. Also I liked to have pupils read their essays aloud. After all, the essay is in part a literary production and only by reading it aloud does the pupil realise how well or badly it reads. I used to take notes as they read their essays and tried to deal with the subject 'by & large', as yachtsmen are said to say. I used to allow twenty minutes for the reading and a full hour for the discussion; starting at 9 a.m. I finished the three tutorials by 1 p.m. But one always made time for the unexpected. That is not the way most tutorials go now. I was, of course, bloody ignorant but they liked the drink I served them.

Sez you, how boring can you get, Corky? True, true, my good Gorgo, and I cease, on the stroke of 7 p.m. I only wish I could help you now. Please accept my dearest wishes.

Yours, George

[note: in the previous letter of 15 October 2013 George had written: 'Of course nowadays 'tis different. Fellows tutor in pairs, & eight hours a week is thought to be a full load leaving sufficient time for their precious articles! Gone are the days of Ronald Syme, who wrote 'The Roman Revolution' in two Long Vacations, a fact which he was prone to mention when a colleague complained about the "burden of teaching". I ask what the heck would happen to us all if there were no undergraduates to tutor; of course, homely duds, like Cawkwell, enjoy the company of the young & cast a sympathetic eye on all they do, but we are rare birds these days.']

9 November 2013

In this letter I repeat myself, a sure sign of decay. I never reread it as I write. Can't read it anyhow. So stop beefing, Irene.

Dear Gorgo,

'Tis incredible, yea incredible (a word not be used 'lightly or inadvisedly' as I think the Book of Common Prayer but 'soberly' etc. – which comes pretty well from a man who is sipping a glass of Auchentoshan given him by a friendly u-grad of Univ, oh God bless him – and anyone who uses the word 'incredibly' when he/she means no more, nor less, than 'very' gets a big silent raspberry from me), yea, 'tis incredible how slow one becomes with age. I mean to write to you each week but the days slide past so slitheringly surely that I am utterly out of date with everything. I am sorry for being so feeble, both physically and morally.

I begin with dreams. As you know the Greeks thought dreams 'real'; those fantasies which come in dreams were thought to be actualities. One really was visited & you had better look out e.g. Xerxes' dream about invading Greece. We are fortunately exempt from this damned folly. The other night I dreamt that RM Dworkin was peeing into my hair-brush; I had my arm round his back & no bad words were exchanged. 'Twas the piss that passes all comprehension.

So the question arises what am I to make of my dream? I lack a Sigmund F. to explain. I am reading a book about the young Kipling by Charles Allen. He mentions you in his preface. But how did you 'get into' Kipling? I admire such of him as I have read, which is 'Plain Tales' and his poetry, and I feel the warmer towards him when I hear colleagues sneer about him as the Imperialist. He certainly admired the

British Tommy, but he had unusual sympathy with and admiration for the native Indians. He was certainly no purblind Brit!

We are half-way through the term. On Wednesday I went to the dinner of the Univ Classicists. On my left sat an outstandingly brilliant young man; on my right was a Greek girl; opposite was a girl and a young man. I immediately remarked that his bow-tie was that of the Christ Church Boat Club. (People don't know ties now, just as they don't wear 'em.) He said his father had been at the House & had actually been to my lectures on Xenophon when doing Greats. (Unlike the very good-looking girl I met at a party, who said she had been to my lectures 'or rather, one of your lectures'.) Anyhow I warmed to a sort of academic connection.

Life goes on pleasantly for me, pretty wretchedly for you. And now Irene has had a car run over her foot. How wretched! Sympathy is not much use, but I am sorry for your misfortunes.

Sorry for all this trivial chatter. My constant sympathy. I would somehow have visited you in person if my hearing were not so awful. *Eheu!* So, better not.

George

25 November 2013

Dear Gorgo,

Horror, shock, surprise, delight! To write my Annual Encyclical (which I have now completed & of which you will receive a copy in due course) I bought me a new pen which makes for unprecedented clarity and, lo, your *Vorleserin* need not be in a sulk with me. More serious, however, is the danger of repeating myself, to which I and other old men are so prone. So please, remember "old men forget".

I don't think I've written much of Univ in earlier letters and I can write therefore without fear of repetition. Univ, of which I became a Fellow in 1949, was, is a very different place from the House. I say nothing disrespectful to either institution. I expect the most striking difference is that Univ is a very friendly place – and neither of us would say the House was 'friendly' in the same way. Of course there were groups of friends, often originating in schools, but 'twas all comparatively formal. E.g. in Univ junior members & porters etc. call me 'George'.

Can you imagine that happening in the world of Trevor-Roper? Of course, we all referred to Robin Dundas as 'D', but not to his face. A man has to be a rank troglodyte not to make ample friends in Univ. I expect it is in large part due to us being middle-class or lower, of which no one gives a damn. But it's also a matter of size. The House was so vast. Meadow Buildings away on its own; in Tom Quad mostly canons and that big shot, the Dean; Peck rather separate; Canterbury Quad, where the peers' staircase was, again separate. But in Univ in 1949 about 200 stuffed into quite a restricted space. There was a communal lavatory called 'South Side' where word was quickly spread (as in the Army; I remember a man I knew saying, on receipt of some private news, 'Jesus, the shit-house Telegraph,' & rumours certainly spread, e.g. 'Madame Chiang Kai-shek is planning to present a kimono to everyone who has fought against the Jap Division that had been responsible for the Rape of Nanking' (? 1936) [in fact 1937]. I'm still waiting for mine). When the College was playing in Rugger Cuppers, practically the whole society went to watch, the sort of 'school spirit' people like you at the House spurned. It was 'dense' in feeling as it was physically. Anyhow, for good or ill it is me. Cp. that line of Plautus, *Homo sum, et nil humanum puto alienum a me.* ['I am a man, and feel nothing human is foreign to me.' Homer nodded here: the author was in fact Terence and the line read *Homo sum, humani nihil a me alienum puto.*]

Outstanding amongst the dons was Giles Alington, the Dean, son of Cyril Alington one-time Headmaster of Eton – but more of him in another letter. Here, since you were tutored for a bit by AF Wells, 'Frederick' as he was to one and all, I will speak of him (rather fearing I may already have done so). He had that wonderful feeling for the Classical languages, particularly Latin, but he also had wonderful feeling for English literature, which he would deploy. E.g. when the Goodharts were retiring from the Mastership in 1963, it was he who provided a bit from Pope to be engraved on a bit of glass the Fellows were giving Cecily (a woman much loved & admired by us all). It ran thus (being the last verse of 'On a Certain Lady at Court'):

'"Has she no faults then (Envy says) Sir?"
Yes, she has one, I must aver;
When all the world conspires to praise her,
The Woman's deaf, and does not hear.'

Wonderfully apt and neat, so typical of Frederick's style. I mustn't go on for I could do so at length. When Giles died in Feb 1956, Frederick became Dean; slightly surprising, since he did agonise over making decisions. But he was a marvellous Dean and the reason for this was his very great humanity. He greatly felt for members of the College who needed above all a wise counsellor. And as I think you will agree, he was for the same reason a wonderful tutor; he understood pupils who were not able readily to comprehend – one of the prime qualities of a good tutor. (We had, later on, that bright star of Philosophy, Gareth Evans, who was not I think a good tutor; he was intolerant of those who did not instantly comprehend and, basically, he was bored with teaching & should have been a Fellow of All Souls. Frederick was quite different, a great Amateur, who loved not only literature but his fellow men.)

This waffle must cease. There were some very gifted Fellows in 1949, and I will continue on this theme next time. Prepare to yawn mayhap. But I dare say that as you lie there you have the comfort of reflecting on your family. So all is not lost. And one of them gave me your telephone number which, after this warning, I propose to use, even if, with your articulation and my deafness, there may not be a true meeting of minds. Anyhow I haven't much mind myself to do battle with.

Dearest wishes from your old friend, George

12 December 2013

Dear Gorgo,

I have not forgotten you, but at this time of year there is a traffic jam of social events, and I try to acknowledge receipt of Xmas cards by returning on that very day my Encyclical letter, which task is very time-taking. I have already sent off nearly a hundred (& will probably have to beg on Hungerford Bridge). I hope you got your copy & that one of your handmaids has read it to you – or as much of it as you were willing to endure.

[From Frederick Wells, recalled in the previous letter] I turn to the Law Fellow who at that time was Estates Bursar, Norman Marsh. He did the College very well by selling investments where dividends were kept down by the zealous Labour Govt. and buying commercial property where rents were left to market forces, and he had other notable merits which deserve to be remembered, but here I will dwell on his eccentricities. He never had matches to light the gas-fire in his room. So he turned on the gas and used a small electric radiator to light his fire, which was not accomplished without an alarming bang; undergraduates were little amused. He was not a good tutor, ahem, and things could happen. A pupil in his Schools term went to him and said, 'Sir we have a paper in x and we've had no tutorials on it.' 'Oh no, Binks, you're wrong.' 'Well, sir, look in the Examination Statutes.' Norman got down his copy of the Statutes and exclaimed, 'My goodness, Binks, you're right.' It couldn't, I hope but I am not entirely certain, it couldn't happen now, but this was just after the War when students were grateful not to be in uniform & they put up with such things.

He was a wonderfully absent-minded person too. The key to the College Library was huge. Indeed it felt like a two-pound trout. In his time Norman 'mislaid' two of them. But if he couldn't find a key, he simply threw himself at the door. He was heavy & strong & doors yielded. At first he lived in Kybald House, sharing with the Wellses and the Strawsons. (Indeed 'twas in the basement of that building that Harold Wilson lived.) When he bought his own house, as he did rather shrewdly, at Upper Farm in Wolvercote, he would, returning home, open the wooden gates by driving into them. (I don't think, however, that he was the hand that added to the graffiti in the toilet of The Plough [a pub at Wolvercote in North Oxford]; on a wall covered with rural crudities and obscenities someone had in a blank space drawn a rectangle in which he had written, 'A merry Christmas to all our Readers.')

I could go on about this Pickwickian figure but here I must add that his wife, Christel, was a German who disapproved of Nazi practices and beliefs and only just got away from the Gestapo. An honourable name she will ever be to me. I may add that they very kindly entertained newcomers like the Cawkwells. I remember him with both gratitude and affection.

Today, as you may not care whether it is or not, is the day of the University Match at Twickenham. I, like other 'colonials' in the 1946 Oxford side, had played first-class Rugby (if not in a first-class way) around the world & when one began on the term, one didn't care at all whether one was chosen to play v. Cambridge at Twickenham, but as the term went on one ardently desired it. Being a Blue was a big thing then. I remember Pat & I, & Simon in arms, were photographed for Tatler (of which appearance Scottish relatives did not necessarily approve). Indeed one was treated with honour, nay reverence. We won in 1946, as we were expected to do, & we lost in 1947, as we were not. *Quel désastre!* To get a Blue & a First was thought to be sublime! Life is more realistic now. (We won today, despite an Oxford player being sent off, which in my whole career I never was save once when I was so frustrated by the nippiness of the Auckland scrum-half that I gave him a boot on the backside!)

I have left no room for a proper account of *Kartoffelnacht*. In a loose moment I boastfully took on outdoing a Greek girl at mashing potato. She came & a couple of witnesses. The contest was on 4 Dec. and I went around quizzing cooks of my acquaintance about how to make/do the Perfect Mash; these included Sophie Grigson, daughter of the formidable Jane G. & Geoffrey G., and I passed without disaster. I remember in the War senior officers would tell one that there are no bad soldiers, only poor officers. *Mutatis mutandis*, that is true of tutors and undergraduates, and I find the young to be most admirable. My writing is becoming tinier as I get to the bottom of the page. 'Tis ever so.

Dearest wishes, George

[This long sequence of George's letters was broken by a letter Gorgo managed to write from Highgate Nursing Home in London on 21 December 2013.]

21 December 2013 (from George Engle)

Dear George,

I have been waiting to write to you for a very long time, ever since my stroke last year, but have not been able to write or type. Vanessa [one of his daughters] is now acting as my amanuensis, as I didn't want any more time to pass before sending you a letter. I have very much appreciated the many letters you have sent me and it saddens me that it has been such a one-sided correspondence. My speech was badly affected by my stroke, so although my intellect is still more or less intact, it has been hard for me to express myself verbally. I spend long hours listening to audio books on CD, which has been a godsend and have enjoyed many books ranging from Dante's 'Inferno' to PG Wodehouse.

About a month ago, out of the blue my speech improved markedly, but unfortunately this didn't last long and more recently I have fallen into a depression, which seems to have caused my speech to deteriorate again. I am finding this very distressing as you can imagine, although thankfully Irene and my three girls are still able to understand me and to sustain a conversation with me. At other times, I am lost for words and talk unintelligible nonsense.

As you know, throughout my life, I have always looked forward to the next meal! Frustratingly, I have now lost my sense of taste and smell and most food tastes to me like cardboard. As a result, I have for the first time in my life lost weight effortlessly. I'm also no longer really able to walk properly, so can only perambulate in a wheelchair. This isn't meant to sound like a litany of complaints – rather to give you an idea of my present situation and its quite severe limitations.

I'm impressed to hear that you still manage on your own and continue to make the most of life. I hope you have an enjoyable Christmas and I wish you good health and continuing independence in the new year. I will be thinking of you.

Your ever-loving friend, Gorgo

27 December 2013

Dear Gorgo,

I was delighted to receive a letter from YOU. 'The tumult & the shouting dies' here and I face the dilemma of an answer. Do I send this to Highgate Nursing Home or, as usual, send it to Wood Lane? I think I will send it via Irene, though I like the idea of Vanessa's part. Say I have a collapse myself and am transported to Highgate Nursing Home. We could write to each other via Vanessa, a wonderful middle-woman. It makes me think of the role played, way back in 1950, by Giles Alington. There had been a bit of a puffle [sic] between Hugh Seton-Watson and the Bursar Norman Marsh, and they were reduced to writing stiff notes to each other. Giles A. took over and wrote letters for each party, olive oil on troubled waters. Somehow the medicine worked. S-W & NSM no longer spoke to each other but they kept their troubled feelings to themselves. At an early stage there was an exchange while each was helping himself to a plate of sausage & mash. S-W said, 'I don't want any Pecksniffian comments from you, Marsh,' and Norman forgoing his plate of sausage mash left the room abruptly, i.e. forgoing his bangers etc. We thought, 'Oh God. That's serious. Norman is very fond of "bangers" ("bangers and").' 'Twas at that stage less serious than we thought. Norman had rushed home to 'Christel, my wife' to ask what 'Pecksniffian' meant. However it needed the balm of Giles Alington to restore calm. Vanessa could write a letter for you to me and another from me to you.

Lunch could be dangerous in Univ. I fear I may have told you this before, but it bears repeating. It concerns the famous Univ murder. Undergraduates all did military training in those War years but there was one Univ pacifist who was ragged for his beliefs & who went off his head and shot, from a point high in the Front Quad, his principal ragger as he came out of Hall. (It's not so many years since the bullet marks in the stonework were removed during refacement work on the Hall.) When the shot rang out, the Fellows were having lunch in the Senior Common Room. The then Domestic Bursar, John Wild, the future Master, rose went out on what was a dangerous quest, went across the Quad, up the staircase, and took the rifle from the poor fellow, generally considered a courageous action. But my colleague, David Cox, liked to adorn the tale. William Beveridge was the Master & he was sitting at the end of the Table. It was the time when The Beveridge Plan [the Beveridge Report of 1942 laying the foundations of the Welfare State] was on everybody's lips, and reports of it in John 'O London or Picture Post were perchance open at the most explicit page on every chair in the Lodgings. (Indeed the Senior Fellow, called 'Farky', i.e. ASL Farquharson, liked to play on Beveridge's vanity and said on one occasion, 'Well, Master. How's Mein Pampf?') So in David Cox's account of the shooting it was said that when the shot was heard, Beveridge, convinced that the Germans had come to get him, got under the Table!

At lunch in those times, Giles, who was Dean & Senior Tutor & Steward of Common Room, a very Pooh Bah, used to hold conversational sway, and he was very good at it. He was a man without academic pretensions. He had taken a Third in Modern History at Trinity, gone off to a teaching post in one of those high-class American 'Prep' Schools, & turned up in Oxford running vacation courses for Army Officers recovering from the damage of War. He was so good at it, so witty, that Arthur Goodhart, the great & good-hearted indeed future Master of Univ (whom I ever revere), was so impressed that he got Univ to appoint him to a Fellowship & so take on all the administrative functions that needed the energy of a young man in a College where the Fellows clinging to the wreckage were all, or almost all, past the sell-by date. Giles was a man whom I have come ever more to appreciate. The undergrads were warm in their admiration. I used to count up about ten Old Members who had named their son 'Giles'. Harold Wilson once told me that he named his son 'Giles' in that mood of appreciation & respect. For a decade in fact Univ was Giles. I would never have voted for him to be Master when we elected Arthur Goodhart (he took office in Michaelmas 1953), but now I'm not so sure, and I think ever more highly of him. As did Arthur G. There is an account of Arthur standing at the bedside of the dying Giles in 1956 and weeping as he said, 'I hoped you would be Master.' In general, Arthur was a very wise person to follow. We made no mistakes when he was Master (1951-63).

I must stop talking about Univ but I dare remark that we have had an ample share of notables, both Fellows & Old Members. When I was first a fellow once a week Douglas Cole (i.e. GDH Cole) would come over the road from All Souls, where he had gone on becoming Professor, and enjoy the homely atmosphere of Univ. Harold Wilson had ceased by 1949 to be a Fellow, but later he liked to come to Univ for which he had great affection. He was an Honorary Fellow when I knew him. Despite what some say of him, I rather liked him. I heard him say in a radio interview many years later that the thing he was most proud of having done was the Open University and he liked the world of universities as I do. (I don't care whether it's a great & famous one or just an ordinary 'red-brick', I always get a thrill from being in such a place; the teaching staff are in general very good and we are all alike in our values.) Later there was Peter Strawson whom you must have met and we had a more than fair share of legal stars. E.g. Kenneth Diplock who read Chemistry & turned to the Law where he was generally greatly respected [becoming a Law Lord in 1968]. He used to go hunting most week-ends and would stay not infrequently in the College on his way to his pleasure. But this is boring & silly perhaps. Every college has its notables.

I apologise to your *Vorleser* for my tendency to become ever more minuscule as the letter goes on. At least I make a sort of contact with your Irene and I can't hear her swearing. But oh George, this a bloody position to have fallen into. Do you remember the last words of Stevenson & Osbourne's 'The Wrong Box'? Someone says, 'Is there then nothing we can do for the man in the cart?' and the answer ends the book, 'Nothing but sympathise.' My love & best wishes to Engles all,

George

2014

4 January 2014

Dear Gorgo,

'Twould be folly to wish you a merry New Year, but I was so impressed with your dictated letter, which seemed to indicate a great improvement in your condition, that I hope this New Year may bring more of the same.

You must be so sick by now of University College that, although I could tell you much much more, I have decided to pitch into another topic. I have just read Alan Johnson's account of his boyhood & teenage years, 'This Boy'. I've always liked him (& a retired senior Civil Servant told me that he was much respected as an honest politician). (Yea, there are some, even in his Party, for whom I have quite a high regard; above all, Frank Field whom I once sat beside at dinner, but Hilary Benn is another such. Indeed I admired his father for his abhorrence of petty mud-slinging; his principles & his views may have been anathema to his colleagues but they were views, not petty slanging of personalities.)

The book is a bit shocking. His mother maintained her family in pretty grim conditions in [London] W10, his father having gone off and done mighty little for the family he left behind. His mother & his sister, a few years older than Alan, had one heck of a struggle living on in slum conditions. To the credit of both of them they did it. But their condition was unusual. What shocked me was the general squalor of the neighbourhood. It was the period of which Harold Macmillan could say, or could be believed to have said, 'You've never had it so good.' A toilet in the back garden used by the whole building! Very inadequate everything else. I wonder if such areas still exist. I fear they do and I don't know what is to be done about it. Is this the inevitable state of misery to be found in all large cities? It's a gloomy prospect for the country at large. Anyhow, I was deeply moved by it all.

In general, housing is an insoluble problem. Think of all those young couples who can't afford to buy a house at present prices. You may well say, 'Ah Cawky, m'boy, you live alone in a house big enough for a family. What are you going to do about it?' I answer, 'I am going to die within, I guess, the next five years and the house will then be on the market.' 'But, Cawky, people need houses *now*, not just in five years. What about that?' 'When I was pondering the renewal of my central heating system, I was warned by wise advisers that a change at the age of 94 would probably secure me an early death.' This house is Pat's, is Pat to whom I was wed for 62 years and having been parted from her once already I don't want another parting. So I will cling on as long as I can – which can't, as I say, be for long. There must, however, be many a bereaved, too old or just unwilling to marry again. So the class of Cawk-wells may be quite large. The Lib-Dems . . . wish to drive us forth into outer darkness, with a swingeing property tax. I shall just have to cash in savings.

Like the Pope, *qui securus judicat orbem*, you happily dismiss all thoughts of the Ashes lost. I don't mind losing as long as we win some. Such are games, which I guess have never troubled you much. But this series in Australia is different. We were beaten in all five games, which happens. But, as far as I can recall, never before have two players left mid-tour. Trott had a fit of depression; understandable, acceptable, for these touring sides playing Test cricket are under immense mental strain. But for a player, fearing or expecting to be dropped from the Test team, to pack his bag, announce he's finished and he ain't gonna play no more no more (which was what the egregious Swann did) is very shocking, at least to me. Sez you, 'How happy am I never to have loved that ghastly game as poor old Cawky loves!' Say I, 'I fear there is not just defeat, but also moral decline, the very thing the game is aimed to prevent.' In the rules of *I Zingari*, a famous cricket club there is, or was, a rule which said 'There shall be no rub'; banged in the balls by a bouncer, one cried in agony, 'Play on.' Is our moral fibre gone? Or is there a temporary infection? What of the 'Lampada Vitai'? All very downcasting for this old man anyhow.

For this joyless letter, may the Lord make us all truly ungrateful. I shall do better next time. Think of Lycidas, your sorrow who is not dead.

> 'And yet anon repairs his drooping head,
> and tricks his beams, and with new-spangled ore
> flames in the forehead of the morning sky.'

Hooray for Milton, hooray for You. Be of good cheer, George

17 January 2014

Dear Gorgo,

'O what a rogue & peasant slave am I.' I am so slow to write these letters! It really is downcasting to be aware of my defects. By way of apology I might dare to say that the last month of 2013 as well as the first of January got taken over by my sending out my Encyclical to all who have sent me a Xmas Card. I have sent about 200 on each of which I write a short personal message, but by the time I have addressed the envelope (and checked the address), time has passed. 'Feeble,' sez you & I quite agree but I cannot omit yet another opportunity to cite that couplet of Fr. Frederic Faber which is so often suitable. 'The old man's eyes were growing dim / The Feast had been too much for him.'

My one-time pupil and enduring friend, Abigail Graham, makes a monthly calendar each year and distributes it to her circle. 'Tis well worth worming one's way into that select band. She is a polyglot. Dutch, German, Hungarian as well as the Classical Languages are there deployed & occasionally bits of French appear. No doubt she would include Italian & Spanish if pressed. Last year's Calendar had for December Noel Coward's 'There are bad times just around the corner' which was an apt prediction. Today my Judy flew off to the Gran Canaries on holiday, marking her 50th Wedding Anniversary on Saturday next. So for two weeks I will have to do for myself. Of course I won't 'do for' myself, but I shall be striving to care for myself and when she returns on 3rd February, I shall be much relieved. Indeed, had I power, I would require *all* males over the age of, say, 55 to have a couple of weeks a year when they take over. That would do more for male respect for women than any wise words. I always knew that Pat was busy but I never realised how busy she was, how uncomplaining, how tiringly she worked, until the 2nd February 2008 when I began to do for myself.

Times may be hard, but my days are not without laughter. I receive, on the computer, Simon's weekly diary of deals & of fears & hopes for the future. They often include a story that is a very good laugh and I am presuming to include a print-out of part of a recent piece. O taste & see! [See below.] But I seize this opportunity to protest that I do not find what is put out on Radio 4 at 11.05 p.m. to make one laugh makes one laugh one bit. The great exception is Pam Ayres, 'an you remember. But silly cackle at not very witty remarks really irritates. I turn it off until 11.30 when Today in Parliament comes on.

One has to endure the horrifying thought that the chances of the Conservatives being re-elected are much reduced by UKIP. I don't know how I would vote if in 2017 there is a Referendum on membership of the EU, but I fear that the boil will not be lanced and Labour will be restored to power, which is a sad thought for a man who has always hoped to die not under a Labour Govt. who always bugger things up, but who will do anything to avoid a Referendum on this matter. It would show that 'tis not only the Conservatives who are divided by this question.

*

It is now 20th January. I have been adding the odd bit for three full days, an elderly fuddler. I went today, after my post-prandial nap, for a walk to Summertown in the course of which I somehow somewhere lost my Bank Debit card. I have rung the Bank and hope the criminal classes have not got hold of it. But I do alarmingly drop & mislay things Of course picking things up is good exercise but the mislaid plans of mice & men cause me a lot of anxiety. How long can it all go on?

Have I previously mentioned the novel entitled 'Stoner' [see letter of 20 September 2013], first published in the mid 1960s? It has had an astounding resurrection. When published, it sold a mere 4000 copies. In this year alone it has sold nigh on 200,000! Nice for the author's widow but it is a remarkable instance of what is common enough in literary history. The poems of John Donne were brought into general esteem after about three centuries. The novels of Barbara Pym had fizzled out until David Cecil in a Christmas T[imes] L[iterary] S[upplement] lauded them and said they were quite undeservedly forgotten. It gives one hope for one's own theories which have sunk without trace. There's always the hope of a new piece of evidence turning up & proving that one was right. For instance, the mighty Mommsen postulated what seemed to all his contemporaries a wildly improbable organisation for voting purposes of the centuries of the Comitia Centuriata. Then in about 1949 the discovery of the so-called Tabula Hebana changed all that, for it showed that Mommsen had been on the right track all along. Think of one's emotion on hearing on one's deathbed that one had been right all along

Novels you will think are different from historians' theories, but 'tis a sweet thought that with one's dying gurgle one could triumph over one's critics. It gives one something to die for! However, returning to novels it seems to me time for a revival of Joyce Cary. I vividly recall the excitement I felt the day I began to read 'The Horse's Mouth', in which Gully Jimson came on the scene. I broke off to go to Chapel and the thrill felt over the first fifty pages never quite resumed, but it was a lovely book indeed. And who now reads Arnold Bennett? *Et alii.*

Sorry for this scrappy letter. I'll try & do better as 2014 gets longer.

Love & best wishes, George

[Printout included with letter]
The railway man: this one got on the overnight train from Euston to Edinburgh, bunged the guard a fiver and stressed that he had to be turned out at Carlisle since he had an important 6 a.m. meeting. He also emphasised that he was a very heavy sleeper and would have to be man-handled from his couch if necessary. In the morning he awoke in Edinburgh. So he strode down the platform and swore at the guard for five minutes who countered with: 'Och, you're a bonny swearer but you're not a patch on the man I turned off at Carlisle.'

29 January 2014

Dear Gorgo,

'Tis infinitely sad to me that Senior Common Rooms are in any real sense extinct. Of the Fellows of Univ, a good many hardly enter the place. Of course they turn up for lunch and a fraction do go and read the papers afterwards, but as for sitting round after dinner and conversing the place is nearly dead save for Emeritus Fellows and Research Fellows. So I treasure memories of evenings in the Senior Common Room & hope for the return of things past, but I will hope in vain.

There are however Common Room chestnuts. At the head of such a list comes the story of JP Mahaffy in Trinity College, Dublin, of the latter half of the nineteenth century. (Oscar Wilde was a pupil in, I expect, the Seventies.) Mahaffy was noted for his colourful but not necessarily fully credible tales. On one occasion he said, 'I was never caned at school save once and that was for telling the truth.' Said the Provost from a corner of the room, 'It certainly taught you a lesson, Mahaffy.' (I apologise if you know it.) Nearer home is the comment of Edgar Lobel, the papyrologist, a great scholar indeed. There was a Fellow of Queen's, just over the road from us, a powerful if unloved figure in that college. At a time when Queen's were about to elect a new Provost, this man declared in Common Room, 'We'll elect X over my dead body.' Quietly from the corner came the voice of Lobel: 'That will solve two problems.'

I'm afraid I can't think of such stories from Univ. When I arrived in Univ in 1949 memories of ASL Farquharson were still alive. In the wrong mouth his playful comments sounded boorish, but, retold by Frederick, they were light & good-humoured. For example, when someone brought JL Garvin [a noted editor of The Observer before the First World War] to dinner, at a time when he was a household name, the 'Fark' opened conversation with him over dessert with the question, "What do you do?"

I have never heard a 'dirty' story told in Common Room. Once, I am told, when Kenneth Wheare was presiding, someone did tell a 'blue' story and Kenneth said bleakly, 'You must tell me what that is about some other time.' But there is one incident worth recounting. The Professor of Chinese was at that time an American who had been a missionary in China before entering academic life, Homer H. Dubs indeed. He was pretty often late for dinner which provoked that crude New Zealander, George Cawkwell, to rib him slightly, but on one occasion he didn't arrive until the last course and he was ribbed thereon more than slightly. Homer quietly endured. After dinner in Common Room Herbert Hart was recounting how, when young, he had been swimming in a somewhat swollen river in France, was swept away and could see before him that he was approaching a bridge the arches of which were already submerged, and he thought, 'I am going to be killed' (but he was sucked under the water and deposited on an internal staircase up which he walked to salvation, thank goodness). At this point, Homer said, 'Death comes at the most unexpected moments,' and afterwards we learned that he had been late for dinner because his (second) wife had just died. (You may remember that Canon Claude Jenkins of Christ Church on his way to Blackwells called into the Porter's Lodge at Tom Gate to say what had happened, viz. that his house-

218

keeper had just died, and that he would be back shortly. Did you know him? A bibliophile one might say.)

(Gentle *Unterleser*, please pardon the minuteness of this writing. I just can't stop myself.)

Back to 1946/7. Playing Rugger for the University I encountered a man from Trinity, Tommy Macpherson. I knew he had had a distinguished War behind the enemy lines in France and had been a very successful saboteur, but I knew no more than that, and people didn't talk about their War if they had really been in the thick of it. I have just read his autobiography 'Behind Enemy Lines' published in 2010. I was astounded by his bravery. He got around in a kilt and might have been killed twenty, nay forty times. At one moment when the Germans caught him, he was put in a line of chaps facing the wall with their hands up, and the end was to be expected. He had tremendous guts. If I had known at the time of playing in 1946, I would not have been able to resist falling down & licking his boots. He was awarded three MCs and a Croix de Guerre! Having done all that, he longed for a Rugger Blue! (His brother, Phil Macpherson, had captained Scotland in 1925 and had become a legend. So there may have been an urge with Tommy to succeed on the Rugger field.) To be personal for a moment, I confess that because I had had so little of a War myself despite coming from a country where anyone was someone only if he had been through it, I did not want to go back there after the War. I had very little indeed and feel very inferior, though Pat, sensible creature, didn't hold it against me. (But oh!, women are wonderful! To have had the loyalty & love of one is the greatest blessing of my life.)

Tim has given me for Christmas a collection of letters by Trevor-Roper. There too you have a hero of a different sort. He writes marvellously and to judge by photocopies here and there he never hesitated or scored anything out. And he must also have written quickly: simply hundreds of letters exist, in which I do not count mere notes, one of which is to be found in my papers. Always witty and never, as far as I must concede my letters are, trivial. They will constitute a precious document of Twentieth-Century Oxford.

There are some juicy footnotes too, emanating often from our old friend Hugh Lloyd-Jones. There is one concerning Enid Starkey, Fellow of Somerville, a striking spectacle in her vivid clothes. She sat beside me in Common Room once and I formed the impression that she was very second-rate. She knew everybody who was somebody and when the Professorship of Poetry was falling vacant & the candidates were getting around seeking support, she got herself nominated and secured more signatures than, in the poll, votes! Anyhow, when Joanna Richardson published a biography of her, AL Rowse wrote a derogatory review, on which I think Hugh L-J wrote to TR, 'Everything he says about that vain, stupid, noisy old trout applies to him.'

My dearest wishes, George

12 February 2014

Dear Gorgo,

Here we are again & pretty late about it you may think. I mean to write you a weekly pick-you-up, but I have become so slow about everything that 'weeks' are a bit like months. I will try harder. I am just reading 'One Hundred Letters from Hugh Trevor-Roper' edited by Richard Davenport-Hines and Adam Sisman (who wrote the excellent biography). It is truly wonderful, perhaps the last of the great letter-writers (for the blasted email is destroying the art, just as, I irrelevantly interject, Amazon is destroying the bookshop). They are wonderfully written; they sparkle with wit; they astound one by the range of his reading. I can't remember when Sisman's biography appeared (and I would have to walk to the Guest Room to verify) but he records that not so long before his eyesight failed and he became practically blind he reread the whole of Greek Tragedy! Some feat! But weighty volumes in German or in French were consumed and are discussed. I can only hope that some of his writings about the Scottish Enlightenment are not reissued, for the Scottish Nationalists would seize on them as proof of English oppression of the Scots. There are also some juicy remarks of Hugh Lloyd-Jones cited here & there, in footnotes and introductory pieces. E.g. Dora Black, daughter of Philosopher Black, was spoken of by L-J thus: 'Dora Russell was one of the most disagreeable women Bertrand Russell ever married.' (You may remember that when she walked out on Russell she did not flush the toilet for quite a time, so that Bertrand R. was left with, if not in, the shit.) It must be maddening for you not to be able to read. I've got fearfully slow at it, but I would be quite miserable if I could not read a stimulating bit each day and I feel for you in this regard most strongly. I can only hope that talking books give some compensation.

I am indeed slow, slow to rise, slow to retire, but also I am beginning to forget. For example, I went down the other afternoon and when I came back I found I had left my shopping-bag at the desk in Marks & Spencer and had to make a second journey to get it, having found that I had neglected to double lock my front door. At least it showed me I was not an elephant. I have not yet gone so far as Sir Arthur Salter in John Sparrow's story. (I can't remember whether I told you this. Pray pardon me if I did.) When John Sparrow was Warden in the 50s and 60s, he went with two fairly Senior Fellows to consult Arthur Salter [1st Baron Salter, politician and academic], who lived I think in London, on some matter of College business. When they arrived, Salter's servant told them that Salter was dressing and asked them to sit and wait. Shortly, Salter entered, dressed in stiff collar and black suit, save that he had omitted to put on his trousers. This did by no means affect the meeting! Sparrow etc. sat unsmiling through the interview, better man than I, for I would not have been able to contain myself. Sparrow rejoiced in the story. I heard him tell it twice at least. (I'm not sure that Salter was not by then ennobled.)

Sparrow's pleasure makes one think of George V whose favourite story, which he called on courtiers to recount, concerned Her Royal Highness Princess X (my memory fails me, but she is well known) on a visit to Sweden. The Archbishop was showing her around Stockholm Cathedral & said, 'Come over here, Your Majesty, and I shall open these drawers and still more wonderful things will be revealed to you.' How the monarch would laugh!

Do you remember the winter of 1946-7, much more severe than the winter of 1962-3 or so it seemed, probably because the heating was so 'economical'? Those were the days, but this year is worse, with those living beside the Thames flooded out. Irene was ever sensitive to cold but so far, despite all the miseries, the temperature has remained comparatively mild. I remember, however, how you liked a heavy load of blankets over you. So 'Are you getting what the doctors may not have ordered?' And yet we somehow hope... I think of you often.

My dearest wishes, George

25 February 2014

Dear Gorgo,

There is good stuff in 'Genesis', as you may have forgotten or even never discovered. For instance, 'remember Lot's wife' – at any rate the version of it given by Alec Douglas-Home's brother, Willy I think, in his Divvers paper (familiar name for Divinity, a paper which all undergraduates were required to take (was it in Responsions?)). He wrote, and got rusticated for his racy theology, 'Lot's wife was a pillar of salt by day and a ball of fire by night.' But it is not Lot & his hot lot which I have been wondering about. I ponder, rather, Noah's Flood, the fellow who took on board & didn't get off until he grounded on the top of Mt Ararat a very menagerie, two of every kind of animal. It must have been no laughing matter, all those animal mates. There is no mention of cages or for provisioning arrangements. Did the apes have to flee the lions of Judah? One would think that unless there were several Arks there must have been lots of Bedlam, nay Cannibalism. But 'tis Noah's bloody Fludde which most concerns me, whereby for forty days & nights the motley crew was bobbing round crying, 'Blimey Earth! Will ye no come back again?' Then a saucy parrot cried, 'Land ahoy! Looks like Ararat to me!' At that sound of -rat, the two cats much in need of rat started scuttling round the ship. The actual rats had long since gone the way of all flesh, gobbled up by the two hungry hippopotami who longed for the Nile as did the crocodile, never fear. But I ask whence & where the story of the Flood. We have of course had it and I definitely don't recommend a stately home on the Thames, but it is now receding and by the waters of Thames as of Babylon we sit down and weep.

But there are stories of Floods, a Flood in Babylon and in Bangladesh and on the Indus I'm told. Was the Biblical Flood recounted on the basis of experience of Floods? Deucalion, you recall, got into Greek mythology. Who was copying whom? There is a hint in 'Genesis' of a dinkum flood. If you and I were making up a story of a Flood, we would fill up our world with endless rain. (Cp. the song at the end of 'Twelfth Night' – "for the rain it raineth every day".) But we would not think of rainwater bubbling up from under the ground. We now know that that is what happens with a dinkum flood. Ask the johnnies who chose to live on the Somerset levels. In 'Genesis' the flood is turned on both in the form of rain and in the underground, which makes me think the Noah story is based on dinkum flood experience. Admittedly the birds sent out to see signs of land saw only the highest, Ararat, but, I ask you, did the birds, only two in number remember, have enough mountaineering experience to chirp, "'Tis plainly Ararat'? 'No, it ain't Pelion on Ossa.' The birds are a difficulty, I concede, but by & large, as they say in yachting circles, Noah's Flood is based on experience.

I concede that your present condition hardly permits you to write at length on this knotty problem, but thank you for that letter dictated to Nell (who also included a card with one of those well-robed girls on the Acropolis, for which I beg you to thank her).

As I told you I am sure, I am now the slowest of slow-coaches (whence comes that word?), but I have finished the selection of letters of your fellow Carthusian. He was the opposite of a slow-coach. His reading was astounding. At one point he says, 'I have not only read or re-read almost all Burckhardt but also most of Nietzsche and much of Ranke, and so I have had no time for more urgent but less interesting subjects...' He was a man of very great powers indeed.

. . . We are all getting steamed up about the question of Scottish Independence. In this week's copy of The Spectator there is a bit by Hugo Rifkind (presumably a son of Malcolm) in which he discusses the silence of prosperous Scots who don't own castles but are 'comfortable'. I guess from conversations I have had that they will nearly all vote 'No'. It's hardly my business but I earnestly hope the result is a firm No. I like Scots and admire them very often and I am a sort of Scot myself. I can only hope.

Satis, nay, more than satis. I think of you often. I wish I could cure you!

Yours, George

12 March 2014

Dear Gorgo,

. . . A story is told in, I think, JL Carr's life (or was it Byron Rogers'? As usual I am too lazy to get the book off my bookshelf in our Guest Room) of the Welsh poet RS Thomas, that austere man. There was only one 'joke' in the book. It concerned an English woman seeking a hotel room in France. Before clinching the booking, she insisted on inspecting the room & having done so she returned to the booking desk and said, 'Mais il n'y a pas un matelot sur le lit. En Angleterre on a toujours un matelot.' The proprietor, overhearing this, said, 'C'est un peuple vraiment maritime.'

I fear I must have told you this before. In my defence I say that one has only a limited stock of stories and one has an unlimited capacity to forget one has told a story before. One can only hope that one has not told it only five minutes earlier.

We are nearing the Centenary of the outbreak of the (so-called by my generation) Great War, which changed the lives of us all. One continues to wonder whether it could have been avoided. Last week there was a dramatised account of the outbreak, on BBC, under the title '37 Days'. I wasn't much taken with the 'drama' but I do wonder whether if we had played our hand differently the Horror could have been avoided. I am really very ignorant of that period but I believe that those are right who argue that the War might have been postponed but could not have been avoided, the view, I believe, of Max Hastings and of Michael Howard (do you remember him at the House?). I watched on TV not only Max Hastings but also Niall Ferguson who takes a rather AJ Taylorish view of it all. I thought Ferguson second-rate & cheap. What stirs it all up is Ukraine. I *fear* that Putin's aim is to re-establish the Soviet Empire. Will he pass from the Ukraine to the Baltic States? The Soviet Union settled great numbers of Russians in Estonia, Latvia & Lithuania. If the formula applied in the Crimea is successful, he'll be ready perhaps to send the Russian Army into each of these in turn, call a referendum & take over, a return to the expansion practised by Hitler. I will, I hope, be dead but it's a poor legacy for one's children. Will there be WWIII at some point? And of course the art of settling by settlements is just what Israel has practised. A war is the only way to settle matters, for the settlements of Russians & of Americans on Palestinian lands is irreversible. I can only shudder.

The Conservatives will not win the Election, certainly not with a clear majority and so there won't be a Referendum on our membership of the EU. The Lib-Dems prevented a reform of the electoral boundaries which might have made a Conservative majority possible. And UKIP will seal it. So we shall be caught in the EU for ever. Simon is supporting

UKIP, his revenge on Conservative politicians whom he holds responsible for loading his life with absurd regulations. So on we go. I just wouldn't know how to vote in such a Referendum anyhow. What a mess! The Recession seems to be passing but the Deficit remains! And I remain full of contempt for the Labour Party and also for the Lib-Dems, but, sez you, I should be contemptuous for the Conservatives also, but I am not, for I am not an Egalitarian and the Conservatives alone do not hold riches to be sinful. But I have to accept that the vast sums bankers & footballers & the like receive may breed social unrest. So everything, myself included, is a Bloody Mess.

I wish I could hear you say what you think about all this, but I could not hear you even if I understood you. I apologise for writing such a messy letter and I will try to do better next time.

Love & best wishes, but what I wish for I am unclear about!

Your muddled old pal, George

23 March 2014

Dear Gorgo,

. . . My mother who was born in 1880 would speak of 'The Drink' as the peculiar curse of many a Victorian family. The Drink was cheap and did for her father and for the happiness of 'Mama'. It was 'the curse'. (Remember Bodger's Whisky at the start of Bernard Shaw's 'Major Barbara'.) Cancer, 'the Dread Disease', came by horrid chance, but the Drink was caused by Evil. So far I have kept my head above water (remember the etymology of Whisky and, I believe, Vodka) but the price of Sobriety is Eternal Abstinence, which doesn't make the heart grow fonder. *Ora pro nobis* when the sinful temptation comes on us.

I find that, with age, abstemiousness comes upon me more & more, probably a sign of the end being at hand. I certainly drink less and I think more of eating less. I take a virtuous little stroll down to the shops in Summertown and I try to walk faster. At least I am not in the condition of that man who walking along Canterbury Rd had his trousers slip to the ground, but I will have to lose a good deal of weight if I am to rival him. I whistle that song of Harry Lauder's, 'Oh the button came off my pants & I didn't know what to do to keep them up.'

But perhaps you are too young to be much informed about that brave Scot. Do you know 'Stop y'tickling, Jock'? When he was touring New Zealand before the First World War, he was called on to open a charitable appeal, which he did ending up with, 'And I'll open things up by contributing Five Pounds to get things going,' and the father of a friend of mine called out, 'And I'll give the same in proportion to my salary.' Seeing that he was but an impecunious law clerk, he was proffering about sixpence.

Mention of Scots arouse thoughts of the Referendum. People here are seemingly not agitated about what may happen & the Scots, or a good number of them, are preparing to vote with their hearts & not their heads. However if Independence wins the mood will change. A 'Yes' Vote will certainly damage the United Kingdom and when this is realised I guess that the mood will change. The Nationalists treat any critical comment of their schemes as English bullying, and there will be no mood of let's be generous to the Scots. I can never forget that review in the TLS written by Neil McCormick, once Law Fellow at Balliol, then Professor in Edinburgh, which concluded thus: 'If I had to choose between being governed from Brussels or from Westminster, I would much prefer Brussels.' If necessary, so be it, and let the mouse taste pitch! But I still hope that the Nationalists will not win.

Your nervous old pal, George

9 April 2014

Dear Gorgo,

Nowadays I am a very idle fellow, and I get very little done. It's partly that what little cooking I do seems to take a great deal of time and when I have done I feel very sleepy. Then there's the shopping. As far as I can, I go every day principally as a means of getting exercise. It takes me the best part of an hour. Heavy shopping, I mean getting weighty bottles of milk, and keeping me supplied with fruit & yoghurt & the like, is all done by my priceless Judy and the bits I buy are trifles, but it all gives me exercise and coupled with a fair number of journeys down the stairs and up again it keeps me going. However time is time & when I have had my post-prandial nap, all in all most of the day is done. Letters pile up & demand my attention which is slowly given, and of course there is all the fussation of emails & the computer generally. So, I prithee, do not think I have forgotten you. I certainly have not.

I think in an earlier letter I talked about the Oxford institution of the Memorial Service. There was another on Saturday, for our ex-Master John Albery. (Did you know his father, Michael Albery, in Lincoln's Inn? I think he was due shortly to assume office as Secretary (or whatever the title of Bencher chosen to preside was) when he died in a car-crash in Wales. (He was a famously reckless driver.)) Alas, I can't remember how much I have told you about him. He started as a Junior Research Fellow in 1962, became a full Fellow in 1963, went off to Imperial College in 1978, & returned as Master in 1989 and left ignominiously in 1997. He was a Chemist of distinction – FRS – and a man of uncommon energy. In particular, he was Admissions Tutor for the last decade of his Fellowship, to which office he applied very great zeal & efficiency and made Univ one of the leading colleges, academically speaking, in Oxford and not just that; he was, unlike Lot's wife (in the Willy Douglas-Home story), never 'a pillar of salt by day and a ball of fire by night'; he was a ball of fire all the time, being half the production of the annual College Revue (those were the days, egad), etc. etc. But, alas, the Bottle took command. So he had to go, and, save for a Memorial Service for a Chemistry colleague, he did not come again until, return of the Prodigal Son, he had a seventy-fifth birthday party on 5 April 2011 when the Hall was full of Chemistry colleagues and others like myself. It was for him a happy evening, & a happy evening for us all, a reconciliation.

In thinking of him, one goes up & down in one's opinion. I used to think he had all the qualities necessary for the Mastership, save for tact, good sense, 'donnish' (as opposed to 'rumbustuous') wit, modesty, but such was his miserable condition for the last two or three years I came much to admire his spirit of endurance. He had cancer of the prostate which spread to his back. It was checked by radiotherapy but this left him paralysed from the waist down. I used to ring him up and came much to admire his spirited refusal to yield. I don't think I could perform like that. There was at his Memorial Service last Saturday an Address by my colleague Leslie Mitchell, which was really first-class, a wonderful sample of the genre. (It may not divert you, but I will send a copy of the Address & one of your women may be kind enough to read it to you. Of course you have to be Univ to comprehend fully but I trust you will see what I mean.)

Minor points to note. John was a resolute atheist. I used to debate within myself whether the atheism came from the Ego or the Ego was a by-product of the Atheism. But the former Chaplain coped. He did not mention Jesus! That was tact. Also, you could see what is happening at and to one Oxford College. Of course, many fellows have begun their fellowships after John 'retired', but there were, are plenty who had been fellows in the 90s. Very few of them attended! *Sinistre fin d'un collège.*

Do you recall the last words of that film, *Some like it hot?* Jack Lemmon (I think), dressed & made up like a woman, was dancing with Joe E Brown (a vagrant millionaire looking for a mate); JL said, 'But I'm a guy,' to which Joe E Brown replied cheerfully, 'No one's perfect' – end of film. Likewise with Masters of Oxford colleges. They *all* have their defects as well as their merits. I have been a Fellow under eight different Masters and experience has taught me that what all Masters need in their middle term is loyalty. They don't necessarily get it and, although when John A. was Master I was no longer on the Governing Body and so cannot exactly say, I wonder whether Albery had the loyalty of certain persons. On the occasion of his seventy-fifth birthday a collection of personal reminiscences was made & at the conclusion of mine I wrote as Kipling wrote of Gunga Din, 'Though I've belted & I've flayed you, / By the living God that made you, / You're a better man than I am.' John Albery, RIP.

My love to you both, to you all, George

4 May 2014

Let your motto be, O Cork, 'Get yourself a new pen.' Sorry Irene.

Dear Gorgo,

No, I have not forgotten you. If you saw my diary you would understand my seeming silence. I do a lot of entertaining both here and in College and people come and go, though not necessarily 'talking of Michelangelo'. Sometime 'twill be Lights Out or, more likely, Lights Dimmed. One becomes ever slower & more confused. E.g. I keep an Account Book, but there are huge discrepancies between my totals and my Bank Statements. Fortunately there is more in my Bank than my Account Book. Confused & stupid!

I am running out of close friends. There is one surviving aged ninety-eight. My oldest school friend has just gone. He was four months older than I. News of his death crossed in the mail with a letter from me. Now, frankly, comes yourself! I consider Fate has played you a scurvy trick, but one can't arrange one's ending. The friend who has just died went to bed feeling rather tired & didn't wake up, lucky bug. Pat got out nice & quickly. I dare not hope.

I have finished the 500-page book about the food supply of countries involved in World War II. ['The Taste of War: World War Two and the Battle for Food' by Lizzie Collingham.] (I mention the '500 page' because I have become very slow in reading. It's all right in the morning but in the evening my vision goes awry. The lines dance about & I quickly nod off & only wake up when it's time to go to bed.) The little war that I had was against the Japanese. One thought of them as the Devil Incarnate. It is now clear that they were rather Hungry Devils. They were dumped on some island without any food supplies and without any special kitchen staff! They had to scavenge & cook for themselves. There was one night of my life when a small party of Japs got into our battalion and I lay all night with my pistol cocked and held over my chest, ready to cope with any stray Jap who came upon my foxhole. I was looking up at the sky, though we were in the jungle, in the hopes of seeing him first. I expect the truth is that he was just looking for grub! We were recipients of tins of rations, edible if not palatable. But the Japs just had to cook some rice for themselves. The trees on Bougainville had their roots in large flanges. The Japes covered over the space between two flanges with a roof of sticks & palm leaves etc, leaving a space beside the trunk of the tree for the smoke to get out, and then they lit a fire on which they cooked. Since they didn't want to betray their position with smoke, they had to wait until after dark. I feel sorry for them in retrospect! But only in retrospect.

. . . Anyhow, this book has been quite an eye-opener. The Ukraine first had their Russian masters taking their food, then when the Germans took over, to the Ukrainians' initial relief, having driven the Russians back, the Germans proceeded not only to take their food but also to murder them to reduce the number of mouths they had to fill, though 'fill' is hardly the word! Now they are getting the Russians back, providentially settled by Joseph Stalin! One fears for the Baltic States, where the Russian settlers were very numerous, 22% in Estonia, 50% in Latvia. No matter! Adolf Putin asserts that he is not stirring it all up. No matter, for the art of hacking is well advanced & the Ukrainians can get the message from Moscow to their 'friends' on the ground.

I'm darned if I can remember what I've said previously. I had the merciful assistance of our new Development Officer in curing my computer of paralysis the weekend before last. I like him very much but now I greatly admire him for his patience & his skill. He had to begin by ringing some number which was of course answered by someone in Bombay; I could never myself have endured his un-English English, but my man was quite calm & polite for a long call, quite unflappable. This put me to think of Unflappable Mac. Macmillan went to a dinner and the doorman said, 'I hope you won't mind me telling you, Sir, but you have omitted to wear your black tie.' Macmillan replied, 'Oh well, they all know I've got one.' Which comforts me as I dress for dinner each Sunday. I know that some time I will be unable to tie my bow-tie. I shall say to the Butler, 'Oh well, they all know I had one.'

Dearest wishes, George

26 May 2014

Dear Gorgo,

Did you ever encounter Lady Trumpington? I can't think how when & where you might have done so. I would like to have done so anyhow. I read recently the Memoir she has written (with the assistance of Ivor & Jill Crewe's daughter Deborah) ['Coming Up Trumps'] & I much enjoyed it. Her husband who had been a don at Eton & became the Headmaster of The Leys School, Cambridge, *postquam nihil*, but she entered political life, first as a member of the City Council in Cambridge, then into the Lords where with ample good sense she seems to have made a useful contribution. (Which prompts me to say that I think you would have made a similar contribution; you are not, I think, passionately political but you are fair-minded and would have done the necessary prep., but by the time John Major was inviting nominations you were, I fancy, too old.) The book contains very engaging snippets.

E.g. Mitterand is reported to have said that Margaret Thatcher had the eyes of Caligula & the lips of Marilyn Monroe – though the Caligula part is just fancy. I don't suppose one would be so silly as to look at the maniac. There is also a bit where Churchill says to Hinchingbrooke who was anti-EU [that] if he continued to oppose the European policy of the Government, he wouldn't get anywhere in the Party. Shocking to me. I don't really believe in Referenda. MPs are elected to *represent* their constituents not to report what most of them want. So if MPs are unable to say exactly what they think, Government becomes the business of a small oligarchy. 'Twas thus under Gordon Brown & indeed every political leader; I think I heard Edward Heath saying that opponents 'must be whipped into line'. (Of course he has got his go-downance this morning, with the success of UKIP; one may be wiser than the masses most of the time, but sooner or later they'll get you.) Anyhow I wish your eyes would allow you to read it for yourself.

I have also read Robert Harris' 'A Gentleman and a Spy', which is, I expect, to be described as a historical novel. It concerns the Dreyfus case, which you may well know about. 'Tis a shocking tale. Not only was Dreyfus condemned and sent to Devils' Island principally because he was a Jew, but also, & here is the really shocking bit, when it was plain to all the French Guards involved that Dreyfus was innocent, they tried to keep him suffering because they didn't want the loss of face that the truth would involve. Justice for a Jew was not to be preferred to the reputation of a mere Jew. I had a vague notion about the trial but I had no idea of the shamefulness of the French Army. Thank Heaven for Émile Zola! His 'J'accuse' named all the villains & he was prepared to suffer for standing up for the truth. I was shocked by the depth of French Anti-Semitism. I read a small book entitled 'Sarah's Key'(I think) ['Sarah's Key: from Paris to Auschwitz, one girl's journey to find her brother' by Tatiana de Rosnay] about the rounding-up of Jews living in Paris in 1942 & their despatch to Auschwitz; I expect the Germans would have done it themselves if necessary but that is no excuse for the French police; they did not need to carry out their sinister task with such zeal. It is a shameful episode in French history.

Sarah has had five days at Tivoli, with her brother Tim & his wife Maggie, and it seems to have been a very happy interlude. They went out by bus to Hadrian's Villa. Have you ever been there? 'Tis spacious! I had thought they might have fitted in a trip to Praeneste (Palestrina) which Pat & I visited in 2005 (but not on the same day as our visit to Tivoli). O golly how I would love to see it all again. Wouldn't you?

For the rest, I struggle on, but this is a miserable thing to say to a man confined by disease. I do, however, think of you a great deal.

Love & best wishes, from your aged pal, George.

31 May 2014

Dear Gorgo,

Last night I took Tim & Maggie to dine in Christ Church. I fear you have never shared my great love & admiration for the House. The root of it is, I think, the way everything, large & small, is done with style. 'Style abides.'

First, we went to Evensong in the Cathedral & I found it all deeply moving. Indeed I was in tears for much of the service (which I hope Tim & Maggie did not notice). In a few days it will be a full sixty-eight years since I first entered the Cathedral, which in itself excited memories, but we were seated in the Stalls of the Choir (I think that is the right term) where Students used to sit and perchance I was seated in the seat I occupied as Pro-Proctor in 1959 at the Memorial Service for Lord Cherwell (on whose staircase I had rooms in 1946-7) and beside me was the space left free for a distinguished visitor. He entered the Cathedral, everyone stood, & he was escorted to that very stall, and so I came perchance very close to Winston Churchill, the nearest to greatness I have ever got, and it triggered memories of my first year in the House and the past flowed before and from my eyes. The Cathedral Choir was having their half-term break but the so-called Cathedral Singers, assisted by the BNC choir, sang wondrously well, to my ignorant ears. You must remember that I had sung in my boyhood parish Choir and any Church music touches me deeply. As a Voluntary we had 'Jesu, joy of Man's desiring', J.S. Bach indeed, who always greatly uplifts me. Then there were the Psalms & the Chants, all to me movingly familiar. I was in quite an emotional state by the end of the Service. There was a Collection Plate into which I slipped a note, for if ever Christ Church asks me for money I will give what I can for I am deeply beholden to the place. Indeed it is a satisfaction to see the glass doors of the Cathedral, through which passers-by can see what is going on inside, and I had given some years before a (for me) ample gift. But in all this you are an outsider, are you not?

The Dinner. I had requested that I (and my appendages) should be got up those spiralling stone stairs, perilous even for young men. So the Assistant Butler got us up them at leisure and we stood at High Table looking down on the assembled undergraduates in the Hall, hardly half as many as in our times but still ample enough, and I thought on the scene in 1946 when the King & Queen dined. We were all in sub-fusc, standing facing inwards as the Royal Party moved up the Hall, followed by the Cathedral Choir, surplices cast aside & in scarlet cassocks, singing madrigals. Then, as last night, a scholar read the Grace, *Nos miseri homines et egeni*, ['We wretched and needy people'] and as ever I thought, 'Not all that *egeni*, egad.' Then dinner, & a lovely dinner it was with very decent wine. To me the blessed House! 'Style abides.'

Sunday morning. Irene is here, sleeping as I write. My days are rigid. She wants to take me out to lunch but I mean to give her one of my picnicky little lunches, then pack her off, then have my post-prandial nap, which lasts anything from an hour to an hour & a half. I wake early & can't get off to sleep again. Hence the length of my post-prandial. I began the custom when I was 18, just having left school, and it was strengthened by my service in the Solomons. So I will decline her blandishments.

I strive to keep on doing things for myself, one of which is cooking little meals. For the rule is universal; use it or lose it. My Judy, who is presently having a holiday on Tenerife, pampers me and would do so even more, if I did not resist. I must collapse some time & perhaps soon. (I've got a possibly cancerous growth on my forehead.) But I will, as long as I can, "strive, to seek, to find, and not to yield". Alfred Tennyson, I think. *Eheu fugaces.*

My dearest wishes, George

16 June 2014

Dear Gorgo,

I went up to London, I proudly announce, last Monday evening to Peter Gibson's eightieth Birthday Dinner in the Old Hall, Lincoln's

Inn. 'Twas a very happy occasion and a lovely dinner (incl. lovely wines) Peter was a pupil in the latter 50s (and so were a number of Worcester men who were present). There was also a Univ man, Nigel Miller, who was one of the first lot I invited to my Dining Club, in Hilary Term 1955; he and Peter had shared lodgings when they first went down. I didn't meet Nigel's wife and when I learnt that she was, is Honor, the daughter of Henry Brooke, the Conservative Home Secretary of the early 60s, I regretted not meeting her. For, I trow my mind does not wander, she had two brothers at least, one a Judge, one the Minister for Northern Ireland and one of these two made me momentarily memorable. In the interval at lunch in a Test Match, he was being asked about cricket at Oxford in his Balliol days. He replied that what he most remembered was 'a New Zealand Rhodes Scholar called Cawkwell, hitting a ball from the Balliol Ground into Jowett Walk, a hefty six indeed'. Pat & I encountered him on the TGV Platform in Lille some time in the Twentieth Century. There's fame for you, fame which faded right quickly; the only person I know who heard & mentioned it was Christopher Pelling. But that is enough. He is now Regius Professor of Greek, hence Student of Christ Church. *Non omnis moriar!* I mention this only out of sheer conceit.)

17 June   My plan had been to take the train to Paddington, tube to Holborn, & then walk to Lincoln's Inn, & get a car to take me home. Peter was uneasy about this & got Francis Reynolds, retired Law Fellow of Worcester, & his wife Susan a notable violinist, to shepherd me. Which they did most handsomely and I have to admit that my initial plan might have been too much. I am much beholden to them. London in the evening is a very hustling place you know right well & I won't again attempt it, not without escort. We rode back to Oxford in the Mercedes they had hired & I slept most of the way.

   Do you ever reflect on what a lot you don't endure by not caring a toot about cricket? You might have been biting your nails during the last day of the Sri Lanka Test at Lord's. Tim & Maggie & Sarah were there last Friday & saw England in good form but the last day, yesterday, was as tense as we cricket devotees know. The strain on the players bodies must be very great, especially on the fast bowlers who bowl with might and main for up to twenty-five overs a day & then prepare themselves for the next crucifixion a few days later. I was a pretty feeble performer but, told that I was to continue bowling, I used to think, 'It will probably do for me.' It didn't & mayhap it contributed to living longer than any ancestor ever has.

But nemesis strikes. I have had a 'growth' cut off my brow. I went to the really wonderful man who attended to me some years ago. BUPA now have a new system & won't pay for me being treated by such a star. The whole thing is costing up to £1000 and I won't be able to repeat it! He tells me that it was a 'low cancer' and he hopes he has removed it. We shall see about that, but he is so good that it must be money well spent. I do feel my aged frame is cracking up. I hope to go up to bed one night & never wake up, an end much to be preferred to months of cancer. So I try to be cheerful as I consider my finances. At any rate, I find I give far too much to charitable causes and am tightening my charitable belt. (Query. Who does your income tax return when you are afflicted as you are? I may need the comfort of your example!)

Love, George

1 July 2014

Dear Gorgo,

Did you in those happy days when you could read come across a book by Anne Fadiman, 'Ex Libris', a collection of beguiling pieces about books and reading? For instance, there is a wonderful bit about WE Gladstone & his booklet entitled 'On Books & the Housing of Them'. (I cannot resist quoting a bit which describes him as a 'thorn in the side of Benjamin Disraeli' who when asked to define the difference between a misfortune and a calamity, replied, 'If Mr Gladstone were to fall into the Thames, it would be a misfortune. But if someone dragged him out again, it would be a calamity.' Disraeli said of him as a parliamentary orator, 'He is inebriated with the exuberance of his own verbosity.') I hope one of your *Vorlesere* (?) will read you bits, e.g. the piece on 'Sonnets'. Of course, Fadiman has read everything & you end up with an inferiority complex.

I write these lines as I await an Old Member who, after my time, read History Ancient & Modern. She was clever & is now a university lecturer. I met her via the Communicants' Breakfast, a College institution, which I used to attend as did the Master when Robin Butler was in power, a warm, pally, & chatty occasion. (When Robin retired, there was such a swingeing increase of price that the Breakfast collapsed.) Anyhow, this Old Member is a delightful person and it raises the old question, 'Do men shy away from clever women?' As far as I know, there is no man in her life and I fear it is just another instance. Should one bring up one's daughters to disguise their cleverness? Very shaming, of course, to male-kind, but we *are* weak, are we not? One needs mothering. That is what Judy has brought *me*. She is my comfort and my strength, as of course was Pat on whom I utterly depended and indeed depend.

'The tumult and the shouting dies / The captains & the kings depart' (to quote my favourite hymn). Term is over & the undergradu-ates are all gone away. I had the last, as it were, to coffee last Sunday, an Italian from Monza (north (?) of Milan). She is much devoted to rowing! When I retired from my Tutorial Fellowship, I did not care to give a piece of silver to the Common Room but gave £1,000 (to which Sarah made an addition of two or three hundred) to establish a prize for the Classics undergraduate 'who, while maintaining a good standard of study, contributed most to the life of the College'. I required that there be no eleemosynary factor; if the richest man in the world best met the conditions, he was to get it (though I privately expected such a man to give to the College). My notion was that there are prizes for the cleverest this or that, but in my time we badly need to bring out the qualities of public service. As a result, there has been a succession of admirable young men & women, who have contributed in a widely varying way. When Pat was alive, we used to have the winner to supper, but now all I do is invite the winner for a drink so that I may know the beneficiary. If there is a woman chosen, I invite her to bring anyone she likes for young women might feel themselves 'vulnerable'. They are not. I am nona-genarian & impotent & too much in the shadow of my upbringing to attempt to play the Rolf Harris (poor fellow) but the young women are not to know it. It has all contributed to my happiness. As I say, 'Anything you can do for the young men & women is infinitely worth-while.'

Another boring epistle.

Love, George

16 July 2014

Dear Gorgo,

I am becoming a very enfeebled correspondent. This envelope has been sitting on my desk, awaiting an enclosure, for a good ten days, but I seem to be getting slower & slower. Did I tell you that I have had a 'growth' cut off, or out, of my head? I'm glad I did, for it was found on examination (biopsy I think that is termed) to have a minor cancer therein. I hope it will be 'purified' now; at least the dermatologist said he hoped he had 'got it' and he is rather a star. But the minor operation of June 6th has demanded two visits a week to Park End Street, down near the station, and owing to roadworks (as usual) I could only reach the clinic by walking down from Balliol. By the time the wound was dressed the excursion had eaten up two hours. That phase is happily past and for my two visits a week to the nurse I need go no further than over the Banbury Road, but even those excursions involve quite a bit of waiting. I am hoping that the job can be declared finished in a couple of weeks' time but we oldies are slow indeed. I have not forgotten you. I do of course have a full social life, which is a blessing but all these visits do take time.

Did you ever read George Eliot's 'Scenes of Clerical Life'? It is a trio of what are now termed 'novellas'. I began it a year ago, but became distracted. Now I have turned to it again and have read two of the stories. She is a witty writer indeed and she gives me a most enlivening picture of nineteenth-century rural life, of social distinctions in general and of the position of the Anglican clergy in particular. Those who were not provided for as younger sons of comfortable families could be poor as church-mice indeed. Have I told you about the 'relative' of Pat (though not really so), Elizabeth Burchfield née Knight? She is a direct descendant of Jane Austen's brother Edward. The Austen family was very poorly off, her father being a clergymen, and, as the habit was, this late brother was adopted by a prosperous cousin & so his name became Edward Knight. (I have no idea how that lot of Knights got to New Zealand, though I'm sure not via Botany Bay!) It may just be fancy on my part, but I always think that Elizabeth writes not unworthily of *the* Austen. David Miers [a former pupil] has a cottage in Steventon, where the Knights lived in some amplitude, & I took Elizabeth to see the

Church etc. The Austens' hard-up-ness was not untypical of the late eighteenth century. Compare the clergy in Trollope. There is no trace or hint of unbelief in that society. All decent people believed and a living was cheerfully conferred (& accepted) on a younger son. Jane Austen doesn't discuss such matters; there was nothing to discuss, though there were theological differences to be discerned. There were, however, cracks in the edifice. 'Scenes etc'. was published first in Blackwood's in 1857, not long before 'Middlemarch' in 1871. She had joined Lewes 'in a union without legal form' in 1854 or so and the 50s & 60s were a challenging time; Darwin's 'Origin of Species' in 1859 was a crisis (Samuel Butler, born 1835, returned to England in 1864 & was the fruit thereof). 'Tis ages since I read 'Middlemarch' but I have the impression that she had by then high morals & low religion. (I'm glad I am not living through it; I fear I would certainly have been on the wrong side of the main arguments, probably a Puseyite. (Oh God, how one has to deplore oneself.))

The nineteenth century is a fascinating period. Did you see that play of Stoppard about AE Housman, the title of which I cannot recall? The something of love, I think ['The Invention of Love'] . . . A good range of worthies of the latter half of the nineteenth century appear, Jowett, Pater, Stead, Bernard Shaw etc. There is one bit I vaguely recall of which I presume to remind you. Shaw (I think) said in response to a long wailing by AEH of all that he had lacked, 'But you had friends?' 'Colleagues,' AEH replied! I'm glad to say that there are some of my colleagues of whom I would not have had to say that in that tone of voice.

Which brings me to local business. The Master is in the Alps, in the Chalet famous as founded by 'Sligger' Urquhart (Univ u'grads go there each year on a reading party – perhaps less of the former & too much of the latter!) The Master has earned great repute by acting as cook for the week he is there. (Can you imagine Goodhart, or Maude, or Goodman etc. doing that?) He had time before he set off for no more than a verbal invitation to a lunch to celebrate my 95th birthday. You & Irene came to our Diamond Wedding in 2005 I think & probably to the others, my 90th [in fact 80th] in 1999 (though that was confused by Pat's motor accident), perhaps the launch of my book of essays, post-mortem of Pat. Pretty decent of the College I think. My longevity is becoming a financial liability. Still, I comfort myself with remembering that I've left the College some money in my will. Only £20k. If I had given it to Simon it might now be 20 million. Sorry for this boring epistle.

Love, George

9 August 2014

Dear Gorgo,

I fear I must have quoted to you before (for with my age repetition is inevitable) the end of Hardy's 'Woodlanders' [see letter of 11 July 2013]. Similarly, though you are not dead, similarly I will not, do not forget you, though I fear you must think I do. My days just tick away, and I sleep as they tick. My memory is much declined. I have, quite simply, largely forgotten all the languages I knew, and I forget names; they have fallen off like leaves in autumn; I scratch around with my boots & occasionally find the lost leaf but in general I have, as they say, 'lost it'. Everything takes so long too. I prepare meals, but that is very time-taking. I shop. I go into College once or twice a week for society – not for food, which has become quite distasteful to me, no one really caring for it and as an Emeritus Fellow I just have to keep quiet and endure. Above all, I snooze. My first snooze is at about 9.30 a.m. I play with my computer, incompetently, I may say. My lunch is plain and my post-prandial nap is for about an hour to an hour & a half. I entertain, in a not very entertaining mode. So it goes on, & then, when I am about to write to my old pal Engle, all is suspended for the Test Matches. How vapid, how idle! But I am on the whole a happy enough chappie. However I apologise for this long silence.

I continue to be in a confused state of mind over the EU. My one time pupil David Edward is a keen advocate of that organisation. He is now playing an important part in the Scottish discussions. His line seems to be that Salmond is wrong to assume that it will be all plain sailing for the SNP. Now he has written for a group called Academics Together, showing that the SNP Government's policy for after a successful vote on Sept. 18th, concerning access to Scottish Universities, is badly flawed. It is, to my ignorant self, a powerful piece. Indeed the more the debate goes on the more Salmond flounders. The public debate between Salmond & Alistair Darling did not turn out as I and the SNP had presumed it would. The general consensus is that Darling won. I begin to hope for a 'NO' victory. (People like to portray Darling as a grey fellow, but I have always admired him. If Brown had not been breathing down his neck, he might have been a successful Chancellor. Of course there will be further debates in which he may not be as successful. But, all in all, I hope.)

All is confusion in the world at large. Putin seeks, I guess, to restore the Empire Russia lost in the late '80s, and those who would try to stop him lack the means to do so. At the least, we are back to Cold War in the steps of Adolf Hitler, & I wouldn't want to live in a Baltic State. But the real turmoil is in the Middle East, and the terrorist government in Gaza is winning the propaganda war. They won't bow down before Israeli might, cost what it may in the lives of citizens of Gaza, and the Israeli just bomb on, losing sympathy with every bomb. The result is an ugly resurgence of Anti-Semitism all round the world. The new Foreign Secretary here, Philip Hammond, is a Univ man. He came from an East London Comprehensive to do PPE. He was the top candidate for that subject for his year, and he proved himself top quality all the way through his time at Univ. There is a nice story told by Leslie Mitchell. He was shaggy-haired & seemingly well fitted to please the PPE tutors. Gareth Evans, the star of Philosophy, said to Leslie after two weeks of term had passed, with evident chagrin, 'He's joined OUCA!' (OUCA is the Oxford University Conservatives Association.) Whenever I hear Hammond speak I am very impressed. He is unflustered & clear-headed and a worthy successor to William Hague who was in his way an admirable Foreign Secretary. (Both of them did PPE, & so did Cameron & Osborne. I expect Miliband also did which rather lowers the praise worthiness of the School. But in general it is I think an excellent preparation for public life, the decline of Greats being right sad I have to confess.) Hammond will need all his wits to cope with the general crisis. Another boring letter ends. I must try harder. It is two years since you had your accursed stroke. I'm so sorry, but what good is that? George

30 August 2014

Dear Gorgo,

I set off on Tuesday (3/9) on my annual migration to East Anglia & will not make the return flight until Monday 8th. Of course I would love to be off to France, but such travel is no longer practicable and I could have as much out of a trip to Suffolk. It is a real holiday. For three days in Aldeburgh I have no bed-making, no cooking, no washing-up, no shopping; I lounge about the Wentworth Hotel obliged to do nothing other than have a stroll along the prom, prom, prom, and though the girls do not sigh or wink the other eye etc. (you know, I trust, the Man who broke the bank at Monte Carlo) I am rich in happiness.

I'm not sure that I told you about my trip to London on 17th August. I went to lunch chez Simon & Anne to meet Ronald Harwood the dramatist. That in itself was sufficient satisfaction, but it was the journey there & back which really gripped me. It was a sunny day and as I went by taxi from Paddington to Chelsea & later back I was moved by the beauty of Hyde Park as well as the sun-lit houses. I thought me of Wordsworth's sonnet, 'On Westminster Bridge' I think it is titled.

'Earth has not anything to show more fair:
Dull would he be of soul who could pass by
A sight so touching in its majesty.'

but I had the feeling that it might be my last trip to the capital, which gave it all a certain poignancy. I was tired when I got home, but like those girls described in Robert Graves' 'Goodbye to All That' who came up to a village for three weeks just behind the Front Line, and plied their trade, and then departed 'pale but proud'. Earlier in the year I had gone up to take Sarah to lunch in the Hotel at St. Pancras Station. So two trips in a year! I expect I'll try again, but may well not make it. London is a very full place in the summer as you well know and one feels quite exhausted.

I am exhausted also by the Scottish Referendum! I watched the debate on TV last Monday & was vexed that the leader of the Nationalists was allowed to keep on talking & to allow Darling no space for reply. Still, I suppose Nationalists are ever so. No one says the thing that many of us demi-Scots feel, viz. that one quite likes the mix of Scottish & non-Scottish. If anyone said that, there would be a noisy Nationalist backlash, and those who do not hate the English have to keep quiet. I shall be greatly relieved when it is, one way or the other, over. It seems to me to have stirred up quite a lot of antipathy in Scotland and here I sense people feel well if they hate us so let them go but let us not make the going easy. But, of course, it will make a very great difference to the rump of the disUnited Kingdom.

'Tis all a trifle compared to the Middle East! One had come to the conclusion that it is best to leave Arabs to Arabs. One is unequal to the complexity of Arab Society. But hideous extremists seem to be too much for the mass of Muslims to cope with. How these Muslims hate one another! If one keeps out, they will go on hating, and now it seems that decent Muslims need non-Muslim help, but America having burned its fingers in Iraq & Afghanistan can't face the task, and we have become too poor to do anything. I greatly fear. One may escape by dying, but one's descendants remain. I certainly fear the return of Labour to power, as seems likely given the effect of UKIP. Labour won't do anything.

This letter is degenerating into a general sulk. I have, however, quite a lot not to sulk about – provided my health holds. You have had two & a bit years of ill health, and it must be a hateful position. But yet one clings on. Life is rarely so awful that one wishes to be quit of it; at least I hope you have that comfort.

My love & best wishes despite all. George

23 September 2014

Dear Gorgo,

I exist you may be amazed to hear. If you could see my diary you would see the reason for my silence. 'Tis the season of the year when people come to Oxford. Gaudies happen in Univ in September. This next weekend, for instance, there is a Gaudy on the Saturday night and a lunch on the Sunday with a quite different set of Old Members. On Saturday morning a girl, nay now a woman, who came to me for tutorials from Corpus, is coming for coffee and on Sunday morning a Univ girl, now aged about 39, is coming likewise. 'Tis not that I am particularly popular, but when people come back to Oxford they like to encounter dons that they have known and since I am such a vapid dud who has nothing to do they call on me. Last Sunday I went to a 'brunch' at Rhodes House, driven there by an old pupil at Univ, where to my pleasure I encountered John Hood, formerly Vice-Chancellor, so the expedition was not unprofitable, but it all takes time!

Having mentioned John Hood who was a New Zealand Rhodes Scholar in the 70s & so is a buddie of mine, & who became CEO of a big company in New Zealand, then Vice-Chancellor of Auckland University (whence Pat and I), I must add that he had what I fancy was an unhappy time as V-C of Oxford. Vice-Chancellors, like Masters of Colleges, need loyalty from their subordinates & they often don't get it. John wanted to change the way the University is governed which raised a hubbub from people who couldn't govern a peanut stall. He tidied up the finances of the University but got nowhere on governance. His successor publicly declared that he thought the governance of the University ought to be changed in the way John H. had proposed but added that he would be leaving the matter alone. It will have to be tackled sometime. When I arrived in 1946 the University consisted of about twenty-seven colleges & a few scientific off-shoots. Now it is a vast empire and dons are not suited to imperial rule. Someone I know told me that he had been on Hebdomadal Council (the Senate of the University in our time) but he resigned because the business was too much for a busy scholar. In John's final report he remarked on the remarkable turnover of members of Council; not surprising, dons are not businessmen! Anyhow John's proposals were received as the Franks Report was in 1966, i.e. virtually rejected before it was read! Mayhap it is not just Oxford but the whole English resistance to change, damnable if admirable.

Having said that some of us are unfit to manage a peanut stall, I cannot refrain from blowing my top about referenda. I remember, when I was young, being told by a senior person, 'You have a point of view, but you don't know what you're talking about.' I don't know whether you have been concerned about the Scottish referendum. Salmond said several times that the best judge of whether Scotland should be independent was the Scottish people itself. I suppose popular vote was the only way of determining the matter, but this admiration for popular opinion is to my mind misguided. There are lots of questions which are beyond the likes of myself. E.g. the death penalty. Popular opinion about whether to hang the villain or leave him in durance vile can sway this way or that according to recent cases, but to judge the matter properly requires knowledge & experience. There are feeble characters who suppose that all argument is to be closed by reference to Democracy. As

Churchill said, it is the worst form of government except for the rest. So one rests content with popular votes, but it is absurd to think that popular votes are 'right'. They can be quite absurd. One wise man's judgment is often wiser than the many. Referenda are to be resorted to only when faith in the judgment of qualified judges has been lost. I am very uneasy about the expected referendum on Europe & the UK. I try & have a point of view but don't know what I'm talking about. The Scottish affair has been very upsetting. I'm very relieved [at the result: 55% of votes cast in favour of No to Independence] but the question has not gone away. If in a referendum on our membership of the EU the vote in favour of withdrawing is the victor, the Scottish question will explode.

These are in general very disturbing times. Being a Tory, I am a bit puzzled as to why Tories are so hated in Scotland and suspect that this hatred was worked up by the SNP as a way of exciting votes for Independence. Margaret Thatcher is blamed for everything but Scottish dislike for England preceded her rise. It is very tell-tale that, when an English team is defeated, Scots in bars explode with joy; hardly good-neighbourly reaction. But Scotland is nothing compared to this 'Islamic State', animals raping, robbing, pillaging, decapitating. I fear we will have to return to Iraq & fight on the ground. Meanwhile one can only hope for accurate bombing and fear for the violence to emerge here. But enough!

There was a rather engaging piece in the latest issue of The Week concerning the Franklin Expedition aimed at finding a North West Passage, one of the ships involved having lately been recovered, or rather uncovered. Are you a member of the Athenaeum? I read that there is a statue of Franklin before that august club. It seems that the exhausted & starving crews resorted to cannibalism, but would we not all in such circumstances? As in the famous Genner story (that fellow of Oriel on his first night, a righteous teetotalist but very fond of his food, helping himself generously to a second helping of trifle, hearing the Provost say, 'Mr Genner, it's the sherry in it that makes it so good,' & exclaiming, 'I'd rather commit adultery,' to which the Provost replied, 'Wouldn't we all Genner, wouldn't we all!') we would all eat each other in such circumstances.

Dearest wishes, George

23 October 2014

Dear Gorgo,

In the space of a few days I have passed from 'elderly' to 'aged'. Getting out of a friend's car on September 16th I somehow contorted my right leg and that misery has spread through all my leg muscles. It slowly improves, but told by the Physiotherapist to stretch myself in bed before I get up I somehow strained a ligament in my left leg & it now gives me heck. Indeed this morning I was crying out for mercy!

What is so troubling is that the College is holding a Cawkwell-fest on 31 October and 1 November and pupils & old members of the College are coming in great number, in total about 200! I *must* be there and I must make a speech and somehow suffer all the excess of urination that the years bring. I don't know how I will manage. On the Friday there is a dinner, which worries me not; by the end of the day I'm settling down. But on the Saturday there is not only a lunch at which I will have to speak, but beforehand there are two lecturettes mostly about Cawkwell, & I deem myself a most unworthy subject. They will be in the Chapel which allows access at about fifty yards distance to a loo! No man is an island but some are more continent than others and old men need to reside in Flushing Meadows. Please think kindly of me on that day.

All this arises from my turning ninety-five on St. Crispin's Day, 25 October, i.e. Saturday next. There will be a family assembly on Sunday 9th November at my house, for which I will have nothing to do save smile benignly upon my grandchildren & their families etc. That will be easy going. But the Cawkwell Fest will be a great strain. 'Tis very generous of the College but I fear that I shall be washed away by floods of emotion and of urine.

I am greatly pampered and on Saturday a couple of women & the Cawkwell Fellow (!) & her husband are coming to the house for a simple dinner. It all warns one against living on! Indeed I long to go up to bed one night & not wake up. Principally I am not keen on myself – for which Pat used to reprove me, but I am me, not she!

. . . All in all, all is not lost but one hopes for Perdition.

Love, George

Undated, 2014

Dear Gorgo,

'The tumult and the shouting dies / The captains and the kings depart.' My ninety-fifth birthday is past. That was the decade that was. It's over let it go.

The College came over very decent. I thought at first 'twould be a lunch only. But no. What if people come from overseas? We must have a dinner the night before the lunch, and if a dinner it would be more than that; people won't come for a mere meal. So it grew & stretched. On Friday 31st October there was a concert in the Chapel, including a couple of chants commissioned in honour of George Cawkwell, no other and no less, and yea 'twas all very beautiful and I did feel proud of the Coll. But it had to be broken up. So I chose two bits of GM Hopkins 'The Windhover' and 'Margaret, art thou grieving?', jolly difficult to read, but read most expertly by the Master of Music (or whatever he is called). Indeed the reading was sublime. Chapel packed full. (God, I wish I could have got half as many to my lectures!) Then drinks, with me seated on a throne; I damaged my leg getting out of a friend's car on September 26th and it all got worse & worse & I just had to stay where I was put, but dinner at 7.15 in a crowded Hall and a jolly decent dinner it was. Speeches from an old pupil and the Regius Professor of Greek in praise of Cawkwell. (As you are thinking I did not deserve it.) Home to bed. Then it all began again on the Saturday. 'Univ in 1949' (the year I became a Fellow). Then George C's contribution to Ancient History. More drinks. Then a superb lunch. Speeches from pupils (including the Lord Butler) then Corky himself. It went off alright, even though I couldn't read my notes. (Must write bigger for my hundredth!) An emotional occasion and I feared I would weep and given aged incontinence I feared I would wet myself. But neither disaster occurred, and I finally got home to peace at about 4 p.m., pampered, praised. So I try to forget I am me! Now letters of thanks, etc. I am wore out, I can tell you but in retrospect I enjoy it more & more. Univ's great merit is that it is a very very friendly place and I certainly had a lot of friendship on Saturday November 1st!

But on Sunday 9th November the family assembled at 8 Moreton Rd. Again kindness & friendship and four little great-grandchildren buzzing about *and* a great niece who bears my sister's name, Alice, the name of my father's favourite sister, and Pol Roger, and wines of high quality laid on by Simon C. They all talked away in a friendly manner & I can tell you I felt and feel uncommonly rich! That was the birthday that was.

So you can see that I have been much occupied with trifles, tremendous trifles as GK. Chesterton said. It is curious but I can endure being abused but I'm not good at putting up with praise. Partly one thinks, 'He can't mean all that,' but partly one's moral powers fail one and one is broken down by kind things said. I found that when I was Vice-Master of the College. One of my colleagues wished to eject me & I stuck it out, but when others spoke kindly I was prone to collapse. So I am relieved that the season of praises is past and I return, 'blissfully safe from joy & pain / As if a rose should shut and be a bud again'.

I am lying very low for the moment. I have my Encyclical letter to compose & despatch, which takes an age. I had thought that ninety-five would be the cut-off point, but people presume it will appear as usual. So you may yet get one, but this tedious scrawl must cease NOW.

Love, George

1 December 2014

My dear Gorgo,

Breathes there a man who loves the English winter? On behalf of all the Oldies of England I spurn & spit upon him. 'Tis the same each year, but what of snow & ice & burst pipes and confinement to quarters? Be ye grateful that within three weeks of the shortest day, though the sun sets before four o'clock, the temperature is not yet below zero. But I do mightily fear what may yet come.

The melancholy truth is that ninety-five has proved a real finale for me. I now pine suddenly to expire. I get very little pleasure out of food or wine. I simply dribble on. I have even lost my zest for the common life of the College. I do not expect ever again to mount those few steps from the High & the food is no longer to my taste. Of course I can get a taxi to Logic Lane and pass in through the little gate by the Master's Lodgings & crawl across the two quads and return home by the same route, but as the late Mrs Cawkwell was fond of saying, 'What a palaver!' Perhaps I'll feel better about it all when the weather improves.

But nonetheless the shades creep on. I have to wear a hat in my study lest the sun strike me by day. And one's circle is diminishing, not so much in numbers but in mind. A pupil of mine has a lady friend whom he brings to a little lunch we have each year & she is definitely losing her marbles. *Eheu!*

Enough of this moping and moaning. Do you recall anything of Dr William Buckland? 'A prominent theologian, he was appointed Dean of Westminster but outraged Christians by gnawing the bones of a long-dead Sicilian saint and declaring them to belong to a goat. When shown mysteriously non-drying drops of blood on a cathedral floor, he promptly dropped to his knees, licked the flagstones and claimed they were not holy relics but urine ... Taste in fact became his ultimate arbiter, when – adding "zoophagist" to his many titles – he resolved to eat his way through the animal kingdom. His hapless guests were regularly treated to menus containing crocodile, panther, scorpion, porpoise & toasted field-mice. Interestingly he considered moles & bluebottles to be "disgusting beyond belief", but when he discovered the preserved heart of Louis XIV, rescued during the French Revolution, in a casket at Nuneham Courtenay near Oxford, he promptly devoured it.'

It all goes to show that science & religion should be kept separate. Buckland was both theologian & geologist, but sometimes the two 'faiths' were in different persons. Damn it! I can't remember the names, but there was a man nurtured in faith & literal belief in the Bible, whose father was a naturalist of note. When the father was told that science was discrediting the Bible and showing that the world was much older than the Bible suggested, he responded by saying that it only seemed so, but God only made it seem so. When the reply came that it was very queer that God should give misleading information, he was very 'pained'. (I wish I could remember all the names of these people, but alas. If I remember them at midnight I will ring you instantly.) (The Geologist I think of was Charles Lyle (?) [a reference to Sir Charles Lyell, Bt, author of 'Principles of Geology', 1830-3] & the fundamentalist 'pained' by that reply was the father of Edmund Gosse (cf. 'Father & Son').) I'm sorry nonetheless for this jagged, untidy story which you may know very much better than I do.

Satis! I have decided that I won't write any more of my Encyclical letters. People profess to enjoy them but I'll have to stop sometime &

ninety-five is a good cut-off point. The addressing of envelopes etc. is a large task (and the postage quite large, £200 or so) & I am not up to it this year. People are begging me to continue but I am hardening my heart.

This pen is failing like its owner. I am very shaky. I have Varicose Eczema; my legs are swollen & I am weakening. So I beg your pardon but I must sign off. Nonetheless I send you my dearest wishes. It's a damned scurvy hand Fate has dealt you. That's all I can say.

George.

2015

14 January 2015

Dear Gorgo,

'Events, dear boy, events.' Why have I been silent so long? Events, dear boy, events. One event is a series of events occasioned by my legs, afflicted as they are by Varicose Eczema. I am now so slow about everything. Then, to crown my feeble performances, last week I tripped on a carpet in my hall. It was not serious in itself but falling I took the fall on my left fist and since my skin is now so thin it split here & there & blood, red unaristocratic blood gushed forth & I had at 10 p.m. to be rushed up to the Hospital by Judy whom I summoned to help me. Bandaged, I return home at 11.30, and since I had banged my head & the doctor declared I should not be alone in case I needed help, Judy slept in the house. I was all right but it made me drowsy & I slept, off and on, for three days.

Enough to go on with? No. My bad leg began to 'leak' & now I have an elastic stocking on top of the dressing, all very slowing up. On Friday Judy & her husband take their annual two-week break in Tenerife & I shall be alone; fearful I can tell you . . . She cares for me wonderfully well & does all sorts of things in a marvellously provident way, but my real lack of her for the next fortnight will be lack of her company. We always have coffee together when I have finished the first part of my breakfast & I hear the chit-chat about her family, which I enjoy in a simple way & she is more of a friend than a servant. You may say that I am not behaving like an Englishman. True. I am a New Zealander & we NZers all get on in a pally way . . . There was always laughter when [people were working] at our house [in Auckland]. So perhaps this is the origin of my unEnglish behaviour . . .

Love & best wishes, George

17 February 2015

Dear Gorgo,

One of the pleasures of old age, if only one could take pleasure therein, is to observe the workings of memory. I dare say I have had a more than commonly good memory. I tutored off my memory all the time with barely a note to prompt me. My mind suffers from what one might term 'slipping clutch'. I am lucky to have got this far without total collapse and I do not complain but it is frustrating. One feature is what I call the Diodorus complex. Diodorus of Sicily kept getting things the wrong way round . . . [see letter of 24 June 2013, page 182]. I noticed this sort of thing in Pat's later days. She might say 'Melleas and Pelisande' and there were various stumbles of a similar sort. (I did not correct her, & if she corrected herself I would assure her that we all make mistakes & that it did not matter, but I think she was privately afraid that she was on the road to Dementia.) But now I stumble. For instance, I have a favourite story about WH Auden which I expect I've told you many a time. It concerns his late practice of making embarrassing remarks. On one occasion he said at High Table in the House to his neighbour who happened to be one of the Canons: 'Do you pee in the wash-hand basin?' – which apparently he regularly did – and the Canon replied, 'Not if there's an open window.' The other evening, however, I told it & got in a tangle & said, 'Do you pee at an open window?' The shades of the prison house close around the ageing man with a vengeance . . .

I did the same [i.e. 'put my foot in my mouth'] at High Table in Univ when I was presiding. I told the story of Mrs Woodrow Wilson in a lull in the conversation. She said, 'When Woodrow asked me to marry him, I was so surprised I nearly fell out of bed.' Most Americans know the story well, & when I told it, the two American women who were seated on either side of me gave a weary nod. People often urge me to write an account of my Oxford life, but I never will. Either I would trot out the old familiar stories or I would make wretched errors. I have heard many stories but so has everyone here. There are pitfalls for upstarts like me!

Yea, the topic of memory is fascinating, if you can remember it. But do you remember Iris Murdoch? I ask because I *think* you once said you had read the proofs of one of her books. She herself is a fascinating topic as is her husband who died in mid-January [John Bayley]. Now there was a queer fish for you! A friend of mine once had lunch with him in St. Cat's, in the course of which admiring words were uttered about the coffee-spoons. As you remember perhaps, that college those buildings, those chairs, those spoons, yea those very coffee spoons had all been designed by the Danish architect, Aarn Jakobson(?) [*sic* – he is referring to Arne Jacobsen]. My pal having expressed admiration for the coffee-spoon he held was bidden by John Bayley to take one for himself. One can hardly credit a fellow of an Oxford college thinking that such behaviour was other than ignorant & shameful. (I am relieved to say that the guest quietly afterwards returned the tea-spoon that he had been bidden to pocket.) But Bayley was a queer fish indeed. You will recall Canon Jenkins in the House going round High Table at the end of the meal – putting away bits of toast left by the diners into the sleeve of his gown. Amiable but harmless, though if I had known about Bayley & the coffee-spoon I would not have been inattentive on the two occasions he & Iris came to my dining club, the Bentham. I remember him being warm in praise of the wine, & I hope he did not walk off with a bottle or two. But both he & Iris were odd. She had been brought up in Ireland but of solid middle-class parents & one would have expected more concern for hygiene than she was said to have displayed. I can't remember who it was, but someone having dinner there was put out to observe Iris spilling the main dish onto a cushion & deftly scraping it back into the pan! Did you read [Peter] Conradi's life of Iris? He recounted that in the course of her affair with Elias Canetti he insisted, & she obliged, on conducting copulations in a large armchair. Their house in Charlbury Road was famously filthy. Whenever I walked a visitor along that road I bade him or her say which was the Bayley/Murdoch house. They never failed. It made me think of a book of my youth, 'Freckles' by I think Stratton Porter, in which the hero just let the whole place go to pot taking delight in this 'natural scene'. (Not unlike the garden of Claude Jenkins in Tom Quad.)

Enough of these memories! Probably unreliable anyhow. Nowadays I do not feel my memories are not my dreams. Bash on regardless playing the scurvy hand you have been dealt. I may fetch up in an adjacent bed tomorrow morning.

George

24 March 2015
Dear Gorgo,

Ah woe is me! Ah lackaday! I who have always enjoyed good health have a melancholy disease, Varicose Eczema, which can be held in check but not cured by sitting long hours in a recliner-raiser chair. I have purchased one at great price and in the least bad times I sit in Pat's Study, as it was once called, but is now the Throne Room, watching TV which I have ever despised. But so much is manageable. One in five oldies of my age suffer & what one suffers is an uncomfortable swelling of the legs which one counters by raising them higher than one's pelvis. This I do & try to come to terms. But, in addition, aye here's the rub, my skin is very thin & dry & when it cracks it does not easily repair, & one has an open sore. Such is now the case with my right leg. It is not really painful but it is not comfortable and I have pretty disturbed nights. So after breakfast I repair to the Throne Room & try to recover the sleep I have lost, in which condition I find it not easy to read and writing letters to my old pal is quite impossible. I go to the nurse at the doctors' surgery to have it dressed & this takes time, for such is the pressure on those good women that I always have to wait and a visit for the trifling business takes about an hour. So, merrily we live. I find in bad periods I wish for death, which is silly and ungrateful. 'Bad periods' implies that some periods are not bad and people are very kind to me. Indeed I know no one who fares, in general, better. So I cease my moaning & turn to the joyous topic of the Election.

As you know, I am a Conservative, registered & fee-paying. I am not sure why. I give as my reason that I am anti-Egalitarian, which I certainly am, but I suspect that I am Conservative by birth. [WS] Gilbert was not merely joking when he said that 'every little boy or girl, that's ever born alive, is either a little liberal or a little Conservative'. One sniff of real poverty would no doubt give me reason to change. But, oh but, I would not consider the Greens & UKIP and the Scottish Nationalists as a natural outcome for anyone. But, whatever the roots of my Conservatism, I care very much about it all & think it crucially important that Miliband and the Band of Despair, the Nationalists egad, do not get into a position where between them the policies of the Scottish Nationalists triumph – not that I know what those policies are, but the aim of the Nationalists is to break up the Union and Miliband wants power & will do and accept anything that seems to adorn him. In short, John Major (whom I have heard talking on two occasions) is the Man for me. Anyhow *odi et amo* & I long for May 8th [the date of the election was May 7th] when for good or ill 'twill all be over.

I don't recall whether I told you that it has been declared, & I have no reason to differ, that I at a mere ninety-five years & five months am the oldest living Scottish [Rugby] International. I played v. France on 1 January 1947 and as the Bishop may have said to the actress, 'Better never than just once.' But I was interviewed by a reporter from the Scottish Telegraph & the Glasgow Herald, & there was an ample article resulting, with some untruthfulness; I was described as a 'Scholar and a Gentleman'. I cannot make much of just the second part but I do know that the first is quite wrong; scholars don't forget everything they have ever learnt, especially foreign languages. Perhaps it should have said 'an extinguished Scholar whose command of foreign languages is a thing of the past'; one should read a bit of each language every day. I have been keeping in the dark my bitter antipathy towards the Nationalist Cause, & in the worst times I transferred my allegiance to Wales; 'twas out of pity and a fear that a victory for Scotland would be turned into more Nationalist gloating. They, i.e. the Scottish Rugby Union, invited me to Murrayfield for last Saturday's match against Ireland, even proposing to fly me. When I turned that down, I was sent a pair of envoys with two Scottish Rugby shirts, i.e. two shirts, which I will give to my wardrobe. I did once have a Scottish cap & a shirt with a thistle embroidered thereon, which I fear Pat must have quietly disposed of. But you can see that I am treated as famous when I should have been given a raspberry for my poor play. Still there was a photograph with me puffing along a couple of yards behind the ball.

Let this vainglorious waffle cease. My dearest thoughts & apologies for going on about nothing much.

Your poor old Corky, George

27 April 2015

Dear Gorgo,

'I will say no word that a man might say / Whose whole life's love goes out in a day' (ACS [Swinburne], don't you know?). Not quite, but your sniffy remarks about TS Eliot really hurt. [It is not clear where those remarks were made.] As I said, we (Pat & I) are of the Eliot generation.

'Twas partly religious, of which disease I was cruelly afflicted; Pat just went along (hers not to reason why, hers but to do & sigh). Eliot was the High Churchman's Vade Mecum. (It wasn't the name, by the bye. Pat had a girlfriend who was courted by an American naval 'loutenant' called Eliot. Her mother, a Mrs Cropper, très anglaise, was not keen on a liaison with a Yank, & he protested to her, 'But, Mrs Cropper, I am an Eliot, an Eliot from Boston, an Eliot with one L & one T.' But Pat was not attracted by such charms.) Eliot was even in our time a Church Warden of a church in (I think) Rochester Row near Victoria [in fact St Stephen's in Gloucester Road], though he didn't show up when I went to a service in hopes of a sight. But I was then a High Churchman, though it gives me a pang to recall yet another folly of my past; I was under the influence of a High Church priest in Auckland. In that country, remarkably free of anti-Semitic feelings, I had no sense of Eliot being anti-Semitic. I know only bits, like 'Burbank with a Baedeker, Bleistein with a Cigar', which don't seem to add up. 'Poems 1909-1925' hardly add up to a hideous crime. In that period there was lots of 'anti-Semitism'; there were hotels on the south coast that had in their heading 'Jews not welcome'. It was the horror of the Holocaust period that really marked people 'anti-Semitic'. So I may be pardoned for not thinking Eliot a great offender or offence.

What appealed to me were those short-lined, four-lined stanzas, as in 'Mr Eliot's Sunday morning service'. I lack the space to write it out for you. So I hope you can recall it. He seems to me to have the verbal skill of Q. Horatius Flaccus. 'Tis not at all easy to write [the third and fourth stanzas]. But I am no poet. I do not know Ezra Pound, who doesn't make much sense to me. I like Alexander Pope & TS Eliot. I prithee pardon me.

A nasty development! One is used to petering out mid-conversation. That is the common experience of us oldies. Sometimes one can be recalled to the point by such of one's company that have not fallen asleep. Today, however, my letter is coming to an insignificant aposiopesis (do you remember the word?). I simply can't remember what I was going to talk about after disposing of Thomas Stearns Eliot. When I sit down to write, I have a vague ration of topics to be touched, but today, Tuesday 28 April, I have drawn a blank. I beg your pardon, there's a hiatus in my garden. There is, of course, the question of what I have written in the past. Irene holds, I am told, the originals of my letters but that's little use when I have to know whether I have discussed the sex-life of the Snails of Acapulco, for instance. She is a good woman but would, I fear, refuse to reread all my letters to search out my views on this searing topic, but of course she could if she would. Now however I have the problem of what I was going to say before I lost my grip on topics to be discussed. Truly old age is not a comfortable business.

In general, I now forget 67% of names, and, since in my heyday I did remember nearly all I tried to recall, I do feel the bite of the Unsaid and Quite Forgotten. What about you? You have been in the Supine since August 23rd 2012. 'Tis a cruel fate for one once so much 'on the ball'. Ah, that phrase stirs me up. I fancy I was going politely to swank about being the 'old [*sic* – he meant 'oldest'] surviving Scottish International'. In due course I'll try, George

[On the envelope:] O Hamlet, what a falling-off was there! I refer to these absurd, tasteless, unbeautiful First-Class Stamps. We must be nearing the point of revolution when such loathsome things are described as 'First Class'.
[The stamp shows a cartoon of three white- and red-striped candles with a smiling face in the teardrop-shaped flame of each one.]

25 May 2015

Dear Gorgo,

I salute thee, though my saluting arm is feeble. I began going to my GP's surgery to have my leg dressed on January 12th, and I have gone twice a week ever since. The nurse I deal with is wonderfully kind & solicitous but, though she conceals it, she must be right bored with me & my leg. I have begun to fear that it will go on as long as I live. I know this is nothing to compare with your long misery. So I apologise for even speaking of it.

You know Hilaire Belloc's lines on a Great Election.

'The accursed power that stands on privilege
And goes with women & champagne & bridge
Shook and democracy resumes its reign
Which goes with bridge & women & champagne.'

(At least, I think Hilaire B. wrote them.) But this Election has changed things. I took the view, as did many, when the Liberal Democrats wanted to institute Proportional Representation, that 'if it ain't broke don't fix it' & so we returned to First Past the Post. Now I regret it. The Scottish Nationalists took nearly all the Scottish seats and seriously diminished Labour and there is no one to speak for those Scots who didn't want Independence. PR would at least have ensured that one million or so of voters would have had MPs to speak up for them. (The Nationalists include a number of pretty nasty types. I saw a letter to the Spectator of which the author said that he used a nom-de-plume because he 'doesn't want a brick through his window'. The brave lad, Jim Murphy, who tried to redeem the Scottish Labour Party, was booed & jostled & unable to get himself heard, not the sort of thing the Scots I know go in for. So it's a right old pickle.) I now see the merits of the French system whereby unless one's party gains 50% of the votes there is a second poll to choose between the two leaders in the first poll. At least it would get rid of the 'sillies'. I used to think that the 'sillies' were catered for; do you remember the Monster Raving Loony Party? (In one election their manifesto promised 'free, heated, lavatory seats for all old-age pensioners'.) It provided for those who held the whole business in contempt. This time, alas, there were parties bent on distracting the voters from the serious debate; though they, UKIP, the Greens, were shut out of the Commons, I think it would have been better to let them say their say in serious debates. Anyhow it's all a b. mess.

I am a Conservative because I am anti-Egalitarian, but I do tremble a bit at Cameron's high-mindedness, which is an English fault. Intervening in Libya was a hideous fault, & I fear the consequences. The hard fact is that Putin was right about Syria, pretending there was nothing to be upset about. I think I would want our PM to be wholly guided by the Foreign Office, which may get things wrong but at least knows enough not to make obvious mistakes.

All this is tedious & trite. Politics is a hard game. Politicians take awful knocks. Some of the Lib-Dems were admirable, people like Danny Alexander. Now all lost & gone (and a mob of Scottish Nationalists are in power). People didn't like [Ed] Balls, but since ('tis said) he helped keep us out of the Euro he deserved our gratitude, but he's out. Quite merciless. And Clegg, who said he had preferred country to party, as he had, is done for. It's cruel, ain't it?

Anyhow, the Great Election is over. Now it's the Great Referendum. I struggle on despite my bloody leg.

My love & best wishes,   George

21 June 2015

[At the head of the letter:] To whomever of the family reads this to George, I heartily apologise.

Dear Gorgo,

. . . Your wonderful daughter brought a photo of you in a wheelchair. I must say you looked as I remember you! . . . [A passage follows referring to a friend 'felled by the bottle', as George surmised.] It has certainly warned me off. I used to have two whiskies a day and a couple of glasses of wine if anyone was sharing a meal but now I have only one whisky if I don't forget to have it and I drink ever less wine, which makes me "sober, steadfast & demure", such is the fear I have of excess. In College I have virtually cut alcohol out almost entirely. It is one of my comforts that I have not so far been a burden to my family. In so far as I can, I mean to keep things that way.

Undoubtedly, longer lives which lead to longer exposure to these debilitating diseases, like Parkinson's & dementia, are the curse of the age; neither can be avoided utterly when they attack. Excess of alcohol and lack of exercise play a major part but with prudence they may be fended off. I walk to Summertown most days and I go up & down stairs relentlessly & dismiss with a grimace those who advocate installation of a stairlift; if I omitted such climbing, I would shortly be unable to ascend without their aid. So I keep going in [to Summertown] as best I can. But one wonders how & when it will all end. It seems too much to hope for the Big Sleep, to go up one night & the day never to arrive.

Of course Vladimir Putin may end us in misery. He is resolved to restore the Russian Empire and that Empire's fringes don't want to return to Russian rule. War may come & we may end our days in a nuclear bomb shelter. 'Twas amazing to me that no one mentioned the possibility no matter how remote during the Election. Comparably, it is notable that of Jane Austen's books no mention is made of war with France, save for the good Captain Wentworth in 'Persuasion', Pat's favourite incidentally. Naval operations in the West Indies do get a mention, but not very seriously. What were the soldiers training for in 'Pride & Prejudice'? Just parades & balls? Is it that the English character thrusts such thoughts aside? Let us keep cool and avoid hot possibilities! Your silly old George

[added on 23 June under the heading 'Contrasts'.] Today I have been inspected by the eye specialist & he predicts five years' life! Tonight I have seen the most horrific scenes on TV of the Yemen.

13 July 2015

Dear Gorgo,

'Here we are again.' Though not, in the song's words, 'happy as can be', I begin to hope this open flesh on my right leg will be covered over by new skin and I will feel comfortable enough to sleep more soundly and so not have to be spending so long each day snoozing in my 'raiser-recliner' chair.

But the Duke of Edinburgh has been heard to use the f word, doubtless to the satisfaction of those who wish to dispose of the monarchy. (The Greens party leader said that she would like to be quit of the Queen, a wild misjudgement electorally one would think. Having said it once, she did not repeat it as far as I know. 'Twas quietly forgotten, one might say. Of course the masses are quietly 'forgetful'. In all the talk about Europe and the referendum & the claim that the Tory party was 'split right down the middle' as if the Labour party was solidly united, the Labour manifesto for the 1997 promised a referendum on membership of the EU. So the Greens' gaffe was not made much of.)

I don't give a 'f***' about the Duke's utterance. I have my own experience of swearing. When I worked during the University vacations in Auckland before the War, I was in the midst of men who 'f'-ed all the time, & I used to mimic them for fun. But there came a day in 1944 when my platoon were engaged in an exchange of fire with the Japs. We got the order to pull out, but my troops were enjoying themselves too much & continued to shoot. Whereupon I, fearing that we would be surrounded, started to swear at them and ever since oaths have come from the depth of my soul. So the army and the rough and tumble of the game I played has done for me.

Of course the Fijians whom I was leading had no sense of impropriety on my part. I can remember hearing my sergeant, when giving instruction in the machine-gun, conclude his lesson with 'bloody fucking machine gun'. He gave no offence. Have I ever been so base as to recount my Pie-shop story? A man went into a bar & said to the girl behind the counter, 'Give me a piece of that fucking pie.' She was affronted and called the manager & the customer said, 'What the fuck's the matter? I asked the fucking girl for a fucking piece of that fucking pie.' So the manager called a policeman. The customer said, 'What the fuck's the matter? I asked the fucking broad for a fucking piece of a fucking pie and she called the fucking manager.' So the policeman took him to court where he said, 'Your fucking Honour, what the fuck's the matter? I asked the fucking broad for a fucking piece of fucking pie, and she called the fucking manager & he called the fucking policeman & here I am in this fucking court.' A voice called out: 'Give him fourteen fucking days,' & the Judge said, 'Shut your fucking mouth.' Thus the meaningless word is infectious & pervasive. Many have laughed at the story – but not Pat I may say. I never heard a swear word come from her mouth. But she was brought up to be a young lady & had not been in the tough and rumble of the War. If the Duke has picked up in the Navy the odd wayward word which slips forth from the depth of his soul, he must be a man for all seasons.

Someone will have to read this to you. Let it not be Irene or Nell, I beg, for my sake, or I shall forever be Foulmouth Cawkwell. Even you have never heard utter a swear word. So I apologise to all who come into contact with this foul letter. And may their vocabulary be not so limited that they had to fill in like this. But they had better keep out of pie-shops.

My dearest wishes, George

22 July 2015

Dear Gorgo,

Did you ever encounter EF Carritt? (Author of 'Beauty' & 'The Ethics of Aristotle', friend of WH Auden etc.) He was Univ's philosopher in the 20s, 30s and 40s and he was kept on *en poste* through the War. He lived on Boars Hill to which house he repaired at weekends. During the week he lived in College. He was a man of the left as of course was his Univ colleague Cole (damn it! I've forgotten Cole's initials. JDH? [GDH] He was Douglas but I forget what else, and he had had a hand in the early days of the Labour Party & he received telegrams from such as Bernard Shaw, one of which I remember bade him to ABOLISH LOCAL GOVERNMENT. He moved to All Souls as Professor but being fond of Univ he used to come over for dinner once a week in term. One night there was discussion of a Greek word & Cole quoted a line of Aristophanes. I expressed mild surprise that he remembered it & he said, 'I haven't thought of it since I was at school!' Although he was of the left, he was a man of fastidious taste. Enough of this rambling parenthesis.) Edgar Carritt, whom I used to drive home a bit to Boars Hill, had a Communist son called Gabriel & I think it was he who featured in a Carritt story. Someone was having dinner who was the Conservative candidate for Slough or some such romantic place. When he announced this in the Common Room over dessert, Carritt said, 'That's interesting. My son is also a candidate. He's the Communist.' This uttered in a flat voice flattened the Conservative!

On one occasion sitting by Carritt at High Table, I said that for me the Utilitarian idea that one must balance the good & ill results of an action in deciding how to act was vitiated by the fact that although pleasures reproduce themselves in the memory the case of pains was different, for one cannot remember pains, and so the balancing of pain & pleasure is quite unreliable; pleasure constantly increases & pain diminishes. Carritt said, 'I think that in general that is true but there are certain sorts of pain that never diminish. Every so often I am struck by recollection of my son, who was killed in the Spanish Civil War, with quite undiminished force; it is as if I have only just received the report that very moment.' Now, I find myself similarly placed. When I recount some sad story, I am overwhelmed by tears. Likewise with poems. I was reading to someone the other day Newbold's 'Lampada Vitaï' (i.e. 'Play up, play up, & play the game') when I got to the regiment surrounded in battle ('The Gatling's jammed & the Colonel dead'), i.e. the third stanza,

I simply blubbed, and this sort of thing goes on all the time with poetry, prose, sad familiar stories blubbing! I remember once reading to the children 'Amahl and the Night Voyagers' [*sic*. The proper title is 'Amahl and the Night Visitors' by Gian Carlo Menotti]. I broke down, much to their embarrassment; children expect adults to be tough. Pat got as near to criticising me as she ever did when she once said, 'You want to watch it.' Indeed I did watch it but 'twas no good. I think I so vividly recall sadness that it breaks my resistance. Wet don't you think? Still Romans, grown-up tough stoical Romans blubbed in court. There is very little with me that lies too deep for tears.

Pat didn't weep. I met her in February 1939 and she died in February 2008 and never did she weep. Upbringing I expect. Like Spartan women, when she had something to weep about she braced up and tried to smile. I was wounded, rather trivially as it proved, in 1944. It was reported in the local Auckland paper. A friend of both of us went round to break the news & she received it without visible emotion. Pretty good when I might have had my legs blown off! She was a very strong person, of whom I was quite unworthy.

The paper is running out. I must stop. Topics have been touched on in this letter, which I will develop some other time. I prithee weep not for me. "Weep not for yourselves but for Jerusalem." Some time I'll try & repair the deficiencies, but, alas, without a printer to record my letters my thoughts are like the songs of Edmund Campion; as my Eng. Lit. book at school said, "The songs of EC are light as thistledown & float away in the wind." Still I'll try to tell you about Univ & William Beveridge. That'll make you laugh.

Love, George

18 August 2015

My dear Gorgo,

I said I would continue with the theme of Univ & the Labour Party but I must begin by commenting on the current election of that party's leader. I don't believe many party supporters will be deterred by the pleas of Tony Blair. Of course sensible people should be moved by the chorus of Kinnock, David Miliband *et al* but before the polls were taken I fancy those who warned against the likely consequences of voting or Jeremy Corbyn would have made their decision and it looks as if Corbyn will win. The reaction to that may not be as drastic as is predicted but the effect on the prospects of Labour winning the next election are surely likely to keep Labour out of office for the next Parliament & possibly the one after that. So back to the 1980s?

In a similar, though minor, way the Conservatives were unable to accept that they had failed to win a majority in 2010 and made their Leader's position constantly difficult by not facing the fact of Coalition. All party politics involve coalitions within parties. Coalitions are not different; both sides must make compromises, as Corbyn will learn.

But enough of this. *À nos moutons!* Harold Wilson got a first in PPE . . . This was at Jesus, whence he moved to Univ as a Research Fellow, the research being in connection with William Beveridge's studies; whence the Beveridge Report. He was not I think much liked by the servants, but later contacts I had with him showed that he greatly enjoyed life in Univ In later times if he could be got off 'HP sauce', as he referred to the banter of the House of Parliament, and, of course, Huddersfield Football Club, he liked to reminisce about 'Farquy' (ASL Farquharson), & Giles Alington, after whom, he once told me, he had his son christened 'Giles', and other worthies like GDH Cole. His accommodation was in the basement flat of Kybald House (where in a room I had presumed to tell you how to win the approval of the examiners in Greats Greek History; I blush to say for I knew practically nothing). After the 1945 election he was less involved, but although many greatly disliked him I did not share their sentiments. Anyhow he was fond of Univ and I quite liked him. I once had a party in my room after a College Garden Party to which he came and promptly engaged in unstoppable conversation with Robin Butler who had worked for him (an experience I was able to use in countering Dworkin's attempts to block Robin's election as Master by saying that Robin was just a Thatcherite lickspittle). When I became Vice-Master I was anxious to secure a portrait of him for the College. When I spoke to Arnold Goodman hoping to interest him in raising the necessary money, Arnold said, 'I'll ask him for one myself.' He did and so we got the Cowan Dobson portrait that hangs in the Hall, & this prompts me to recall a story I fear I may have told you. Mrs. Cowan Dobson, widow of the painter, wanted to view her husband's portrait *in situ*, & Mary Wilson (whom again I rather

liked) brought her to view it. In the course of the viewing, if Mrs. CD
said once she said ten times that the painting should have a label pro
claiming the artist's name. 'It's not the subject that matters. It's the
painter.' Clarissa Avon, widow of Antony Eden, was staying in the
Master's Lodgings, so I invited her to join the party which included
lunch in the Senior Common Room during which Mrs CD continued
not to impress. Afterward Clarissa A. wrote me a bread & butter letter in
which she said, "What a riveting performance from that woman! No
doubt the inspiration for her husband's second-rate paintings." I apolo
gise if I've told you this before. (CA deserves another note. Perhaps I will
remember to tell you in another letter, perhaps on the subject of
Arnold's Guests.) Anyhow there was much not to dislike in Harold
Wilson. When Margaret Thatcher had been in office for a while &
Harold was visiting the College, I asked him how she was doing. He
said, 'She's doing the right things.' (But right for what, I wondered
Right for the country or right for the ruin of the Conservative Party
Harold was very adept in answering questions! An excellent parliament
arian, I thought.) *Satis*. What a bore I am!

 Love, George

31 August 2015

Dear Gorgo,

 I promised to talk about Univ's Master from 1937 to 1945
William Beveridge, Lord B. of the Beveridge Report which has so greatly
changed life in England. For all his defects he was a great man. When his
election at Univ was announced in the LSE, they clapped their hand
with joy & a Senior Fellow of later time, EJ Bowen, found Beveridge "an
impatient man of insatiable energy, well aware of his abilities", a nice
donnish statement. Indeed, vanity was Beveridge's undoing. The Fellow
got pretty sick of him being constantly away in Parliament and thing
came to a head at a meeting at which Beveridge was brought to say that
if he was re-elected in the coming General Election he would resign
"But, Master," said CK Allen, "you are sure to be re-elected." So Bev
eridge resigned on the spot. It all taught him a sharp lesson. He was no
re-elected & Beveridge was out on his neck from both Parliament & the
Mastership. But Beveridge remained a sweet old silly. He came & lived

in Oxford, reforming zeal undiminished. He used to drive in to the City by the Woodstock Road at 29½ m.p.h. & he took the number of any car that passed him & sent it to the Police & was puzzled & put out by their taking no notice! But he was a good old man & genial as the portrait of him in the Hall shows.

The date is now 11 September! I fear [I] have told you some of this before, and I have made no reference to the real horror of the Beveridge period, to wit, his secretary & later wife. The Fellows deplored her [see letter of 9 August 2013, page 192]. Her name was Janet Mayer [*sic*. Her surname was Mair]. They went away for a weekend & returned man & wife. The undergraduates gathered outside the   Lodgings & sang, 'The old grey mare, she ain't what she used to be.'

I spend most of my time snoozing, for I don't sleep very well at night, and I continue to visit the doctors' surgery to have my leg dressed, the sore being now pronounced to be an ulcer. *Eheu!* I'll try & do better next time.

My dearest wishes, George

28 September 2015

Dear Gorgo,

When, ah when will I the bucket kick? How long can the present state of affairs go on? In less than a month I shall be ninety-six & when I ascend to bed each night I ask myself whether this is the night? It all raises the flavour of the age. What about assisted suicide? Do you remember interesting me in Living Wills? I made one, & I have renewed it several times but I realise that it is little use. The matter was debated in the Commons recently and the hopes of all those seeking a happy issue out of all their afflictions were dashed.

The simplest sort of 'assisted suicide' was displayed by Peter Brunt. He had been told, 'Die now or in six months.' He had no close relatives; he wanted to die; he was a firm atheist. But he was required to live on until nature removed him. He had a right to choose whether he stayed or went. So why not let him have the pill he asked for. However, there are all sorts of cases not so straightforward. Quite apart from the 'polite pressures' families could put on there are irrational pressures. When I was discussing the topic in a general way with my daughter-in-law, Maggie, she said, 'If you committed suicide, we would feel we had failed you'! How so? But we are irrational creatures. Cf. the feelings people have about abortion, sensible until put to the test. So one has to battle on.

I say I would like to die, but one irrationally clings on to life. The other night I felt I must be approaching death. I woke up at 3 a.m., panting & wheezing. It went on for a good hour. I thought, 'This must be the old man's friend, pneumonia.' I wondered how I felt about the approach of death, & came to the conclusion that though I have no particular desire to live on & on I have great unease about dying, as opposed to death. I bethought me of Pope's "The dying Christian to his soul": 'Tell me, my soul, can this be death.' Then I remembered what a former undergraduate had told me. She said, 'Dairy products can produce uncomfortable quantities of phlegm,' and I felt 'twas not yet death but the ill consequences of having had a large & unusual lot of yoghurt as the base of the pudding I had made myself for dinner. Crisis over! I have, the while, given up yoghurt and returned to normal.

But one is going on rather long, isn't one? No member of either my father's or my mother's family has lived this long. Long lives keep us suitably placed for Alzheimer's, Dementia, Parkinson's, MS & the like, & the world is becoming a more miserable place. Is it diet? I used to be tallish, but now I am constantly reduced to average height by the great number of tall young men.

And another sniffy remark, my dear Gorgo. I am not what the masses call a real democrat. I am agonised about how to vote in the coming referendum on membership of the EU. I care about it greatly. 'Twill be a most important decision affecting all my descendants who are the light of my life. But I don't have any confidence in my judgment. To me, government is to a considerable extent a matter for experts. Remember the Syracusan leader in Thucydides summing up (6.39.1) thus: 'I say . . . the rich are the best at looking after money, men of intelligence are best at taking counsel, the masses are best at making a judgment when they have heard . . .' I am a believer in Representative Government; those suited to understanding are a minority; only when a government gets it wrong do we need a judgment of the people. This fellow Corbyn thinks that we should be governed by a series of a sort of popular decisions. That way we will go to pot. His naïveté is sublime.

We should not fight the Islamic State; we should argue with them. He omits to say what sort of arguments are effective in dissuading them from cutting off the heads of those who do not agree with them. It's just a way of postponing action when action is necessary. The silly throng are all clapping their hands. I hope he never gets power! Sorry for this rotten letter.

Your feeble Corky, George

21 October 2015

Dear Gorgo,

As you must have realised, I am a man of uncommon patience but there are some things I can by no means tolerate. For instance, the word 'incredibly', which in most cases means no more than 'very'. From the Prime Minister downwards (& upwards) it is spewed forth and whenever I hear it, I swear and accord the loose-lipped lout a large GAMMA. I never interrupted an undergraduate reading out an essay save when he/she wrote bad English; if he/she did, I became (for him/her) incredibly furious, for they can't believe that I should become furious about such misuse. Likewise, I near vomit at the sound of the word 'proactive'. What the devil does it mean if it means more than 'active'? Indeed I publicly reproved the author of the Butler report for using it therein. (By 'publicly' I mean 'at High Table'.) He tried to excuse himself by saying that the Report was a joint effort. I indicated that he should feel ashamed of his being associated with such colleagues, whereupon he became credibly silent. Great harm is being done in these times by 'texting' on mobile phones. Will English survive? I can only rant. The good old accusative 'me' is going fast. 'Whom' is nigh dead. *Ego, me, mei, mihi, me* have lost their power to influence English tongues. 'Ask none for whom the bell tolls; it tolls for' our lovely language. Cads continue to din into our ears that there ain't no rules and whatever is generally said is OK. 'KO' sez I.

But my rant is not ended. In fact, it is at its most ranting whenever I hear the word 'Democracy'. People think that they have only to use it and argument ceases. It doesn't for me. China has a population of one & a half billion and only a bloody fool supposes that they could become a democracy like us or the USA or even India. I say, the bigger the less.

Then Zionists say that 'Israel is the only democracy in the Middle East'. True enough, but so much the worse for Democracy. If a democracy votes to snitch other people's farms & fix a great wall to stop the poor devils trying to regain it, that is a nasty snitch. It suits Netanyahu to continue with his 'settlements'. The population of the settlements is now so large that no Israeli government, even if they wanted to 'unsettle' them which I don't believe they do for a moment, could act in any way that didn't please the settlers. It is no surprise that the dispossessed resort to murder. 'Democracy' is an indecent slogan. As I must have said before, & I apologise for repeating it, the golden merit of Representative Government is that it can get rid of an unpopular government. Beyond that, popular decision of policies [*sic*] is just a load of cow dung. (You should hear what is being said about the coming Referendum!) Rant over!

I spoke above of the reading of essays. Nowadays tutors take them in & read them before the tutorial. I liked pupils to read them out, because I wanted them to hear them themselves. An essay is a literary production & should be heard. Some day some slick u-grad will produce a marked essay in a court of law & want his tuition fees back if the tutor has failed to criticise all the points in the essay that he is told by someone else should have been criticised! I held & hold the view that the essay should be heard & discussed as a whole without nit-picking.

By heck, Heracles! Books unread pile up. I have a hefty & important book by Christopher Tyerman entitled 'How to Plan a Crusade'. One couldn't write 'How Xerxes Planned the Invasion of Greece'. So the book is suggestive for under-informed Ancient Historians.

This letter is a bore. I concede it. Please pardon me. I must try harder, as Hanging Judge Jeffries perhaps said.

Dearest wishes. George

1 December 2015

Dear Gorgo,

I sit upon the Dunces' Stool, and there are frequent fallings off. Please do not think I have forgotten you. I do not sleep well and so have to sleep during the day. 'Our life is but a sleep,' but not a forgetting, but all my days are rounded with a little sleep, as was said by our Bard. Then oo there is much for me to think about, currently Syria principally. If I could I would wipe Arabs off the slate of my mind, but we'll have it for as long as I live and after.

But my life has taken a turn for the better. I got for Pat the creature called a Rollator [a walker with three wheels] and I have taken to using it. At first I felt myself between Triumph and Humiliation. I had tried to avoid the use of it, but when the leaves fell thickly and the rain made me fear to slip & slither I humbled myself and found it a magically supportive machine. I try not to be caught out after sundown, but I can now accept that with prudence it supports me all the day long of this miserable winter. I no longer fear but walk cheerfully to Summertown & back as the daylight fails, and I can do the journey in a mere forty or so minutes. It has a container fixed on it and I no longer have a weight on my shoulders. So 'think of that, Hedda'.

Have you ever had anything to do with Longfellow? He was a very Victorian taste. My father was particularly fond of 'King Robert of Sicily, Brother of Pope Urban'. Indeed that poem contains one sublime verse. King R. was a haughty monarch of Sicily who was taught a humbling lesson; he was shut out of his palace when he returned from Vespers, an angel of the Lord having anticipated his return & himself taken over. But during the service he noted with dissatisfaction the way the choir sang, 'He hath put down the mighty from their seat and hath exalted the humble & the meek,' and Robert said, ''Tis well such things are said within the Latin tongue,' a line I am prone to quote over Grace in Hall, to my mind a good line indeed. (I haven't looked it up, but that's it or near it; I was given a prize at my Prep. School with all the Longfellow, 'Hiawatha' & all.) However I have myself been humbled. I occasionally do a reading of a poem for some smart possessor of a smartphone or an I-camera or the like, and you would even hear me reading on YouTube. I just sit at my desk & a zealous young one records me reading a poem which he/she then sends in an email to some pals. So when I was asked by the Development Office to read a bit of Long-fellow for the College's Christmas Greeting I fearlessly said 'Yea' & I went into College yesterday to record it. But the smart girl running this operation laid me low. I had to look the camera in the eye & could not look down at my text. Old men do not memorise. They are done for. She wanted me to do it line by line & I simply couldn't remember the line she read out. I did it quite wretchedly, though she was very polite to me.

The bit of Longfellow I was put to 'read' was a Sonnet entitled 'Holidays'. Now 'holidays' is not a word dons of my generation used. We had 'Term' & 'Vacation' and spurned 'holidays'. My colleague, John Mackie, worked every day including Christmas Day. Indeed when I was collecting material for the address I had to deliver at his Memorial Assembly, a friend of his told me how at 10.30 one Christmas Eve John called on him to discuss some philosophical problem. Of course, Mackie had no religious views to detain him but it might have been thought that he should leave the masses to their Masses. But holidays and holy days were nought to him. (I admired him greatly. I once said to Herbert Hart that I was amazed that John had not acceded to the Wykeham Chair [of Logic]. Herbert said, 'Don't be crazy. [Michael] Dummett is a genius,' and I was reproved thereby, but Mackie was scholarly and wonderfully rational, which was not how Dummett struck me when I encountered him on the Lit. Hum. Board. Anyhow I will always treasure my memories of John M.) Anyhow anyone who used the word 'holiday' got a big (secret) raspberry from me. Indeed I fought my private battle against Christmas 'holidays'. I founded the Scrooge [Club] devoted to limiting Christmas to 10 a.m. to 6 p.m. on 25 Dec. There were not many takers. Only one in fact, but a blow had been struck. (I have a penchant for secret societies. I and a single undergraduate have a society called the 'Aberlourian' devoted to the enjoyment of the Malt Whisky called 'Aberlour'. We recently admitted one other person but it's nice & elitist a word that gives the masses the gripe. All in the spirit of Chesterton' 'Man who was Thursday'. D'ye ken? So let it be firmly proclaimed decent dons don't have 'holidays' and revile the word.) A recent Master was prone to using the cursed word, but I respected him so much that let the nasty usage pass.

'Tis melancholy to reflect that, though in time past I worked hard all the vacation, now I do nothing for most of the day but sleep. Age certainly wearies me. I have taken to forgetting names, & having lived for 90 years on my memory I am now 'helmless in middle tide'. But haven't forgotten you. Pray do you likewise not forget me. Fate has dealt you a scurvy hand. I remember hearing some woman journalist (name forgotten, as usual) [Katharine Whitehorn] who ended a talk about Muslim women thus: 'No doubt the day of arranged marriages is past but we must hand it to Muslim women. They do play the hand as dealt.' *

My warmest greetings & good wishes, George

[* Whitehorn's words read strictly: 'Probably there is no place for arranged marriages in the West, but Oriental women do earn my admiration for the way in which they play the hand as dealt.']

2016

18 January 2016

Dear Gorgo,

My birth may not have been 'a sleep and a forgetting' but certainly now my life is largely a sleep. As old men will I sleep a good many hours of the day. This is in large measure because I have rather wakeful nights & when day comes I can only compensate by sleeping. But I do not forget 'ee, I assure you. I try to walk a bit but in this weather I have to go gently and I sleep, sleep, sleep, and that gives me little time not to forget . . .

(It is now 23 January! Nigh on a week has fled away since I began this letter, a good example of how I live!) I can't remember what I said about the coming referendum. Indeed I remain very divided about it. I wouldn't want the future of Great Britain to depend on me. It is a complicating factor that the Scottish Nationalists will in the case of a Vote to leave the EU demand another referendum on Independence. I am so sick of the SNP that I would like to get rid of them & endure the ill consequences. But the consequences would be ill and one struggles on. Labour affects great unity on the matter of the EU. They didn't always. But the divisions in the Conservative Party have made Labour united. Such are politics!

There was a Univ man who as an undergraduate was a great rabble-rouser. (It is now 8 February! I just fall asleep whenever I sit down to do anything!) The other day he astounded me by saying that democracy is now, for him, a dirty word! I am of my unflinching opinion that the best form of government is what we have, viz. oligarchy, but he said he is now in favour of monarchy! How to get rid of individuals like Mugabe & Assad and a dozen others he did not add. All single rulers go off the rails & need to be got rid of & that is why I think that our system of Representative Government which makes it possible to throw out unpopular rulers is precious. An oligarchy, however, consisting of a small number of people competent to judge, who skilfully pretend that they are doing what 'the People' want, is best. They have to put up with a lot of silly talk about 'democracy' but, as long as by 'democracy' they mean not pure democracy which rules by referenda, the least harm results.

This muddled paragraph had best be forgotten. I am half asleep as I write it. Let me do better by quoting a letter I have received: '... the story about Martin West sharing tutorials with someone who subsequently won a Nobel Prize in physics ... reminds me of a story about Sean Connery who was briefly a milkman on a Glasgow horse-drawn float before becoming James Bond. These floats needed two men, one to keep an eye on the horse. Connery was teamed with a driver who subsequently became general secretary of the British Communist Party. The horse, so it was said, went on to win the Derby.'

Not only I but our whole world is in a muddle. Are you aware of it, as you lead your bookless newspaperless life? If you are not, that is one tiny advantage of your miserable condition. You were 'struck' on, I think, August 23, 2012. So you are in your fourth year of being half incommunicado, which I think is quite cruel. I can only curse Fate or the Deity or whatever. You were always so gentle & reasonable & kind, & I feel for you more than this muddled pen can say.

I am sorry to write such a messy letter & must now yield yet again to the embrace of Sleep.   My dearest wishes, George

No date but sent after 3 March, read out 14 March 2016
Dear Gorgo,

You may, but then you may not, recall the letter of Tiberius Caesar to the Senate (Tacitus 'Annals' 6.6) which said, in Latin mark you, 'What I can write to you, conscript fathers, or in what manner I am to write or what I am absolutely not to write to you at this time, may the Gods & Goddesses give me a worse fate than I daily feel myself to suffer, if I know.' (The poor fellow was in a pretty distraught state, & his Latin suffered for it. For I must at this point warn you that Tiberius is my favourite emperor & I feel great sympathy for him. If he had died before his son Drusus, he would be generally well thought of. He did go to pot in his last years, though I'm a bit sceptical about stories of his misbehaviour on Capri. He was just sick of coping with his damned countrymen. Victoria had a bad period after Prince Albert snuffed it; & monarchs are bound to get cheesed off with the whole lark. I once intimated as much to Ronald Syme who despised such talk but Syme is somewhat in trouble these days. His picture of Tiberius is a bit too much like Syme himself. Waffle, waffle, digression over. So wake up! In any case I don't fail to follow the throng in thinking Sejanus was a bastard. So please don't think Corky is going off the boil.)

What Tiberius wrote in 32 AD is, *mutatis mutandis*, the sort of thing I am minded to write about myself in 2016 AD. I simply can't remember what I said to you in previous letters. E.g. did I recount what a former pupil, now my great friend, said in a letter about Martin West OM? [See previous entry.] *Or* did I tell you what my pupil Willie Hall remarked when someone said in the College Beer Cellar, 'My father's house in Leicestershire is being taken over by the Ministry'? [See letter of 3 June 2013.] (I repeat this often, for it deserves immortality.) I know I didn't report to you the National Tragedy of Carr's Water Biscuits, for I still have the cutting from a newspaper which I meant to send you so that you could weep over it (which I now enclose if I don't forget). [Enclosed was a cutting from the Daily Mail/Express: FLOODING IN WATER BISCUIT FACTORY. With comment: 'Gorgo, ain't it tragic!'] Carr's factory is in Carlisle and the recent floods put a stop to their production but I am relieved to read that 'our team is working tirelessly to get your favourite water biscuits back on the table'. So Jacob's Cream Crackers will not quite soon monopolise the biscuit barrel of our lives. But you can see how Dementia has seized my letter-writing.

However, I am glad of the opportunity the Sean Connery story has given me to discourse on the subject of Coincidence. As a historian one was constantly saying, 'This is unlikely to be mere coincidence; there is probably a causal connection.' But in one's own life one is constantly encountering coincidence. I used to cite the story of a Greats Examiner who picked up the first script in his pile which proved to be a brilliant set of answers by A Andrewes. He then picked up the next, similarly distinguished, by JL Austin and the next by AJ Ayer, and the next by I Berlin. I was once intending to launch a tirade in a lecture about those who refuse to take seriously real coincidences. So I thought I would look up the lists in the OU Calendar for that period & find which year it was. I found that though they all took their Finals in roughly the same period these celebrated performers did not all take Finals in the same year. A lesson indeed, & end of tirade.

Alas the names of Austin, Ayer, Berlin, Andrewes are now forgotten by many u'grads, & one must be careful. Peter Brunt, the Camden
Professor [of Ancient History], found himself sitting in a bus beside a
pupil of mine. He inquired of the young man what he was doing, &
learning that he was reading Greats, Brunt said that he had no doubt
been to his lectures. The young man said No, he hadn't. So Peter said his
name was Brunt & the young man did then say he had never heard of
him. A good lesson for the Professor, indeed.

And did I ever tell you this story concerning Lord Beveridge?
[Concerning Beveridge and A.S.L. Farquharson – see 27 December
2013.] But I vaguely recollect telling you this story some time ago, I
apologise.

O Gorgo, *dein Kampf* goes on, & you nobly endure. But what
else could you do? It is 6.11 p.m. on the 3rd of March. 'Very soon, very
soon, I say bluff March.'

My dearest wishes, George

20 March 2016

Dear Gorgo,

When I became a Fellow of Univ in 1949, it was customary for
newcomers to the Faculty to be invited by established members of the
Faculty to dinner which is how I came to know a bit about Hertford
College. The Ancient Historian of that college was Charles Hignett [see
pages 56-8] whose book on the Athenian Constitution may not have
come your way. Indeed, now I think of it, that book was not published
before you took the Schools. Not everyone found it a light read but it
was exact and in various ways original. In, I suppose, Hilary Term 1950, I
was invited by Charles to dinner and there was a similar entertainment
by each of us either annually, or even each term. So I gleaned quite a bit
of information about that, at that time, archaic institution . . .

Hertford was fixed a century or two back. They were sadly short
of money, & at a time when the University gave what was called a
'Common University Fund' to each fully confirmed Fellow but to
Fellows only. Hertford however had somehow wangled a C.U.F. for
their Principal [N Murphy]. He was not among the leading thirty philo-

sophers of Oxford, though he had written an article on 'the Line and the Cave' (if you remember your 'Republic'). We know now 'how many attended how many of his lectures', to borrow a phrase from Dundas' obituary of Canon Jenkins. Certainly his tutorials were unusual. When the pupil had read his essay, Murphy would offer him a cigarette and would sit ready to answer any questions the young man cared to put to him. This method did not lead to long tutorials. One u'grad however posed a problem. His essays were so short that there was an embarrassing gap between the end of the essay and the expected end of the tutorial. But Murphy dealt with that, as he explained to my friend, Peter Brunt. ' set him five essays a week.' Indeed, Murphy was not a man without resource. His rooms were chilly & draughty. So without opening mail he put it all under the carpet to cover up the cracks. In this way, 'tis said, a generous offer from M Besse, the man whose money got St. Antony' going, was 'carpeted'. So Hertford remained poor. Charles was the College Librarian and controlled all purchases of books for the Library and indeed did their classification. Hertford in their way had quite a small library. It was the college in which Evelyn Waugh found himself in the Twenties, snobbishly longing to be with the toffs of Christ Church (amongst whom we could not be numbered), but the more is learned about Hertford in those times the more I rather sympathised with Waugh. That was in the Fifties. Things are quite different now, or so I hope . . . God bless you Charles, and Principal Murphy, & all the rest of that gallant Fellowship!

And God bless you Gorgo! Your aged pal, George

16 April 2016

Dear Gorgo,

I, you, we all cling to life. Speaking for myself, I cling despite doing absolutely nothing of any use. I hope that one night I will go up to bed and not wake up, as do many oldies I suspect, but one wakes up & waits for the Big Bang. I got a notice from an insurance company headed: 'One simple step to beat rising funeral costs...' I could beat them at their game with a 'bare bodkin' as the Bard remarked. Anyhow exist & wonder how long this improbable persistence will go on. Pupils whom I highly regarded die but I go on. And the horrible fact is that I quite enjoy myself!

I had the widow of Merton Atkins to stay for a couple of nights this week. I have known her for *sixty* years. She, as I, waits for lift-off in our Space Rockets. The machine is waiting. What really keeps one here is one's family, who are indeed good to one, and to give them things is great pleasure. So when Jeremy Corbyn declared on the Andrew Marr Show, that he would like to abolish inheritance of money (I forget his precise phrase), he wants to deprive us old men of our last pleasure. He is a good man but a great ass, is he not?

One pleasure one could gladly forfeit is this damned referendum. There are those who blame Cameron for having any such thing, but to my mind this is unfair. He was bound to give in to those who sought a referendum. It was promised by Labour in its Manifesto in 1997 and repeated in discussion of Liberal Democrats [*sic*] in 2000 (at least I remember Menzies Campbell [leader of the Lib-Dems] saying, again on the Andrew Marr Show, that he didn't want a referendum on the Lisbon Treaty & that what he wanted was a referendum on the whole question of whether we wanted to stay or withdraw from the EU, & Cameron had to let the Eurosceptics in his party have what they insisted on as the only solution, a referendum.)

But the repercussions will be severe. If the Brexit movement get majority support, I expect Cameron will soldier on for a bit to try & make the best of a bad job, but the Tory party will be divided for a decade or two. I have forgotten about the repeal of the Corn Laws, but I seem to remember that it took quite a time to reunite the party. Osborne may already have discredited himself by ill-judged measures in the last budget but in any case his firm assertion of the case for not leaving the EU will have made it unlikely that he will become Leader. Johnson just seems unsuitable. So another must be found. Perhaps Gove; at least he is said to be a very clever man. But it is not beyond imagination that Corbyn will win the next election, in which case it will be wise for a lot of richer people to pack up & get to Europe.

Whatever his merits Corbyn seems to me a political lightweight. In Labour's exploitation of the Panama papers, he was arguing that, although there had not been illegal conduct by the mass of those with shares in a Panamanian company, it was 'immoral' for people to put their money into such enterprises even if they paid the due taxes. Everyone I know makes the effort to pay no more than he/she legally must. Not a penny more, not a penny less. So to start labelling such investment 'immoral' is proof of a mind that is unfit for high office. Of course, there are shabby enterprises plainly established to avoid liability & it is the job of government to legislate & prevent, if they can. (Personally, I know of only one such but no doubt they exist, & efforts to prevent must go on endlessly.) But in politics generally the word 'morally' so dear to English ears should be jeered out of usage in Parliament. Corbyn is not suited to lead. (I always admired Tony Benn, in a way, and his son, Hilary may well be the best chance for Labour's resurrection.) 'Tis all chaos & confusion.

I remain agonised about which way to cast my vote, but on the whole I incline to favour 'Remain'. There are still two more months to go & much may happen to strengthen the hostility to immigration. As you will recall, the Ugandan Asians were admitted *en masse* & I fancy they were an asset to this country. It is very downcasting that having had the miseries of the Protestant/Catholic struggle to endure we now have to endure a couple of centuries of Shia/Sunni conflict. (And is it all due to a silly wrangle about who is descended from the Prophet? I fear human beings just like such nonsense.)

It's all interesting & disquieting, is it not? One would like to close one's eyes with hope that one's family will live as comfortably as one has oneself. For we, having survived the War, have had a pretty easy time. But I fear that it will not be so for one's tribe. Hooray for the wit of John Wilkes. I must have cited this a thousand times before, but here goes yet again. [See letter of 1 September 2013.]

My dearest wishes, George

[On the envelope:]

> 'Dear me!' exclaimed Homer,
> 'What a delicious aroma!
> It smells as if a town
> Was being burnt down.'

I hope you remember such Clerihews.

9 May 2016

Dear Gorgo,

I trust you know the story of Jowett on a visit to Edinburgh, when an Edinburgh sage said to him, 'And what do you think of us in Oxford?' to which Jowett replied, 'In Oxford we don't think of you at all,' a good vote-loser for referenda to come. But I am no Jowett. I do think of you a great deal, but ever more and more I sleep and sleep. I don't sleep very well in the night and after breakfast I ever more & more slip off to slumber when I should be getting on with the business of life. I used to have a good post-prandial but now it's four hundred and forty forty winks [*sic*] after I have my toast y-taken. There's no good me saying that I will repair my ways. I sleep on & on and sleep for ever more. Indeed I become a sleeping beauty or, rather, brutey. I go less & less to College.

(But it is now 16th May! So life drags on.)

Did I tell you that at some date in late April I had a fall! I got up to go to the loo rather in haste, took hold of my Zimmer frame, set off for the loo, fell on to my bed, tried again, fell again & bounced on to the floor whence I could not get up. I was barefooted and the carpet was slippery and I could not get up. I pressed my alarm aid. My chosen neighbours were not 'in town', one family was in Morocco, another in their house in France, another had switched off their phone to try & get rid of cold callers. So there I lay. Fortunately my blessed Judy was at home & when the alarm aid called at 2 a.m. she & her husband rose, dressed & hurtled down the by-pass from Littlemore, arrived here at 2.35 & got me up & saved the day, but 'twas a shocking experience. I could still be there awaiting salvation! But clearly I had to avoid a repeat if only for Judy's sake.

I now have a pot *on* the table by my bed and I keep a pair of crepe-soled shoes to wear when I get up in the night and I hope the situation will not recur. But then two forceful ones, Tim & Sarah, wanted more cover than mere hopes provide. So now I have professional cover all night from 10 p.m. to 7.30 a.m. It comforts the family and also Judy and also myself and there is general all-round relief for each & all of us. The cost is of course horrific and I don't want to live on into this black night. I've always thought that Dylan Thomas' line, 'Do not go gently into the dark night [*sic*]. Rage, rage against the dying of the light' was the silliest bit of Eng. Lit. I have encountered. What would Aristotle say of such folly? One quietly hopes for death. Much better is the humour of Pope's 'The Dying Christian to his Soul': 'Tell me, my soul, can this be death?' One doesn't believe that one has a soul which is a hangover of the pre-Christian world, though until life becomes plainly intolerable, one endures contentedly enough, and I expect one would face the news of imminent death with a bit of a flutter, but I have done pretty well and will greet death with relief. It's dying one fears, but let us hope for the good sense of Stoics & be gone.

(But it is now 25th May!) One's troubles are petty but they obsess one, do they not? I am very delighted that Sarah is very contented in her new house, whence she walks forth healthily. Alas I shall probably never get the chance of seeing inside it but it cheers me to know that Sarah is so happy there. It gives me a lean excuse to talk about my academic life. In general it is a detestable fault in a don to show special feelings for a pupil. But one can't avoid having such feelings. In general I have liked my pupils but there have been a smallish number I have specially liked. For instance, I will never forget the effect made on me by a girl who entered my room for interview in December 1983. 'Twas friendship at first sight and we have been friends ever since. I speak of Abigail Graham, daughter of New Zealand parents, whom I don't think you have ever met. Then too there is to be remembered Michael Milner who once stayed with us as he recovered from illness whom I see constantly. Etc. etc. but I must not go on for there are too many it would be unjust to omit. But one recent disaster may be mentioned. I continued to tutor after I had ceased to be a member of the Governing Body of Univ. Pupils came to Moreton Road [where George and Pat lived] and it was a very happy chapter of my life. One in particular gave special pleasure [Rebecca Williams]. She was the daughter of a Birmingham University lecturer/Professor. I don't know why exactly, but I derived the greatest pleasure from tutorials with her. I don't precisely remember why I felt this, but it was all such fun. I hope I didn't ruin her chances by my excess of laughter, but we laughed & laughed & it is a great sorrow that she died of cancer at the age of forty-two. When I was told I did just weep. Powerful, quick-witted, kind & generous, she will ever hold a special place in my memory. *Manibus date lilia plenis.* ['Give lilies with full hands.'] I have just been very lucky to have known such people. I have always referred to my Univ pupils as *La crême de la crême*, or 'the Quality'.

Well love to you. It's a pleasure to me that Sarah & Nell seem to get on so well with each other, a proxy friendship.

Yours, yours ever, George

30 June 2016

Dear Gorgo,

> 'Yet once more, O ye laurels, and once more
> Ye Myrtles brown, with Ivy never-sear...'

Beware! I am having a back-to-Milton attack, not necessarily infectious but one may be reminded of things past. When I was at school, I had to learn bits of 'Lycidas', 'Il Penseroso', 'L'Allegro' (did you too?), and they have taken to floating up to the surface of my mind. Thus the other day I suddenly wrote, 'Yet once more, O ye laurels,' believed it was Milton, was too lazy to go to my book-shelf & verify, so I rang a neighbour who chances to be the Wharton Professor of English. He is ever ready to settle my uncertainties by recourse to works of reference, but in this case without delay he referred me to the opening of 'Lycidas'. (If he can't find something, like as not I have made a muddle of something. But there is one poser neither he nor other learned chums have been able to satisfy. I can't have dreamed it and I remember somewhere I read the very Miltonic line, 'Lean on our fair brother, Christ,' but no one has ever been able to pin it down. 'Twas only eighty years since I read it I think. Can you help this aged silly?)

Yet once more indeed, we are reminded of our old friend Tully [Cicero]. He warned (don't ask me where) against making the state *biceps* ['double-headed'] or I think he did. One had better avoid two sources of authority like the *plebs* and the *patres*, but that is just the clash we have in the Labour Party. The popular vote is one source and the Parliamentary Party the other. The P.P. must be the really important power, for they have to work with the Party leader day by day and so their judgment is all-important but the popular choice claims the equal authority, and Jeremy Corbyn bases his claim to continue in power in whichever part appears to support him. What a how-de-do! And there is another point. One had better make sure that the popular vote is not composed of voters who are not welcome to exercise power, but Miliband (Ed) opened it to anyone who pays a mere £3. So Simon C. & his like is free to join in voting for a mere £3 fee and he plans to join in the fun just to contribute to the chaos when it comes to a new vote. Miliband, in short, has run his Party onto the Rocks.

Poor Miliband, puppet of the Unions. He never looked the part and, alas, in such matters looking the part is mighty important. I say this with Michael Gove in mind. He is reputed to be *very* clever. My once pupil, David Edward QC, & still my friend, for 'tis a paradox that one's ignorance is never held against one, though I must confess that modest potations in my room did a lot for good relations. He is the source of my report. Gove comes of very humble stock & went on a scholarship to some 'good' Scottish school, where he shone academically. When he was introduced to David, David was told that 'Gove is just about the cleverest boy to have attended the school'. So, sez you, is he headed for the leadership of the Conservative Party? (As you are well aware, we Conservatives are savvy enough to draw on Scots to lead them. Both Blair & Cameron are Scots, both to my mind clever, and Gordon Brown should not be forgotten if one forgets his psychological troubles. Labour has called on 'em e'en though some have been reviled – I think of Ramsay MacDonald much admired by my mother, & George V pronounced him 'his favourite Prime Minister'. Let me not go on. That clever brat Nicola Sturgeon is in the mould. In fact I think she may well be seduced into forgetting her Nationalist aspirations and giving herself to ruling the Brits. She clearly enjoys her reputation, does she not?) But to return to Gove. He has the brain & the ability and Simon Cawkwell has his money on him. (However, there is a streak of petulance there, & a wildness of judgment, & I guess he won't make it, principally because he doesn't look like a leader of men I fear.)

The date is 25 July; i.e. it is almost a month that I have been drivelling on (or driveling). I have been sleeping by day not having slept by night. So an epistle that was to find a new leader to the Conservatives and mildly to grieve for David Cameron, whose final Prime Minister's Questions was a triumph. But Theresa [May] did wonderfully well on her first outing, did she not?

I must desist from politics. It has been a fascinating time and a sadly worrying time for old codgers like me. *Satis eventuum, satis casuum.*

Have you ever met our Master, Ivor Crewe, whom I greatly like? He has got only two years before retirement. His wife Jill has been in every way marvellous. I was saying the same as Jill Butler went away and you may be a bit sceptical about praises from me. Indeed all the Masters of my time have done us wondrously well in this respect, but latter-day wives have a great deal more to do & have done it with the greatest care. Still I won't, can't be here for ever. I have already had to avoid my part in the College. It's so exhausting for a 96-97 year old. Do you think I'm going soft? I am greatly pampered by all, staff, colleagues, even taxi-drivers who do not dump me at my door but walk me into the front door of my house. But, oh golly, how long can it all go on? I expect they want to encourage me, but the two doctors who have recently predicted I will live for five more years downcast me! Still, I labour on; for what else can I do?

This is a shamefully ragged letter & I apologise. It has had about a month in the gestation. I blush to reflect. But I do think of you off & on constantly. Perhaps we'll arrive there together.

George

25 August 2016

Dear Gorgo,

Late in time behold I write. My slumbering has become ever more disgraceful. After breakfast I retire to the room that once was Pat's study, now the Television Room where I snooze, making up for sleep lost in the night, a mere hour or two, after which twice a week I await the moment when I must set off for the Nurse's room in the Summer-town Health Centre, whence I return at 11.30 meaning to get on with what I should have got on with at 9 a.m. I make a simple lunch and have my post-prandial nap after which I set off for Summertown to shop. Not much remains before I set about preparing my supper, after which I get the washing up done, & too late for anything else, I watch television until I prepare for bed. That is a dog's life, lived by a dog. Pray despise me, for I deserve it.

It is the life of Napoleon Buonaparte on St. Helena. Not, mark you, on Elba. He got away from that & could dream of action. No, it is sheer vacancy. How I despise myself. (I came across this pad on which I can write on distinct lines, but there's not much room for me to make plain my thoughts. I beg your pardon.)

I don't know whether to go on about the political capering I have to witness. I rather think you would be on the side of Remaining in the EU. You have a house in France which generally makes a Brit into a European. I am done with referenda, egad. The Welsh chappie who aspires to displace Jeremy Corbyn says he wishes to have another referendum, which he says is a way to erase the performance of JC. Theresa won't have it and the only way of having it would be for her to call another election. So we will have to go ahead with what we've got. I mope on.

Part of my moping is due to the fact that the Senior Common Room of Univ has collapsed, if by 'Senior Common Room' one means dinner & leisurely conversation. Of course we have lunch, a meal for which I have little inclination. The food is decent enough, indeed it is much improved. But there is little in the conversation to enliven one. However I mean to try it again and my one visit for a long time on Tuesday last went off well enough. We have an Australian librarian whom I greatly like and she looks after me in most kindly fashion as do indeed the staff if I should fetch up on my own. But I look back on many years of dinners in Oxford Common Rooms. The only college in which I have not dined is St. Peter's. I would like to repair this deficiency but my range of acquaintances shrinks year by year. Maddeningly I don't recall what I have said in these stodgy letters, but there are one or two evenings that stick in the memory, such as an evening in Magdalen with CE ('Tom Brown') Stevens at which Jack Bennett and CS Lewis were present. ('Tom Brown', because he was reputed to have arrived as a new boy at Winchester wearing Rugby uniform, credible enough.) The evening that really sticks in the mind was in Univ itself. The Regius Professor of Medicine who had been a Fellow before he moved to Christ Church wanted Univ to consider for membership of Common Room a man who was not greatly at ease & brought him to dinner. Peter Strawson was present & his guest was Gilbert Ryle. Gilbert's brother [nephew, Martin Ryle] was, I think, Astronomer Royal and the Regius Professor's guest was so unwise as to make adverse comment on Gilbert's brother. This greatly riled Gilbert who set about putting him down. Gilbert spoke to him at length & ended up by saying, 'You're a donkey, sir,' & turning to the company at large said, 'The man's a donkey. Let's leave him out of the conversation.' 'Twas the end of the Regius Professor's effort to have the fellow made a member of Common Room! Gilbert was amiable in general and I recall a special affection for Jane Austen. He was a Student [i.e. Fellow] of Christ Church before he became the Waynflete Professor [of Metaphysical Philosophy] and had been a leading spirit in the Ch. Ch. Boat Club. You may say that was improbable for a philosopher but rowing provides thought for Platonists and Aristotelians. In Plato's 'Republic' all the members of the team did the same but did they serve the Golden Mean in the way that Aristotle required? At least I used to have such thoughts but, frankly, though such ideas are only seventy years past, I'm darned if I know what I had in mind in 1946. One never, by the bye, wondered what such a man as Gilbert Ryle thought about sex life for dons. There were of course those who kept a lady for an out-of-term pastime. Freddy Ayer did not wait. Perhaps Gilbert had a lady on the side line of Philosophy. Certainly Bradley did. Nowadays they often can't wait until the end of the tutorial!

But I digress. When Gilbert was Censor, he forbade RH Dundas to continue his sex talks. I know this because Dundas said so in his retirement speech. I fancy there was a good deal of suppressed sex in those times (as in monasteries? Let us leave this uncertain subject). Devotees had to make the best of things with an indiscreet use of the cane, & take their opportunities there. A friend of mine was at Shrewsbury, in Chenevix Trench's house. He is a scientist and found the Latin language hard going. So he went to Chenevix and asked for his assistance. Ch. gave him two hours of highly enlightening & enlightened instruction for which the boy was very grateful, but Chenevix rounded it off with 'a caning to rub the lesson in'! When he told me, he manifested no dissatisfaction with such 'tuition', though nowadays it would be illegal. You may remember that when Ch. Tr. retired from Eton, or rather got the sack, there was a rhyme in a Sunday newspaper which ran thus: 'When caning is waning, it must be a wrench for Chenevix Trench to be beaten by Eton.' Another version of the methods of Dotheboys Hall.

By the bye, Nell sent me a little note to say how appreciative you are of my letters. I can only think that the quality has much declined. It's a bit difficult keeping up a one-ended correspondence & I beg you to be patient & forgive me my decline.

Someone gave me a copy of the autobiography of John Christie who was Headmaster of Westminster School (& subsequently Principal of Jesus, Oxford). On the cover is a photo of him in conversation with our own RH Dundas, in a gown. I expect D was on the Board of Governors. But it reminds me of that strange fellow. I couldn't make out what he was saying, but if perchance I did I didn't make much of it all. He had a considerable reputation as a tutor. I wondered why. His choice of topics for essays was bizarre. How could one cover early Greek History without essays on the constitutional development of Athens & also of Sparta. He just missed all that out. It had the great merit of making one think one had better get on & do it for oneself. Which I did. So paradoxically he was a good tutor if being a good tutor moves pupils to get on & do it for themselves. On the other hand he certainly took good care of those in his charge & I'm not sure that that is not more important than conventional instruction. His style of language was sublime . . . I wish I had kept all the cards I had from him. They were brilliant.

Good night, good friend. I'll try & do better. Your aged friend, George

This was George's last letter to Gorgo, for Engle died on 14 September 2016. The following note from Engle to Cawkwell is undated, so it is not clear when exactly he dictated it to his daughter Eleanor. It was found last in the batch of the letters.]

Dear George,

Memento mori. The best thing is you die in your sleep. Remember what Wittgenstein said: death is not lived through.

My Uncle Albert died in his sleep on Christmas Day without a moment's warning. It's difficult to arrange this.

Your letters are the best. I for one am very glad you are still alive even though your last one has a moribund feel to it.

Much love,

George

[George Cawkwell died 897 days later, on 28 February 2019.]

INDEX

ABOUT SFORZINDA BOOKS

Tim Cawkwell is a freelance writer on film, cricket and travel, with three poetry booklets to his name as well. From 1968 to the 1980s he was a film-maker working initially in 8mm and then in 16mm. His dvd LIGHT YEARS – THE FILM DIARIES OF TIM CAWKWELL 1968 TO 1987 was released in 2018. More recent short films can be found on Vimeo. His essays on the cinema can be found at www.timcawkwell.co.uk

Except where indicated all the titles listed are published by Sforzinda Books, the name of his self-publishing venture. These books are available on Amazon; the poetry books can be ordered through a bookshop only, or direct from the author.

- *The World Encyclopaedia of Film* (co-editor, 1972, London: Studio Vista)
- *Temenos 2012*, a diary about the Temenos film festival in Greece in 2012 (digital only)
- *From Neuralgistan to the Elated Kingdom: a personal journey inside Sicily* (2013, digital only)
- *Between Wee Free and Wi Fi: Scotland and the UK belong surely?* (2013, digital only)
- *The New Filmgoer's Guide to God* (2014, Leicester: Troubador Press)
- *A Tivoli Companion* (2015)
- *Cricket's Pure Pleasure: the story of an extraordinary match – Middlesex v. Yorkshire, September 2015* (2016)
- *The Tale of Two Terriers and the Somerset Cat: the County Championship 2016* (2017)
- *Belaboured. Bats Broken. Britain Shaken: a personal account of the 2017 General Election* (2017)
- *Compleat Cricket: eight days in September* (2018)

- *Bittering, Norfolk, Lost and Found* (co-authored with Joan Norton, 2018)
- *Film Past, Film Future: an enquiry into cinema and the imagination* (2019)
- *Cricket on the Edge 2019* (2019)
- *Infelicities: poems in an age of declinism* (2020)
- *In These Torrid Times*, poems (2021)
- *The Battle of Trafalgar Square*, poetry pamphlet (2021)
- *In the Shadow of the Pandemic*, poems by Mervyn Wilson (2022)

He was born in 1948 and lives in Norwich in the United Kingdom. Email: cawkwell200@gmail.com

Printed in Great Britain
by Amazon